MW00584328

Volume 2

Dr. Karen C. Fuson
and
Dr. Sybilla Beckmann

This material is based upon work supported by the
National Science Foundation
under Grant Numbers
ESI-9816320, REC-9806020, and RED-935373.

Any opinions, findings, and conclusions, or recommendations expressed in this material are those of the author and do not necessarily reflect the views of the National Science Foundation.

Teacher Reviewers

Kindergarten
Patricia Stroh Sugiyama
Wilmette, Illinois

Barbara Wahle
Evanston, Illinois

Grade 1
Sandra Budson
Newton, Massachusetts

Janet Pecci
Chicago, Illinois

Megan Rees
Chicago, Illinois

Grade 2
Molly Dunn
Danvers, Massachusetts

Agnes Lesnick
Hillside, Illinois

Rita Soto
Chicago, Illinois

Grade 3
Jane Curran
Honesdale, Pennsylvania

Sandra Tucker
Chicago, Illinois

Grade 4
Sara Stoneberg Llibre
Chicago, Illinois

Sheri Roedel
Chicago, Illinois

Grade 5
Todd Atler
Chicago, Illinois

Leah Barry
Norfolk, Massachusetts

Grade 6
Jean S. Armstrong
Austin, Texas

Cheryl Van Ness
Dunellen, New Jersey

Credits

Cover art: (wolf) Lynn Rogers/Photolibrary; (branches) Matthias Bein/dpa/Corbis

Photos: 237 Photodisc/Getty Images; 238 Corbis; 311 (t) Robert Glusic/Photodisc/Getty Images; (c) David Ponton/Design Pics/Corbis; (b) PhotoDisc/Getty Images

Printed in the U.S.A.

ISBN: 978-0-547-56740-2

1 2 3 4 5 6 7 8 9 10 0868 20 19 18 17 16 15 14 13 12 11

4500308259 A B C D E F G

VOLUME 2 CONTENTS

Unit 5 Expressions and Equations

Unit 6 Volume of a Rectangular Prism

Unit 7 Ratios and Rates with Fractions, Decimals, and Percents

VOLUME 2 CONTENTS (CONTINUED)

Student Resources

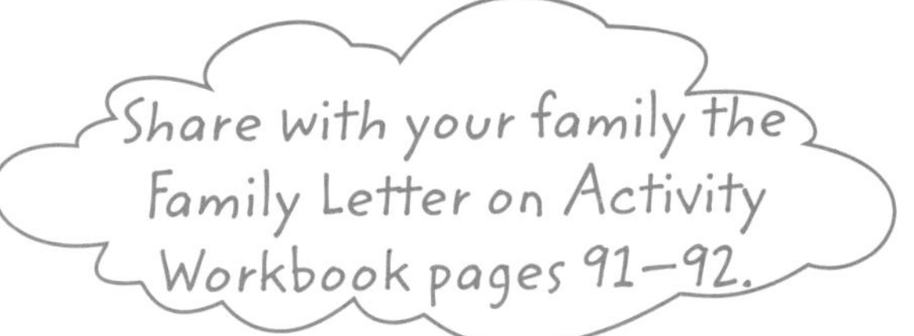

Share with your family the
Family Letter on Activity
Workbook pages 91–92.

Dear Family,

In our math class, we are studying algebra. We will study

- algebraic expressions,
- how quantities vary together, and
- solving equations.

These concepts are important for your child's success in middle school and high school math and science.

An *algebraic expression* summarizes a calculation in a concise way. For example, we can write the calculation "subtract 3 from a number and then multiply the result by 5" with the algebraic expression $(s - 3) \bullet 5$. The letter s is a *variable* that stands for "a number." We can substitute any number for s and evaluate the expression to get a value.

To help students interpret numerical and algebraic expressions, we relate them to math diagrams that indicate quantities.

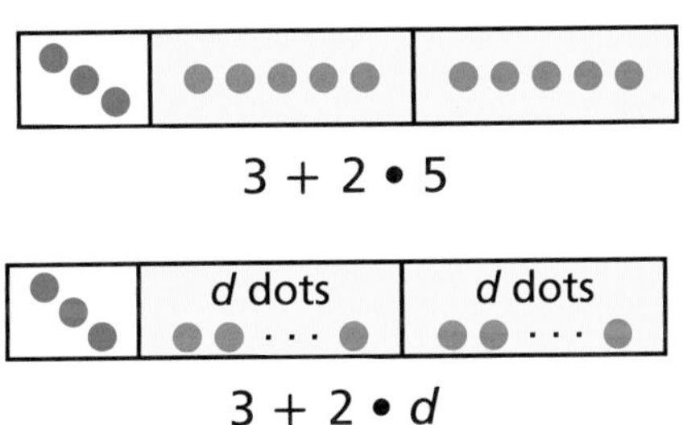

In this unit, we will study quantities that *vary together*. For example:

- The weight of potato salad and its cost vary together.
- The distance a person has walked and the time that has elapsed since the person started walking vary together.

To show how quantities vary together, we will use double number lines, tables, graphs, diagrams, and equations. Here is a double number line that shows distance and time varying together for a person walking at a constant rate of 3 feet per second.

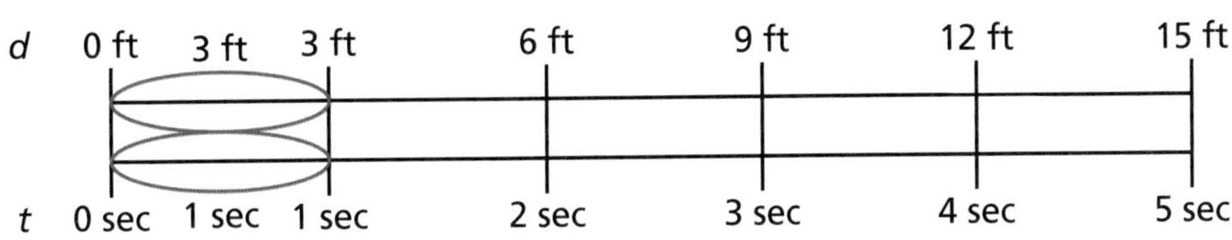

continued ▶

In this unit, your child will also study solving equations. To *solve an equation* means to find the numbers that make the left side of the equation equal to the right side. Students find solutions of equations in several ways.

- They check numbers to see if they make the sides of the equation equal. For example, $x = 12$ is a solution of $7x - 1 = 83$ because $7(12) - 1 = 84 - 1 = 83$.
- They reason about what number makes the two sides of an equation equal. For example, both sides of $14 + 72 = 72 + x$ have an addend of 72. Therefore, the other addends must also be equal. So, $x = 14$.
- They use the inverse operation to write a related equation that is easier to solve. For the addition equation $32 + x = 51$, we can write the related subtraction equation $x = 51 - 32$. Now it is easy to see that $x = 19$.
- They apply the same operation to both sides of an equation to get an equivalent equation with the variable alone on one side. For example, multiplying both sides of $\frac{1}{2}x = 5$ by 2 gives the equation $x = 10$.

If you have any questions or comments, please call or write to me.

Sincerely,
Your child's teacher

This unit includes the Common Core Standards for Mathematical Content for Expressions and Equations, 6.EE.1, 6.EE.2, 6.EE.3, 6.EE.4, 6.EE.5, 6.EE.6, 6.EE.7, 6.EE.8, 6.EE.9, Number System 6.NS.4, Geometry 6.G.1, 6.G.4, and all Mathematical Practices.

Muestra a tu familia la Carta a la familia de las páginas 93 y 94 del Cuaderno de actividades y trabajo.

Estimada familia,

En la clase de matemáticas estamos estudiando álgebra. Aprenderemos acerca de:

- las expresiones algebraicas,
- cómo algunas cantidades varían juntas,
- cómo resolver ecuaciones.

Aprender estos conceptos es importante para su hijo, ya que son la base para los cursos de matemáticas y de ciencias en la escuela media y en la escuela media superior.

Una *expresión algebraica* resume un cálculo de una manera concisa. Por ejemplo, podemos escribir el cálculo "restar 3 de un número y luego, multiplicar el resultado por 5" usando la expresión algebraica $(s - 3) \cdot 5$. La letra s es una *variable* que representa "un número". Podemos sustituir s con cualquier número y resolver la expresión para obtener un valor.

Para ayudar a los estudiantes a interpretar expresiones numéricas y algebraicas, las relacionaremos con diagramas matemáticos.

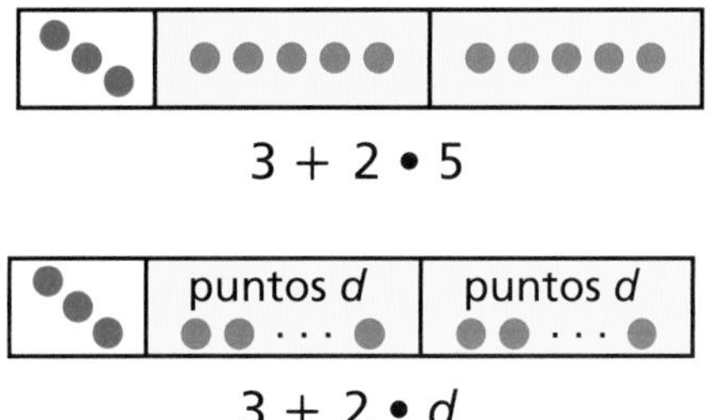

En esta unidad, estudiaremos cantidades que *varían juntas*. Por ejemplo:

- El peso de una ensalada de papas y su costo varían juntos.
- La distancia que una persona camina y el tiempo que transcurre desde que comienza a caminar varían juntos.

Para mostrar cómo varían juntas algunas cantidades, usaremos rectas numéricas dobles, tablas, gráficas, diagramas y ecuaciones. La siguiente es una recta numérica doble que muestra cómo varían juntos la distancia y el tiempo cuando una persona camina a una velocidad constante de 3 pies por segundo.

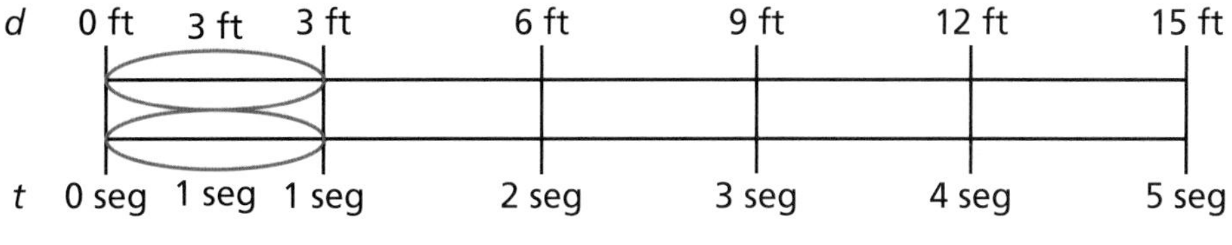

continúa ▶

En esta unidad su hijo también aprenderá cómo resolver ecuaciones. *Resolver una ecuación* significa hallar los números que igualan el lado izquierdo con el lado derecho de la ecuación. Los estudiantes pueden hallar soluciones para las ecuaciones de diferentes maneras:

- Probando números para ver cuáles igualan ambos lados de la ecuación. Por ejemplo, $x = 12$ es una solución para $7x - 1 = 83$ porque $7(12) - 1 = 84 - 1 = 83$.
- Razonando para determinar cuál número puede usarse para igualar ambos lados de una ecuación. Por ejemplo, ambos lados de $14 + 72 = 72 + x$ tienen 72 como un sumando. Por lo tanto, los otros sumandos, también deben ser iguales. Entonces, $x = 14$.
- Usando la operación inversa para escribir una ecuación relacionada que sea más fácil de resolver. Para la ecuación de suma $32 + x = 51$, podemos escribir la ecuación relacionada de resta $x = 51 - 32$. Ahora es fácil ver que $x = 19$.
- Aplicando la misma operación a ambos lados de una ecuación para obtener una ecuación equivalente que tenga la variable sola en un lado. Por ejemplo, al multiplicar ambos lados de $\frac{1}{2}x = 5$ por 2 se obtiene la ecuación $x = 10$.

Si tiene alguna pregunta, por favor comuníquese conmigo.

Atentamente,
El maestro de su hijo

Esta unidad incluye los Common Core Standards for Mathematical Content for Expressions and Equations, 6.EE.1, 6.EE.2, 6.EE.3, 6.EE.4, 6.EE.5, 6.EE.6, 6.EE.7, 6.EE.8, 6.EE.9, Number System 6.NS.4, Geometry 6.G.1, 6.G.4, and all Mathematical Practices.

▶ Variables, Expressions, and Terms

Vocabulary

variable
expression
term

A **variable** is a letter or symbol used to represent a number.

In Unit 2, you worked with variables in area formulas. For example, in the formula for the area of a triangle, $A = \frac{1}{2}bh$, the letters A, b, and h are variables.

1. Write another formula that includes variables.

An **expression** is made up of one or more numbers, one or more variables, or both numbers and variables. An expression also often includes one or more operations, but does not include an equals sign. Some examples of expressions are shown below.

$4 \qquad n \qquad x - 9 \qquad 3z \qquad b + 2 - a \qquad \frac{1}{2}bh$

2. Circle the expressions.

$p \div 7 \qquad 13 \qquad z = 6 - x \bullet y \qquad t \qquad 7 + 4 = 11 \qquad 0.5 \bullet (k + s)$

3. Write an expression that includes at least one number, at least one variable, and at least one operation.

Terms are parts of an expression that are added or subtracted. Some examples of terms are shown below.

y	$+$	9		g	$-$	$2g$		$\frac{3}{4}a$	$+$	b	$-$	1
↑		↑		↑		↑		↑		↑		↑
term		term		term		term		term		term		term

4. Write an expression that consists of two terms that are numbers.

5. Write an expression that consists of three terms.

Vocabulary

numerical expression
Order of Operations
algebraic expression
evaluate

▶ Simplify Numerical Expressions

A **numerical expression** includes only numbers. Follow the Order of Operations to simplify a numerical expression.

Order of Operations

1. Perform all operations inside parentheses.
2. Multiply and divide from left to right.
3. Add and subtract from left to right.

Simplify each expression by following the Order of Operations.

6. $36 - (2 + 9) \bullet 3$

7. $20 - 8 \div 2$

8. $3 \bullet (26 \div 2) + 11$

▶ Evaluate Algebraic Expressions

An **algebraic expression** is an expression that includes one or more variables. An algebraic expression summarizes a calculation in a concise way. For example, $(n + 3) \bullet 5$ is a short way of saying "add 3 to a number, and then multiply the result by 5."

To **evaluate** an algebraic expression means to substitute given values for the variables, and then simplify by following the Order of Operations.

Example Evaluate $x \bullet (5 - y)$ for $x = 8$ and $y = 3$.

$x \bullet (5 - y)$	Write the given expression.
$8 \bullet (5 - 3)$	Substitute 8 for x and 3 for y.
$8 \bullet 2$	Perform the operation inside ( ).
16	Multiply. The expression simplifies to 16.

Evaluate each expression for $a = 3$ and $b = 6$.

9. $24 - 15 \div a$

10. $12 + 6 \div b$

11. $10 \bullet (b + a)$

12. $b + (2 + a) \bullet 3$

13. $2 \bullet a + 4 \bullet b$

14. $18 \div a - b \div 2$

Vocabulary
power
base
exponent

▶ Powers

Some numerical and algebraic expressions and equations include powers. A **power** is an expression that includes an exponent and represents a repeated multiplication. An example of a power is 4^3, which is read "four raised to the third power."

A power consists of a base and an exponent. In a numerical expression, the **base** is a number, and the **exponent** tells how many times the number is used as a factor.

In the expression 4^3, the base is 4, and the small raised 3 is the exponent. The exponent tells you to use 4 as a factor 3 times.

$4^3 = 4 \bullet 4 \bullet 4$ $\quad$ $4 \bullet 4 \bullet 4 = 64$ $\quad$ So $4^3 = 64$.

In an algebraic expression, the base is a variable. In the expression r^5, which is read "r raised to the fifth power," the base is r and 5 is the exponent. The exponent tells you to use r as a factor 5 times.

$$r^5 = r \bullet r \bullet r \bullet r \bullet r$$

Remember, whenever you work with powers, you are working with expressions that represent repeated multiplication.

Write each expression as a repeated multiplication.

1. $6^2 =$ ▢
2. $11^3 =$ ▢
3. $13^2 \bullet 4^4 =$ ▢
4. $2^3 \bullet 5^2 =$ ▢
5. $a^5 =$ ▢
6. $a^3 \bullet a^2 =$ ▢

Use an exponent to write each repeated multiplication.

7. $2 \bullet 2 \bullet 2 \bullet 2 =$ ▢
8. $b \bullet b \bullet b \bullet b \bullet b =$ ▢
9. $2 \bullet c \bullet c =$ ▢
10. $4 \bullet 10 \bullet 10 \bullet 10 =$ ▢

▶ Exponents and the Order of Operations

In the Order of Operations, powers are simplified after operations inside parentheses and before multiplication and division.

Order of Operations

1. Perform all operations inside parentheses.
2. Simplify powers.
3. Multiply and divide from left to right.
4. Add and subtract from left to right.

Simplify. Follow the Order of Operations.

11. $4 + 3^2 =$ ▢
12. $5 + 5 \bullet 2^3 =$ ▢
13. $4 \div 2^2 + 1 =$ ▢
14. $(7 - 2)^2 =$ ▢
15. $1 + 6^2 \bullet 2 =$ ▢
16. $3^2 + 3^3 =$ ▢

Evaluate each expression for $a = 5$ and $b = 8$.

17. $3 \bullet a^3$
18. $9^2 \bullet (b + 1)$
19. $(b - a)^2$

▶ What's the Error?

Dear Math Students:

My friend said I did not simplify the three expressions shown below correctly.

$2^6 = 12$ $10^4 = 40$ $5^2 \bullet 2^3 = 60$

What error did I make? Please help me understand how to find the number that each expression represents.

Your Friend,

Puzzled Penguin

20. Write an answer to Puzzled Penguin.

5–2
Class Activity

Use Activity Workbook page 95.

▶ Squares and Cubes

Solve.

21. Write a power to represent the area of a 5 meter by 5 meter square.

area = ________ m^2

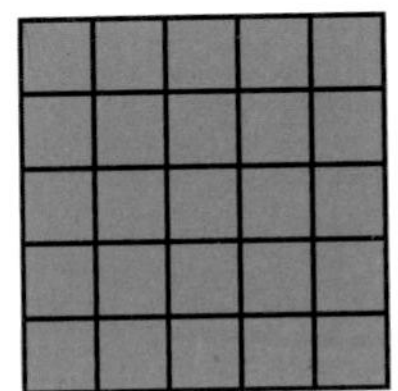

22. Write a power to represent the volume of a 5 cm by 5 cm by 5 cm cube.

volume = ________ cm^3

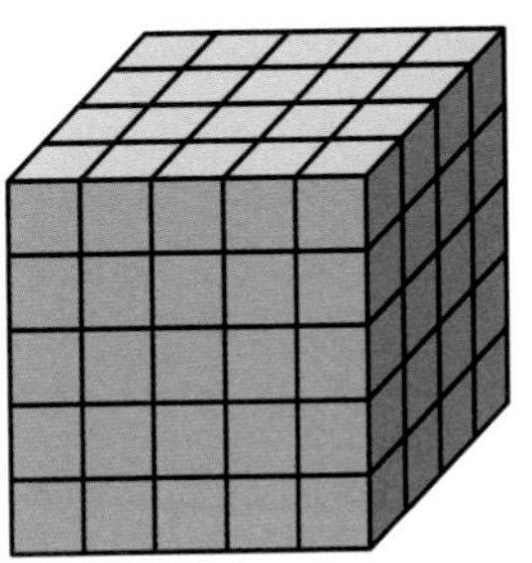

Solve.

23. On the grid at the right, use a straightedge to draw a ten by ten square.

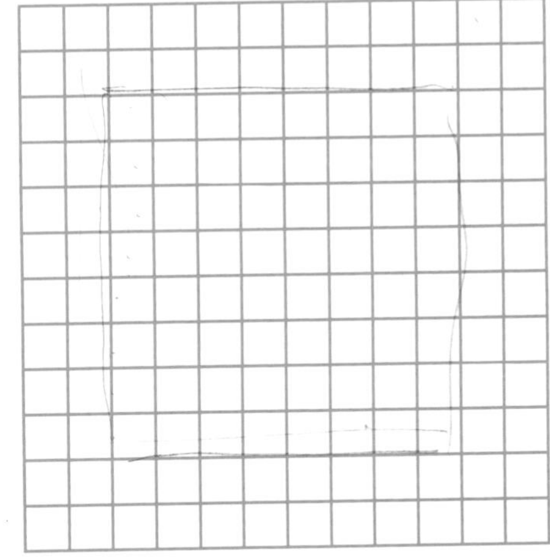

a. What repeated multiplication represents the area of the square?

b. What power represents the area of the square?

c. What is the area of the square?

24. The answer for Exercise 21 is often read as "five squared," and the answer for Exercise 22 is often read as "five cubed." Explain why it makes sense to read the answers in this way.

Write your answers on Activity Workbook page 96.

▶ Matching Parts of Expressions and Figures

Match the terms of each expression to parts of the figure. Then simplify the expression to find the total number of dots or cubes.

25. total: ________ dots

$4^2 + 3^2$ dots

26. total: ________ dots

$7^2 - 2^2$ dots

27. total: ________ cubes

$2^3 + 4^3$ cubes

28. total: ________ cubes

$3 + 3^2 + 3^3$ cubes

Write an expression to represent the shaded area of each figure. Then match terms of the expression to parts of the figure.

29.

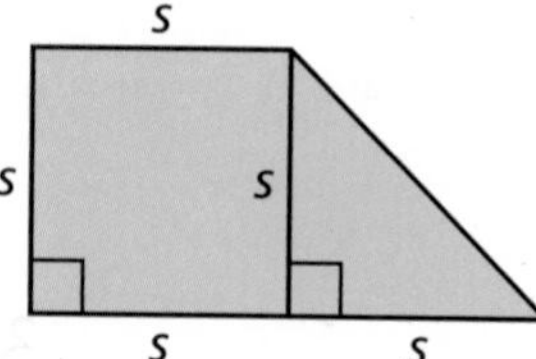

____ + ____ square units

30.

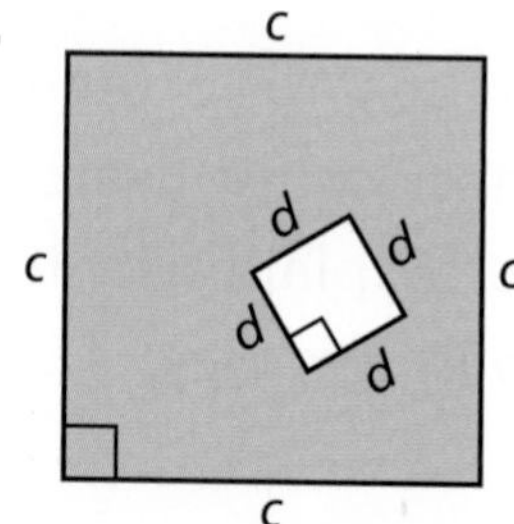

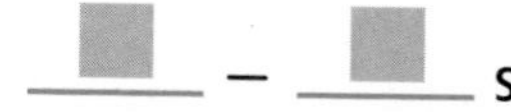

____ − ____ square units

5–3 Class Activity

Write your answers on Activity Workbook page 97.

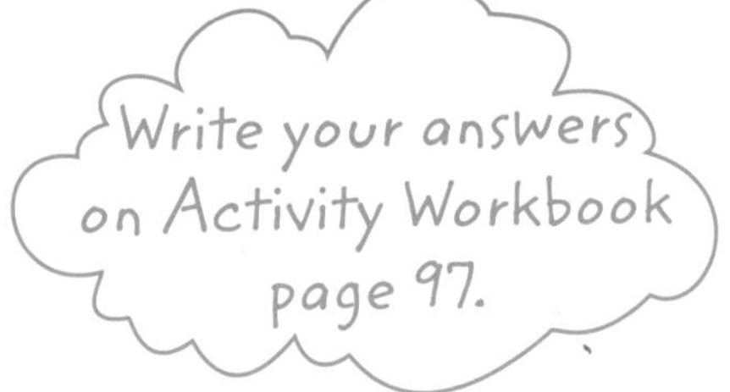

▶ Language of Expressions

Complete the table.

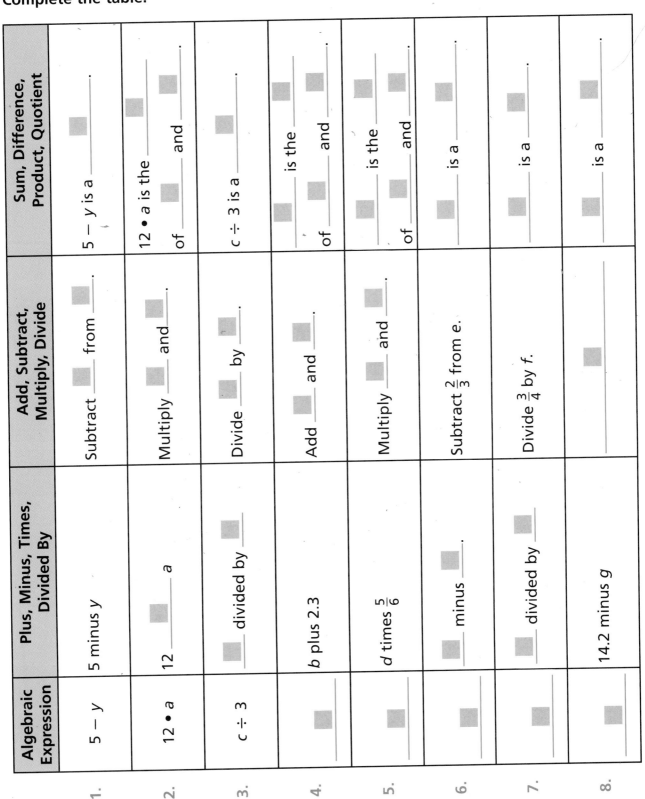

	Algebraic Expression	Plus, Minus, Times, Divided By	Add, Subtract, Multiply, Divide	Sum, Difference, Product, Quotient
1.	$5 - y$	5 minus y	Subtract ___ from ___.	$5 - y$ is a ___.
2.	$12 \bullet a$	12 ___ a	Multiply ___ and ___.	$12 \bullet a$ is the ___ of ___ and ___.
3.	$c \div 3$	___ divided by ___	Divide ___ by ___.	$c \div 3$ is a ___.
4.	___	b plus 2.3	Add ___ and ___.	___ is the ___ of ___ and ___.
5.	___	d times $\frac{5}{6}$	Multiply ___ and ___.	___ is the ___ of ___ and ___.
6.	___	___ minus ___.	Subtract $\frac{2}{3}$ from e.	___ is a ___.
7.	___	___ divided by ___	Divide $\frac{3}{4}$ by f.	___ is a ___.
8.	___	14.2 minus g	___	___ is a ___.

▶ Analyze and Describe

To analyze an expression, we follow the order of operations and circle parts of the expression at each step.

Order of Operations
1. Perform all operations inside parentheses.
2. Simplify powers.
3. Multiply and divide from left to right.
4. Add and subtract from left to right.

Example

Analyze $7 \bullet (a - 5) - a^2$.

Step 1: Look for parts of the expression inside **parentheses**. Circle them.

$7 \bullet (a - 5) - a^2$

Step 2: Look for **powers**. Circle them. (Remember, a power includes the base *and* the exponent.)

$7 \bullet (a - 5) - a^2$

Step 3: Look for **multiplications** and **divisions**, as they appear from left to right. Circle them.

$7 \bullet (a - 5) - a^2$

Step 4: Look for **additions** and **subtractions**, as they appear from left to right. Recall that parts of an expression that are added or subtracted are terms. Circle any terms that are not already circled.

The two terms, $7 \bullet (a - 5)$ and a^2, are already circled.

Once you have analyzed an expression, you can make a simple diagram to show its structure. The diagram for an expression shows the terms and indicates whether each term is a number, variable, product, quotient, or power.

Here is a diagram for $7 \bullet (a - 5) - a^2$.

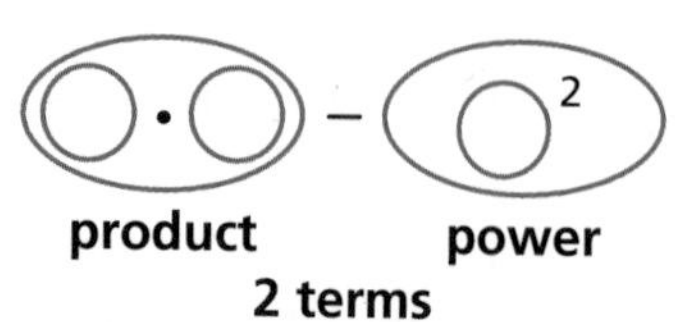

The diagram shows that the expression has two terms and that one term is a product and the other is a power.

▶ Analyze and Describe (continued)

9. Follow the steps to analyze $18 \div 2 + 4 \bullet p^2$.

$18 \div 2 + 4 \bullet p^2$

Step 1: Look for parts of the expression in **parentheses.** Circle them.

Step 2: Look for **powers**. Circle them.

Step 3: Look for **multiplications** and **divisions**, from left to right. Circle them.

Step 4: Look for **additions** and **subtractions**, from left to right. Circle any terms that are not already circled.

10. Below is a diagram for $18 \div 2 + 4 \bullet p^2$. Discuss how it matches the expression in Exercise 9.

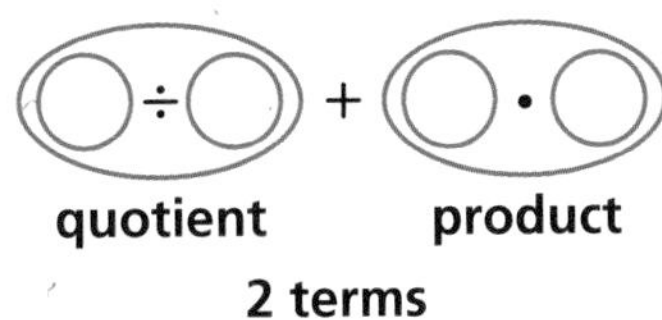

Analyze the expression. Then match the expression with the diagram that describes it.

11. $12 - 4 \bullet (c + 1)$

A. •

product
1 term

12. $7 \bullet 8 - 5 \bullet d$

B. • – •

product product
2 terms

13. $2 \bullet (e - 3 + 9)$

C.

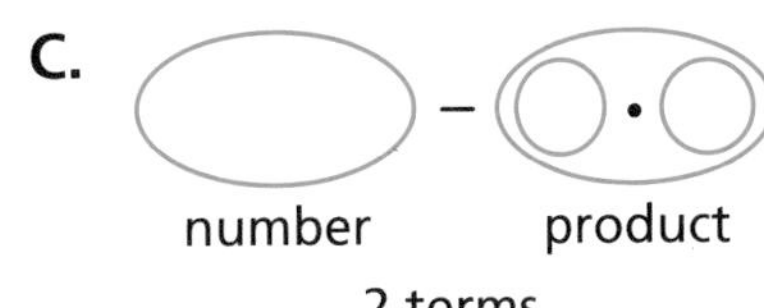

number product
2 terms

Write your answers on Activity Workbook page 99.

▶ Analyze and Describe (continued)

Analyze each expression. Then make a diagram to describe it.

14. $7 + 2 \bullet (a - 3)$

15. $b^2 + 5 \bullet b + 6$

16. $(c - 3) \div 4 + \frac{1}{2} \bullet c^2$

17. $m \bullet (4 + m)$

▶ What's the Error?

Dear Math Students,

Here's how I analyzed $m \bullet (4 + m)$. Did I do it right? If not, help me understand what I did wrong.

Step 1: I circled the part in **parentheses**. $m \bullet (4 + m)$

Step 2: There are no **powers**, so I didn't do anything. $m \bullet (4 + m)$

Step 3: I circled the **multiplication**. $m \bullet (4 + m)$

Step 4: I looked for **addition** and **subtraction** and circled the terms. $m \bullet (4) + (m)$

Your friend,

Puzzled Penguin

18. Write an answer to Puzzled Penguin.

Use Activity Workbook page 100.

▶ Relate Expressions and Models

Analyze each expression. (That is, follow the Order of Operations to circle the parts.) Then match the terms of the expression with parts of the dot diagram.

1. $3 + 2 \bullet 5$

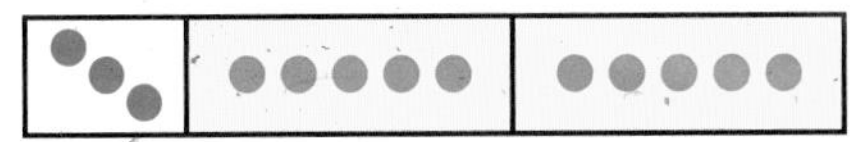

2. $3 + 2 \bullet d$

3. $4 \bullet 5 - 2$

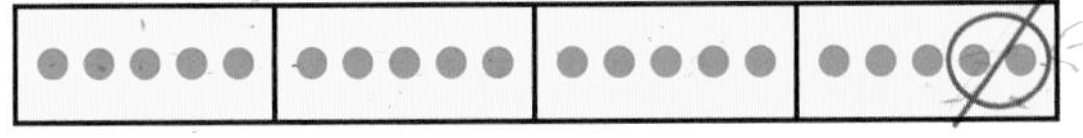

4. $4 \bullet c - 2$

c dots | c dots | c dots | c dots

5. $3 \bullet 5 + 3 + 5 \bullet 2$

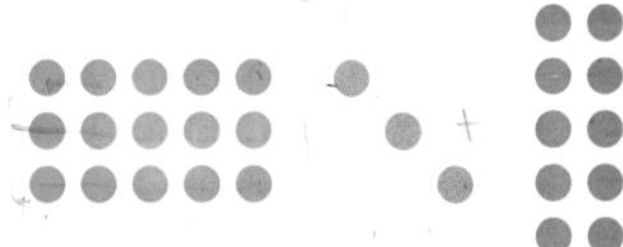

6. $3 + 3 \bullet (4 + 4)$

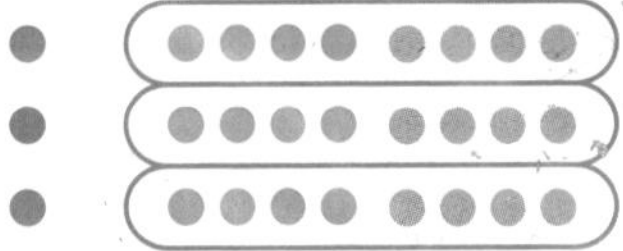

▶ Simplify Expressions

To simply an expression, first analyze it. Then perform the operations for each term from the *inside out*. Finally, combine the terms. For example, here is how you would simplify the expression in Exercise 6.

$3 + 3 \bullet (4 + 4) =$	Analyze the expression.
$3 + 3 \bullet 8 =$	Compute the inside part of the second term.
$3 + 24 =$	Compute the outside part of the second term.
27	Combine terms.

You analyzed the expressions below in Exercises 1 and 5.
Use your analysis to help you simplify each expression.
Compare your answer to numbers of dots in Exercises 1 and 5.

7. $3 + 2 \bullet 5$

8. $3 \bullet 5 + 3 + 5 \bullet 2$

▶ Match Models to Expressions

Put a check next to the expressions that tell the number of dots in the diagram. Look for more than one expression for each dot diagram.

9. 

$(5 + 3) \cdot 7$

$5 + (3 \cdot 7)$

$3 \cdot (7 + 5)$

$5 + 3 \cdot 7$

10. 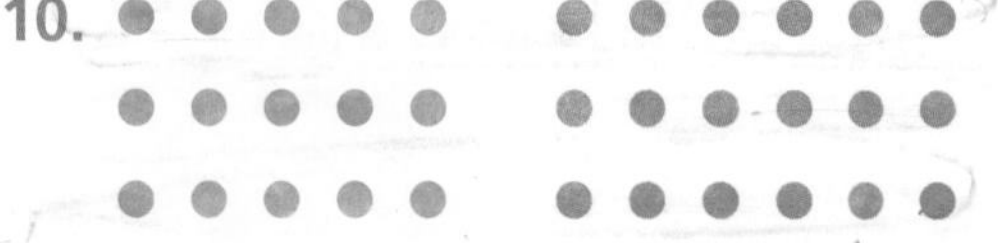

$3 \cdot (5 + 6)$

$3 \cdot 5 + 6$

$3 \cdot 5 + 3 \cdot 6$

$(3 \cdot 5) + 6$

11.

a dots	a dots	a dots	a dots	
●● · · · ●	●● · · · ●	●● · · · ●	●● · · · ●	● ●

$4 + a + 2$

$a + a + a + a + 2$

$4 \cdot a + 2$

12. 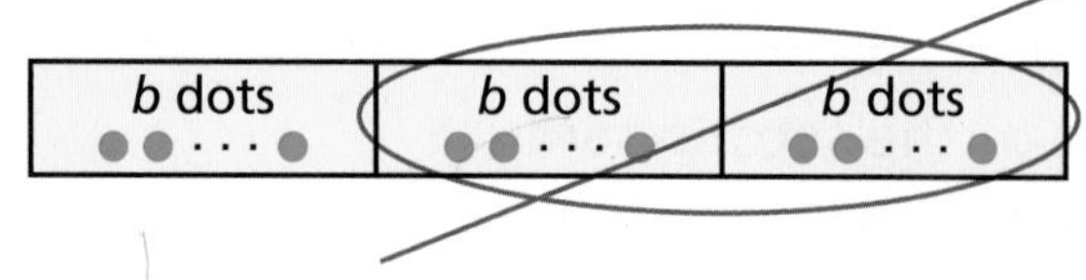

$3 \cdot b - 2$

$3 \cdot b - 2 \cdot b$

$b + b + b - b - b$

▶ Write and Simplify Expressions

Write an expression for the number of dots. Then, analyze the expression and simplify it. (Simplify terms from the *inside out*. Then combine the terms.)

13. 

Write an expression and analyze it.

Simplify the expression.

14. 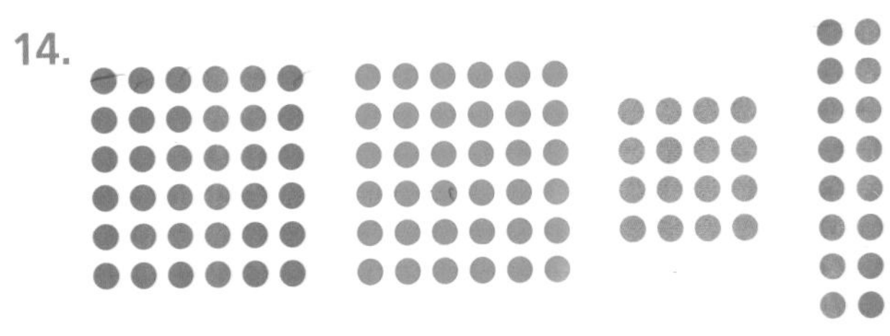

Write an expression and analyze it.

Simplify the expression.

15. 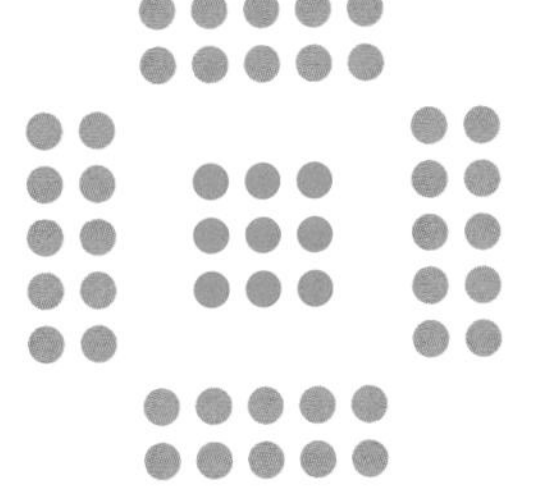

Write an expression and analyze it.

Simplify the expression.

16. 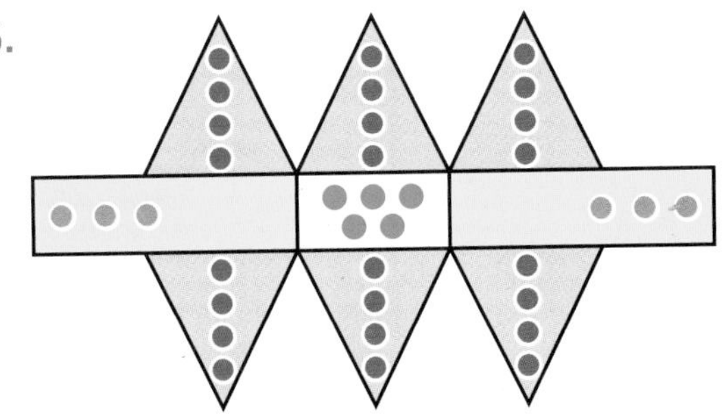

Write an expression and analyze it.

Simplify the expression.

▶ Write and Evaluate Expressions

17.

d dots	*d* dots	*d* dots	●●

Write an expression and analyze it.

Evaluate the expression for $d = 7$.

18.

a dots, *a* dots, *a* dots
b dots | ●●●●● | *b* dots
a dots, *a* dots, *a* dots

Write an expression and analyze it.

Evaluate the expression for $a = 2$ and $b = 7$.

▶ What's the Error?

Dear Math Students,

I tried to simplify $3 + 4 \cdot 5$. I added $3 + 4$ and got 7. Then I multiplied that by 5 and got 35. My teacher said this is not correct. What did I do wrong?

Please make a dot diagram to help me understand how to simplify the expression $3 + 4 \cdot 5$.

Your Friend,

Puzzled Penguin

19. Write a response to Puzzled Penguin.

Write your answers
on Activity Workbook
page 102.

▶ Area of a Floor Plan

The figures below show a floor plan for a room. Keiko, Alex, and DeShun each found a different expression for the area of the room.

Analyze the expressions. Then discuss with your partner how the student might have thought about the area. Describe how the parts of the expression relate to the diagram.

1. 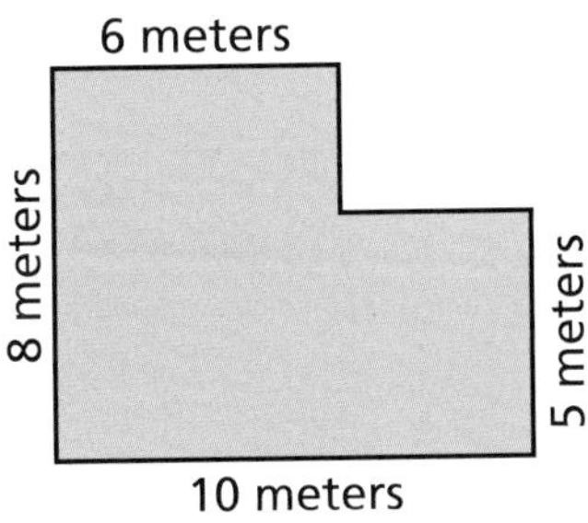

Keiko's expression: $5 \bullet 10 + 3 \bullet 6 \text{ m}^2$

2. 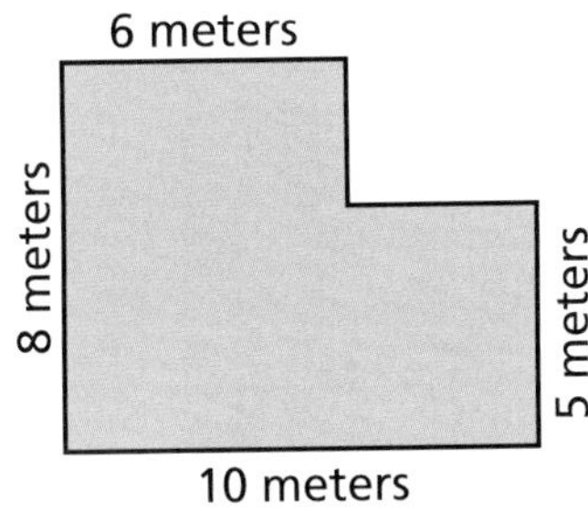

Alex's expression: $8 \bullet 6 + 4 \bullet 5 \text{ m}^2$

3. 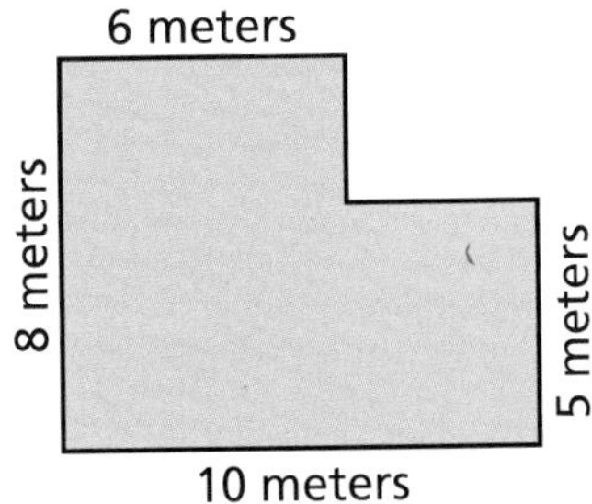

DeShun's expression: $8 \bullet 10 - 3 \bullet 4 \text{ m}^2$

▶ Find Surface Area Using a Net

Below is a net for a rectangular prism with a height of 5 centimeters and a base that measures 4 centimeters by 3 centimeters. Visualize what the prism would look like.

4. Write an expression for the surface area of the prism, using only the numbers 3, 4, and 5. Show your expression to another student, and explain how the terms of the expression match parts of the net.

5. Simplify your expression.

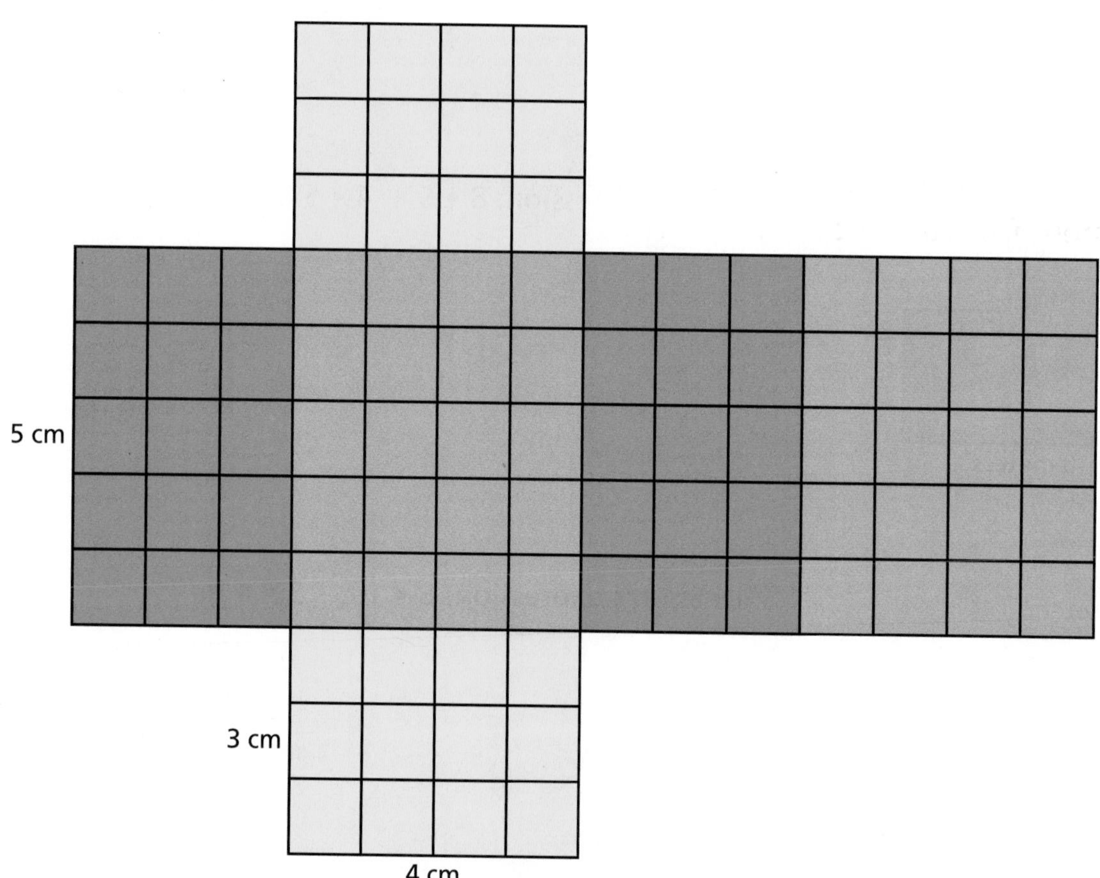

▶ Write an Algebraic Expression for Surface Area

Visualize nets for rectangular prisms with heights of z centimeters and bases that measure x centimeters by y centimeters. These prisms might be short and wide or tall and narrow or any shape in between. Here are a few examples:

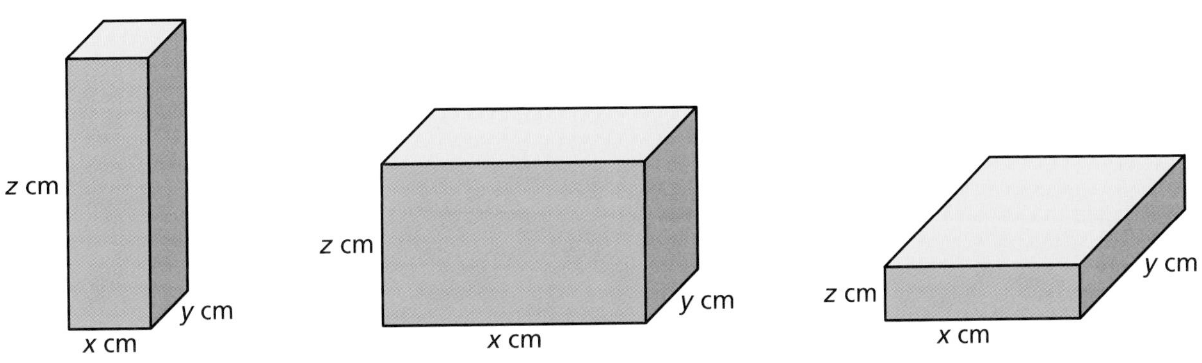

Think about how the nets for these prisms would be similar to and different from the net on the previous page.

6. Sketch and label a net for one of the prisms above.

7. Write an expression for the surface area of a prism with an x centimeter by y centimeter base and a height of z centimeters.

▶ Different Ways to Express Area

8. A construction company builds 5-foot-wide walkways around square gardens of different sizes. Write an expression for the area of a walkway around a g foot by g foot square garden.

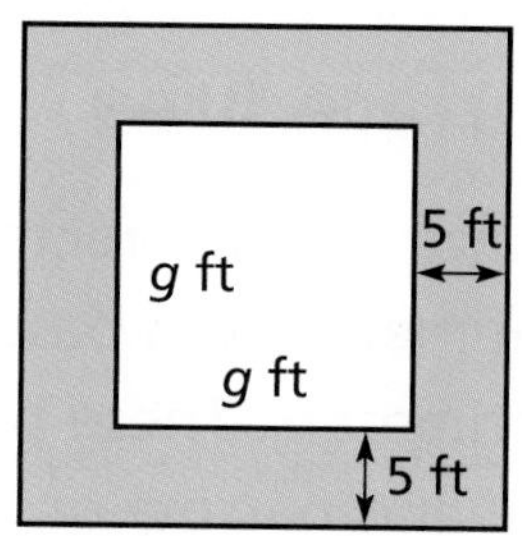

9. Each small square in the diagram at the right is 1 square unit. Write an expression for the total area of the blue part of the diagram.

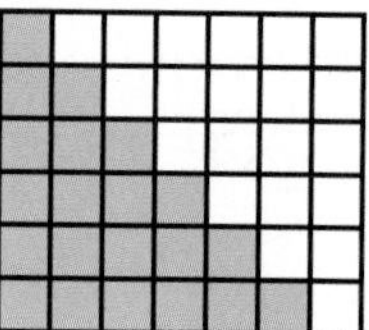

Marla, José, and Sue each wrote a different expression for the blue area in Exercise 9.

Marla's expression: $1 + 2 + 3 + 4 + 5 + 6$

José's expression: $(6 \bullet 7) \div 2$

Sue's expression: $\frac{1}{2} \bullet (6 \bullet 7)$

10. How do you think each student found his or her expression? Are all the expressions correct?

11. Simplify each student's expression.

12. Whose expression was easiest to simplify?

Write your answers on Activity Workbook page 103.

Vocabulary

equivalent expressions

▶ Introduce Equivalent Expressions

Equivalent expressions always have the same value.

$a + 2 + 3$ and $a + 5$ are equivalent expressions because $a + 2 + 3 = a + 5$ for all values of a.

$a + 5$ and $3 + 4$ are *not* equivalent expressions because $a + 5 = 3 + 4$ *only* when a is 2.

As you learned in Unit 2, the multiplication symbol can be dropped as long as it is not between two numbers.

$3c$ means $3 \bullet c$ ab means $a \bullet b$ $4(p + 6)$ means $4 \bullet (p + 6)$

Complete the table.

	Situation and Diagram	With +		With •		Without •
	Example A Three identical packages weigh $\frac{1}{5}$ gram each. [$\frac{1}{5}$ | $\frac{1}{5}$ | $\frac{1}{5}$]	$\frac{1}{5} + \frac{1}{5} + \frac{1}{5}$	=	$3 \bullet \frac{1}{5}$	=	$\frac{3}{5}$
	Example B Three identical packages weigh a grams each. [a | a | a]	$a + a + a$	=	$3 \bullet a$	=	$3a$
1.	Two boxes hold b books each. [b | b]		=		=	
2.	Four bags hold c peaches each.		=	$4 \bullet c$	=	
3.		$d + d + d + d + d$	=		=	

▶ Use Algebra Tiles to Model Expressions

Write the expression that the model represents.

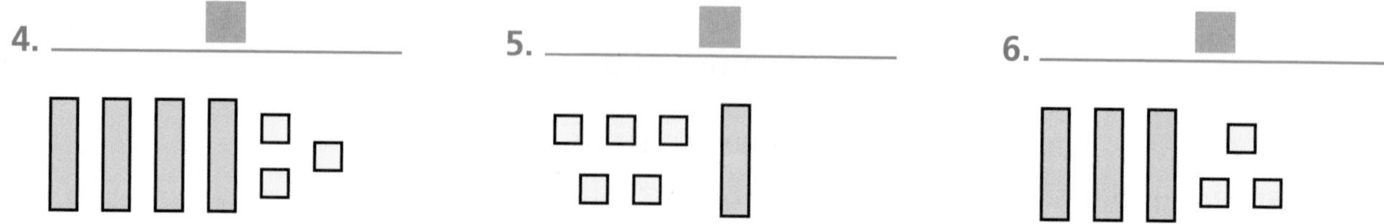

Use your algebra tiles to model each expression. Make a quick drawing of your model.

7. $x + 6$

8. $4x + 1$

9. $3 + 2x$

10. Make a quick drawing of algebra tiles to help you explain why $5x - x$ is not equivalent to 5.

11. Make a quick drawing of algebra tiles to help you explain why $3x + 3$ is not equivalent to $6x$.

▶ Use Diagrams to Model Expressions

Drawing diagrams and thinking about real world situations can help you find equivalent expressions and understand why expressions are *not* equivalent.

Example 1	**Example 2**
Consider the expression $3a - 3$.	Consider the expression $4b - b$.
Situation: Three boxes each contain *a* apples. William takes three of the apples.	**Situation:** Hannah has four stamp albums with *b* stamps each. She gives one album away.
Diagram 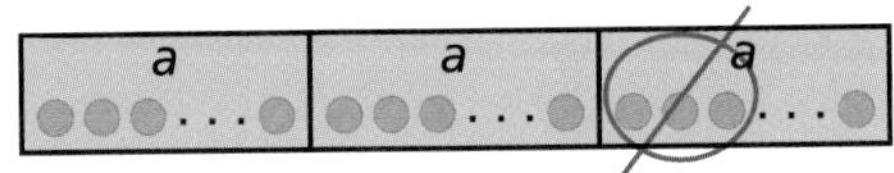	**Diagram** 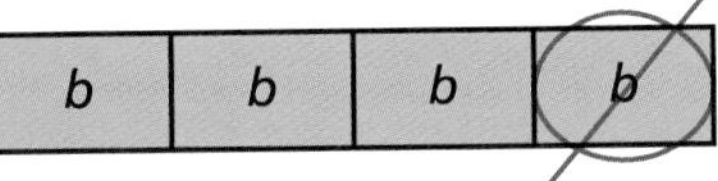
Equivalent expressions: $3a - 3 = 2a + (a - 3)$ $= a + a + a - 3$	**Equivalent expressions:** $4b - b = b + b + b + b - b$ $= 4b - 1b$ $= 3b$
Non-equivalent expression: $3a - 3$ is *not* equivalent to *a*.	**Non-equivalent expression:** $4b - b$ is *not* equivalent to 4.

For each expression, describe a situation and make a diagram. Then circle the equivalent expression(s).

12. $4 + 3d$

Situation:

Diagram

Circle the equivalent expression(s).

$7d$ $\quad$ $4 + 2d + d$ $\quad$ $4 + d + d + d$

13. $2e + e$

Situation:

Diagram

Circle the equivalent expression(s).

$(e + e) + e$ $\quad$ $2 + e + e$ $\quad$ $3e$

Use Activity Workbook page 105.

▶Use Diagrams to Model Expressions (continued)

For each expression, describe a situation and make a diagram. Then circle the equivalent expression(s).

14. $5 + 1 + 2c$

Situation:

Diagram

Circle the equivalent expression(s).

$6 + (2 \bullet c)$ $8c$

$6 + c + c$ $6 + 2c$

15. $3g + 3 + 3$

Situation:

Diagram

Circle the equivalent expression(s):

$9g$ $3g + 6$ $g + g + g + 6$

Think about how the situation and diagram model the expression. Then circle the equivalent expressions.

16. $\frac{1}{3}f$

Situation: One third of the f students at a school take Spanish.

Diagram

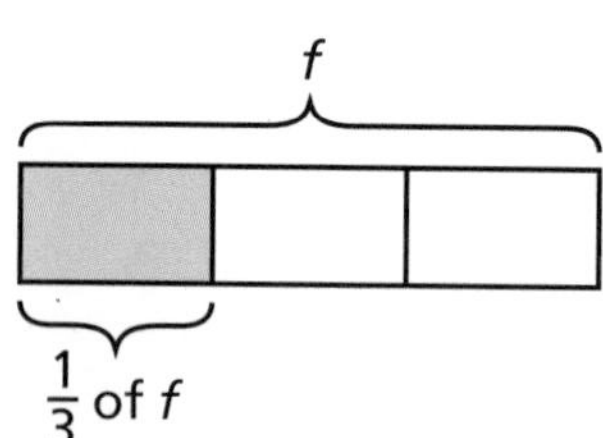

Circle the equivalent expression(s).

$\frac{f}{3}$ $3f$ $f \div 3$

17. $2f + 2 + 1$

Situation: Rachel bought two boxes of f golf balls. She also found 2 golf balls in her car and 1 in her golf bag.

Diagram

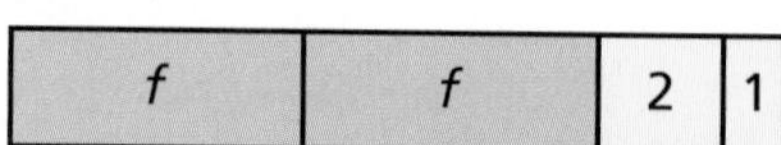

Circle the equivalent expression(s).

$5f$ $2f + 3$ $f + f + 3$

Write your answers on Activity Workbook page 106.

▶ Modeling with Expressions and Diagrams

Make a diagram for each situation and write two equivalent expressions for the total.

18. There were 200 children already at summer camp. Then three buses arrived with g children each.

Diagram

Expressions

________ = ________

19. A restaurant received a shipment of five crates of glasses with g glasses in each crate. The manager dropped one crate, breaking all of the glasses inside of it.

Diagram

Expressions

________ = ________

20. Describe a situation for this diagram, and then write two equivalent expressions.

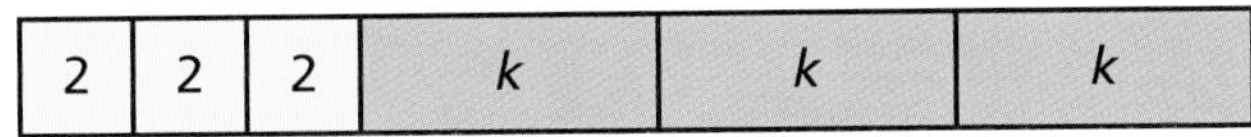

Situation

Expressions

________ = ________

▶ What's the Error?

Dear Math Students,

I just had a math quiz about equivalent expressions. Here are two problems I got wrong:

$4x + 3 = 7x$ $\quad\quad$ $7x - x = 7$

Can you explain why my answers are not right and help me find correct equivalent expressions?

It might help me understand if you use a model or make up a situation.

Your Friend,

Puzzled Penguin

21. Write a response to Puzzled Penguin.

▶ Practice

Write an equivalent expression with fewer terms if possible. Make quick drawings or use tiles if you need to.

22. $6m - m = $ ▒

23. $8 + 3t = $ ▒

24. $7w - 7 = $ ▒

25. $4s + 4s = $ ▒

Vocabulary

Associative Property of Addition
Commutative Property of Addition

▶ Properties of Addition

For each example, discuss how the situation, diagram, and expressions are related.

Example 1

Situation

Joey earned a dollars in the morning and b dollars in the afternoon.

Arianna earned b dollars in the morning and a dollars in the afternoon

Diagram

Joey: | a | b |

Arianna: | b | a |

Equivalent Expressions

$a + b$

$b + a$

The bars are the same length, and the expressions are equivalent.

Example 2

Situation

Clare earned a dollars and another b dollars in the morning. She earned c dollars in the afternoon.

Matteo earned a dollars in the morning. He earned b dollars and another c dollars in the afternoon.

Diagram

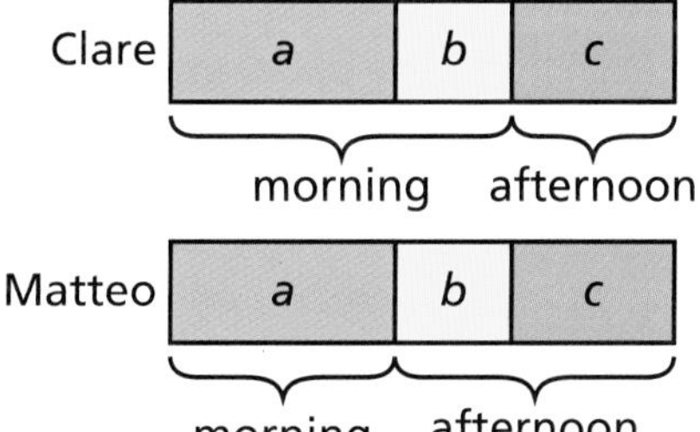

Equivalent Expressions

$(a + b) + c$

$a + (b + c)$

The bars are the same length, and the expressions are equivalent.

The examples above illustrate two important properties of addition.

Commutative Property of Addition	Associative Property of Addition
For any numbers a and b, $a + b = b + a$. For example, $5 + 2 = 2 + 5$.	For any numbers a, b, and c, $(a + b) + c = a + (b + c)$. For example, $(3 + 4) + 1 = 3 + (4 + 1)$.

Write your answers on Activity Workbook page 107.

▶ Combine Terms with Algebra Tiles

Model each expression with algebra tiles. Then rearrange the tiles to model an equivalent expression with fewer terms. Write the new expressions. Make quick drawings to record your work.

1. $6 + 2x + 1 + x = \square$

Model of Original Expression

Model of Rearranged Expression

2. $3x + 1 + 1 + 2x = \square$

Model of Original Expression

Model of Rearranged Expression

3. $x + 2 + x + 4 + x = \square$

Model of Original Expression

Model of Rearranged Expression

Vocabulary

like terms
simplify

▶ Simplify by Combining Like Terms

Like terms are terms with the same variables raised to the same power. (Number terms are like terms, even though they do not have variables.)

In $6 + 2x + x^2 + 1 + x$, 6 and 1 are like terms and $2x$ and x are like terms.

You can **simplify** an expression—that is, make it shorter and simpler—by combining like terms.

Example 1	**Example 2**
Simplify $2a + 3 + a + 4$ by using a diagram. **Step 1:** Model the expression. | a | a | 3 | a | 4 | **Step 2:** Rearrange the model so the *a* pieces are combined and the number pieces are combined. | a | a | a | 3 | 4 | **Step 3:** Write an expression for the new model. $3a + 7$	Simplify $2a + 3 + a + 4$ by using properties. $2a + 3 + a + 4 = 2a + a + 3 + 4$ (1) $= (2a + a) + (3 + 4)$ (2) $= 3a + 7$ (3) **Step 1:** Use the Commutative Property to swap *a* and 3 and get like terms next to each other. **Step 2:** Use the Associative Property to group the terms. **Step 3:** Combine like terms.

4. Use the diagram to help you combine like terms.

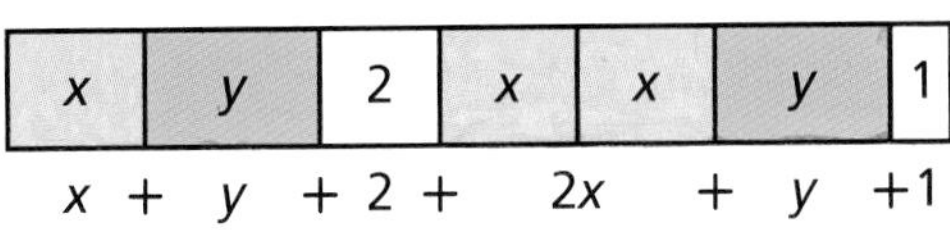

$x + y + 2 + 2x + y + 1 =$ ▢

Simplify each expression by combining like terms.

5. $3x + 4 + 2x + 1 =$ ▢

6. $d + 2e + 3 + e + 2 + 3d =$ ▢

7. $y + 7 + 4y + 3 =$ ▢

8. $1 + x + y + 3 + 2y =$ ▢

Vocabulary

Associative Property of Multiplication
Commutative Property of Multiplication

▶ Properties of Multiplication

For each example, discuss how the situation, the diagram, and the expressions are related.

Example 1

Situation	Diagram	Equivalent Expressions
A rectangle has side lengths a cm and b cm. If the a-cm side is the base, then the area is $a \cdot b$ cm^2. If the b-cm side is the base, then the area is $b \cdot a$ cm^2.	b cm, a cm; a cm, b cm	$a \cdot b$ $b \cdot a$

Example 2

Situation	Diagram	Equivalent Expressions
There are a trucks. There are b boxes in each truck. There are c soccer balls in each box. Here are two ways to find the total number of soccer balls: number of boxes • number of balls in each box number of trucks • number of balls in each truck	b boxes in each truck; c soccer balls in each box; a trucks	$(a \cdot b) \cdot c$ $a \cdot (b \cdot c)$

The examples illustrate two important properties of multiplication.

Commutative Property of Multiplication	Associative Property of Multiplication
For any numbers a and b, $a \cdot b = b \cdot a$. For example, $4 \cdot 7 = 7 \cdot 4$.	For any numbers a, b, and c, $(a \cdot b) \cdot c = a \cdot (b \cdot c)$. For example, $(6 \cdot 2) \cdot 5 = 6 \cdot (2 \cdot 5)$.

5–7
Class Activity

Vocabulary
coefficient

▶ Identifying Coefficients

When a term is a number times a variable or a number times a product of variables, we call the number the **coefficient** of the term. In each example below, the coefficient is shown in blue.

$3a$ $7x^2$ $8xy$ s^3 (hidden coefficient of 1)

In algebra, we usually write the coefficient in the front of a term. If a term is not in this form, you can use the Commutative and Associative Properties of Multiplication to rewrite it.

Example 1		**Example 2**	
Rewrite $(4x)5$ so the coefficient is in the front of the term.		Rewrite $(6x)(3x)$ so the coefficient is in the front of the term.	
$(4x)5 = (4 \bullet x) \bullet 5$		$(6x)(3x) = (6 \bullet x) \bullet (3 \bullet x)$	
$= 4 \bullet (x \bullet 5)$	Assoc. Prop.	$= 6 \bullet (x \bullet 3) \bullet x$	Assoc. Prop.
$= 4 \bullet (5 \bullet x)$	Comm. Prop.	$= 6 \bullet (3 \bullet x) \bullet x$	Comm. Prop.
$= (4 \bullet 5) \bullet x$	Assoc. Prop.	$= (6 \bullet 3) \bullet (x \bullet x)$	Assoc. Prop.
$= 20x$		$= 18x^2$	
The coefficient is 20.		The coefficient is 18.	

Rewrite the term so the coefficient is in front.

9. $(2y)8 =$ ____

coefficient: ____

10. $7(8a) =$ ____

coefficient: ____

11. $\frac{1}{2}(\frac{3}{4}b) =$ ____

coefficient: ____

12. $(\frac{2}{3}c)\frac{4}{5} =$ ____

coefficient: ____

13. $(2a)(3b) =$ ____

coefficient: ____

14. $2(3x)(4x) =$ ____

coefficient: ____

▶ Simplify Expressions

You can use all the properties you have learned in this lesson to simplify expressions. Simplifying an expression can include writing the terms with the coefficients in front, combining like terms, and doing all possible computations.

Example

Simplify $2(3x) + 4 + (5x)4 + 1$.

$2(3x) + 4 + (5x)4 + 1 = 6x + 4 + 20x + 1$	Rewrite terms with coefficients in front.
$= 6x + 20x + 4 + 1$	Put like terms together.
$= 26x + 5$	Combine like terms.

Simplify each expression.

15. $2x + 5(6x) + 1 =$ ▒

16. $2(8x) + 3 + 4(2x) + 4 =$ ▒

▶ What's the Error?

Dear Math Students:

I had to simplify this expression on my homework.

$$5 + 3(2x) + 4x(2) + 2^2$$

I didn't see any like terms, so I just left this like it is. I got the problem marked wrong. Please help me understand what to do.

Your friend,

Puzzled Penguin

17. Write a response to Puzzled Penguin.

▶ Examples of the Distributive Property

Discuss what the examples have in common.

<table>
<tr><td>Example 1

Qing said, "If I forget what 7 • 8 is, I can think of it as 5 eights plus 2 eights."

5 eights + 2 eights = 7 eights
40 + 16 = 56</td><td>Example 2
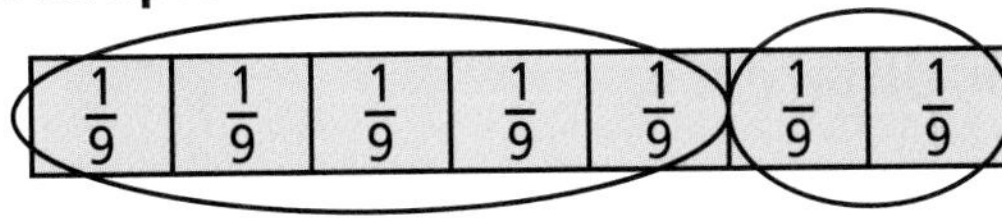

$\frac{5}{9} + \frac{2}{9} = \frac{7}{9}$</td></tr>
<tr><td>Example 3

5 boxes with c books in each box plus 2 boxes with c books in each box make 5 + 2, or 7, boxes with c books in each box.</td><td>Example 4
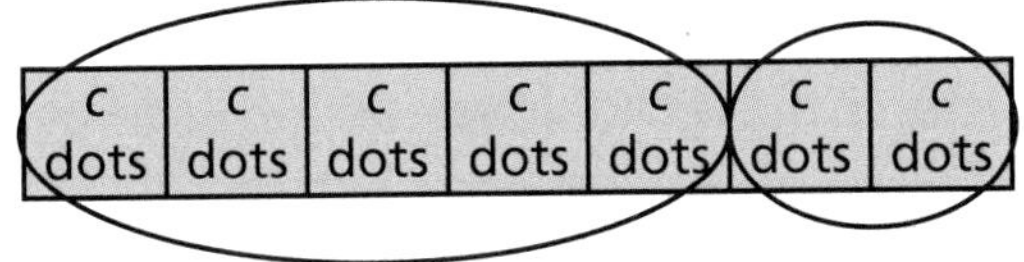

$5c + 2c = (5 + 2)c$</td></tr>
<tr><td>Example 5

a boxes with c books in each box plus b boxes with c books in each box make (a + b) boxes with c books in each box.</td><td>Example 6

a c's plus b more c's make (a + b) c's.

$ac + bc = (a + b)c$</td></tr>
<tr><td colspan="2">Example 7

Mariah said, "The area of the big rectangle is the sum of the areas of the smaller rectangles."

Dave said, "The area of the big rectangle is its base times its height."

Mariah said, "That means $ac + bc = (a + b)c$."
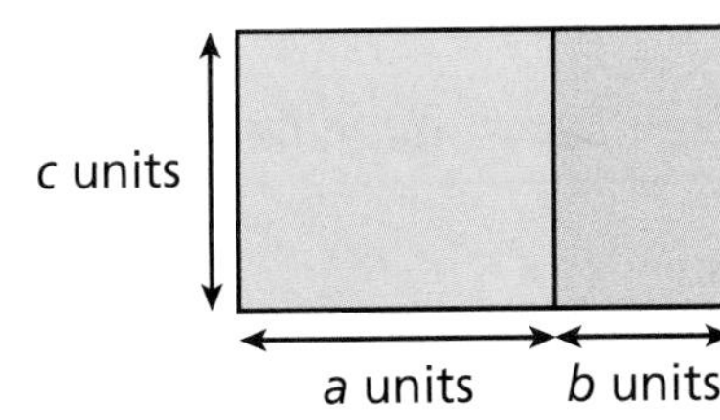
</td></tr>
</table>

1. In Example 7, explain why $ac + bc = (a + b)c$.

Write your answers on Activity Workbook page 108.

Vocabulary

Distributive Property

▶ Two Ways to Use the Distributive Property

The **Distributive Property** gives us two opposite ways to transform expressions into equivalent expressions.

- We can distribute a factor to the terms of a sum or difference.

  $(5 + 2)c = 5c + 2c$ c is distributed to 5 and 2.

- We can pull out a common factor from the terms of a sum or difference.

  $5c + 2c = (5 + 2)c$ c is pulled out of $5c$ and $2c$.

Use the completed rows as a guide to help you fill in the blanks. Draw arrows to show how a factor is pulled out or distributed.

	Distributing	Pulling Out a Common Factor
2.	$(a + b)c = ac + bc$	$ac + bc = (a + b)c$
3.	$(2 + 3)x =$ ▢	$2x + 3x =$ ▢
4.	$(y + 2)x =$ ▢	$yx + 2x =$ ▢
5.	$(a - b)c = ac - bc$	$ac - bc = (a - b)c$
6.	$(x - 3) \bullet 7 =$ ▢	$x \bullet 7 - 3 \bullet 7 =$ ▢
7.	$(7 - 2)x =$ ▢	$7x - 2x =$ ▢
8.	$d(e + f) = de + df$	$de + df =$ ▢
9.	$5(x + 2) =$ ▢	$5x + 5 \bullet 2 =$ ▢
10.	$6(3 + y) =$ ▢	$6 \bullet 3 + 6y =$ ▢
11.	$d(e - f) = de - df$	$de - df =$ ▢
12.	$x(y - 4) =$ ▢	$xy - x \bullet 4 =$ ▢
13.	$4(x - y) =$ ▢	$4x - 4y =$ ▢

▶ Writing Equivalent Expressions

Sometimes you can apply the Distributive Property to part of an expression to write an equivalent expression.

<table>
<tr>
<td>

Example 1

Consider $3 + 2(a + b)$. We can apply the Distributive Property to $2(a + b)$.

$$3 + 2(a + b) = 3 + 2a + 2b$$

We can model this with diagrams.

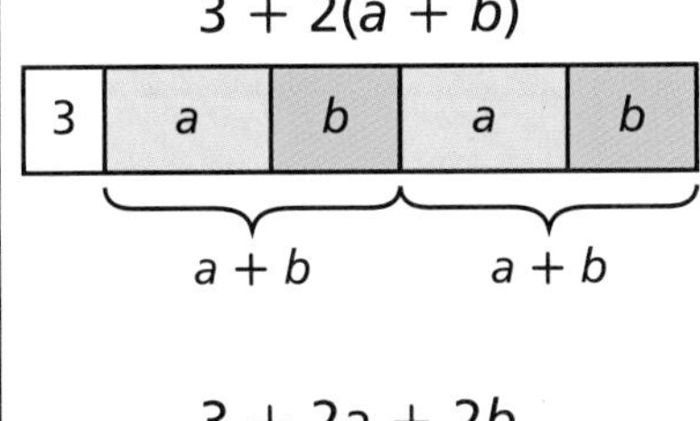

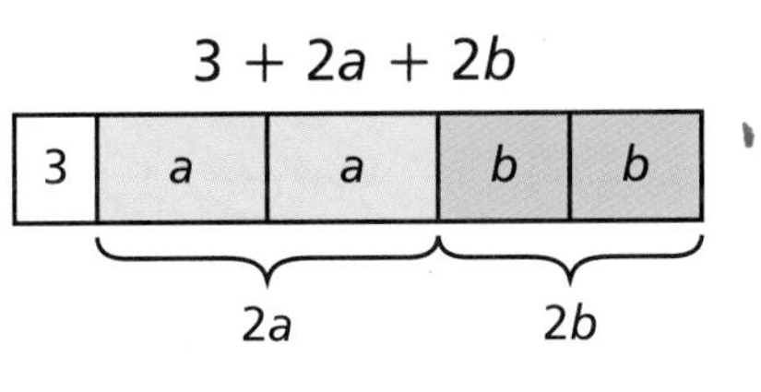

</td>
<td>

Example 2

Consider $3a + 2a + b$. We can apply the Distributive Property to $3a + 2a$.

$$3a + 2a + b = (3 + 2)a + b$$
$$= 5a + b$$

We can model this with diagrams.

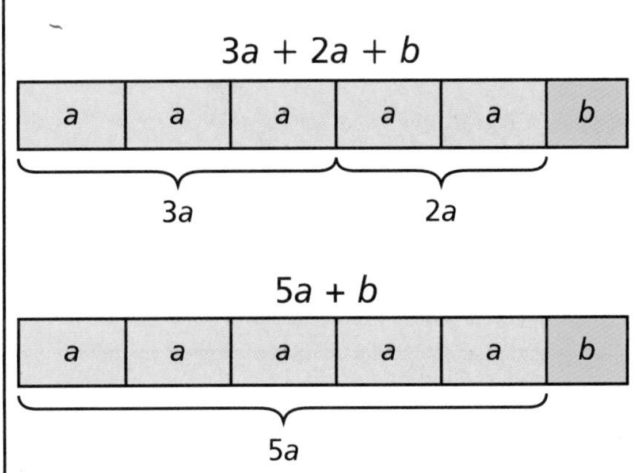

</td>
</tr>
</table>

14. Look at Example 1. Use the diagram to help you find a third expression that is equivalent to $3 + 2(a + b)$ and $3 + 2a + 2b$.

Apply the Distributive Property to part of each expression to write an equivalent expression. Model the equivalent expressions with diagrams.

15. $3(c + d) + 6 =$ ▢

16. $7 + 2e + 2f =$ ▢

5–8
Class Activity

Vocabulary

greatest common factor

▶ Are They Equivalent?

Tell whether the expressions are equivalent.

17. $5 + 3(a + b)$ and $5 + 3a + b$

18. $5 + 3(a + b)$ and $5 + 3a + 3b$

19. $4 + (2c + 1)$ and $(4 + 2)c + 1$

20. $4 + (2c + 1)$ and $4 + 2c + 1$

21. $3 + 2f + 4$ and $2f + 7$

22. $3 + 2f + 4$ and $5f + 4$

▶ The Greatest Common Factor (GCF)

The **greatest common factor (GCF)** of two or more numbers is the greatest number that is a factor of all the numbers.

Example

The factors of 48 are 1, 2, 3, 4, 6, 8, 12, 16, 24, and 48.
The factors of 32 are 1, 2, 4, 8, 16, and 32.

16 is the greatest number that is a factor of both numbers.
So, 16 is the GCF of 48 and 32.

Find the greatest common factor of the numbers.

23. 12 and 15

24. 24 and 36

25. 21 and 26

26. 42 and 56

27. 30 and 48

28. 30, 45, and 75

▶ Use the GCF and the Distributive Property

Write each sum or difference as a product by using the Distributive Property to pull out the greatest common factor. Show all your steps.

29. $63 + 36 = 9 \cdot 7 + 9 \cdot 6 =$ ▒

30. $63 - 56 =$ ▒ • ▒ – ▒ • ▒ = ▒

31. $7x + 35 =$ ▒ • ▒ + ▒ • ▒ = ▒

32. $24x + 18y =$ ▒ • ▒ – ▒ • ▒ = ▒

▶ Simplify and Evaluate Expressions

Simplify. Follow the Order of Operations.

1. $16 \div 2 + 6 \bullet 3$
2. $7(5 + 4)$
3. $3 + 3^2$
4. $3^2 - 2^3$
5. $11 + 4 \div 2 + 6^2$
6. $48 - 4^2 \div (6 - 2)$

Evaluate each expression for $x = 3$ and $y = 5$.

7. $4x - 6$
8. $15 \div (y - 4)$
9. $10y + x^2$
10. $4y + 2(x + 2)$
11. $(x + y)^2$
12. $y + 2 \bullet x^2$

13. Write two equivalent expressions to represent the number of dots in the drawing below.

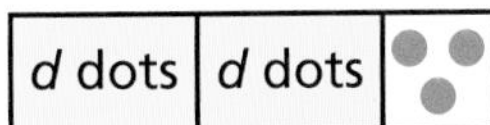

Evaluate one of your expressions for $d = 12$.

_______ dots

14. Write two equivalent expressions to represent the number of dots in the drawing below.

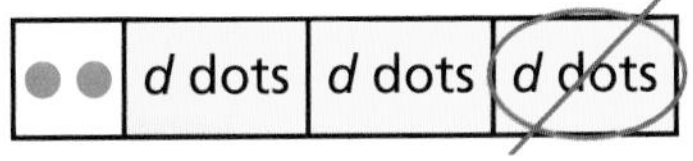

Evaluate one of your expressions for $d = 9$.

_______ dots

Use Activity Workbook page 109.

▶ Connect Expressions, Diagrams, and Situations

For each expression, describe a situation and make a diagram. Then circle the equivalent expression(s).

15. $4x + 2$

Situation:

Diagram

Circle the equivalent expression(s).

$6x$ $x + x + x + x + 2$ $6 + x$

16. $2m - 1$

Situation:

Diagram

Circle the equivalent expression(s).

$m + m - 1$ m $2(m - 1)$

17. At a restaurant, Maria and Sam each paid d dollars for their food, and each left $3 for the tip.

Draw a diagram to represent the total amount Maria and Sam paid.

Write three different, equivalent expressions to represent this situation.

▶ Expressions for Real World Situations

18. Fatima made m batches of 12 muffins. Her children ate 5 of the muffins.

    Write an expression for the number of muffins that were left.

    Evaluate your expression when $m = 4$.

    _______ muffins

19. Rebecca had $47 in her savings account at the beginning of the year. Then she added $6 a week for the next w weeks.

    Write an expression for the number of dollars in Rebecca's account after the w weeks.

    Evaluate your expression when $w = 20$.

    _______ dollars

20. Dale had a square piece of paper with sides 6 inches long. He cut out a square with a side length of s inches.

    Write an expression for the area of the paper that was left.

    Evaluate your expression when $s = 3$.

    _______ square inches

▶ Properties and Equivalent Expressions

Tell whether the expressions are equivalent.

21. $(3x)(3y)$ and $3xy$

22. $6b + b$ and $7b$

23. $4m - 4$ and m

24. $5(a + b)$ and $5a + b$

Simplify each expression. Be sure to do the following:

- **Do all the computations you can.**
- **Write each term with the coefficient in front.**
- **Combine like terms.**

25. $6 + 4x + 2(7x) + 1 =$ ▒

26. $m + 2n + m + 3n =$ ▒

27. $3y \cdot 3 + 4^2 + y + 5 \cdot 2 =$ ▒

28. $x + 2x + 3x + (7 - 1)^2 =$ ▒

Use the Distributive Property to write an equivalent expression.

29. $5x - 15$

30. $ab + ac$

31. $(7 - p)2$

32. $y(4 + y)$

33. $x^2 - 10x$

34. $r(p + 3)$

Write each sum as a product by using the Distributive Property to pull out the greatest common factor. Show all your steps.

Example: $24 + 32 = 8 \cdot 3 + 8 \cdot 4 = 8(3 + 4) = 8 \cdot 7$

35. $42 + 35 =$ ____ • ____ + ____ • ____ = ____ = ____

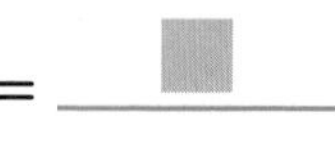

36. $36 + 48 =$ ____ • ____ + ____ • ____ = ____ = ____

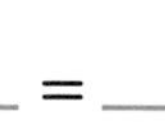

Vocabulary

double number line

▶ Quantities That Vary Together

If you buy potato salad at a deli, your cost is related to the amount you buy. The more you buy, the greater your cost. The amount and the cost *vary together*. In other words, as the amount of potato salad changes, the cost changes.

We can use these variables to represent this relationship:

Let p be the number of pounds of potato salad a person buys.

Let c be the cost in dollars for that number of pounds.

Each variable above includes a unit of measure. The variable p represents the number of *pounds* of potato salad, and the variable c represents the cost in *dollars*.

A double number line can be used to illustrate the relationship p and c share. A **double number line** is a pair of number lines that show how two variables relate to each other. The double number line below shows how p and c vary together.

Buying Potato Salad by the Pound

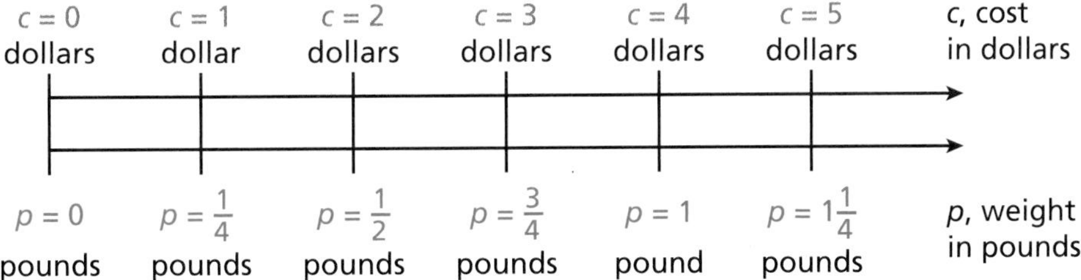

Discuss these questions with your class.

1. Why are two variables needed to represent this situation?
2. Why do we need to specify a unit of measure when we define each variable?
3. What is wrong with the following definitions of p?
   - Let p be the potato salad someone buys.
   - Let p be the weight of the potato salad a person buys.

5–10
Class Activity

Use Activity
Workbook page 110.

▶ Define Variables

Motor vehicles require fuel. Suppose a gasoline pump dispenses gasoline into the fuel tank of a car at a rate of 1 pint per second.

There are two quantities in this situation. The two quantities vary together—as one changes, the other changes too.

4. What two quantities vary together in this situation?

5. What units could you use for these two quantities?

6. Define two variables for your quantities in Exercise 4.

   Let ______ represent ______?______.

   Let ______ represent ______?______.

7. Label this double number line to show how the quantities vary together.

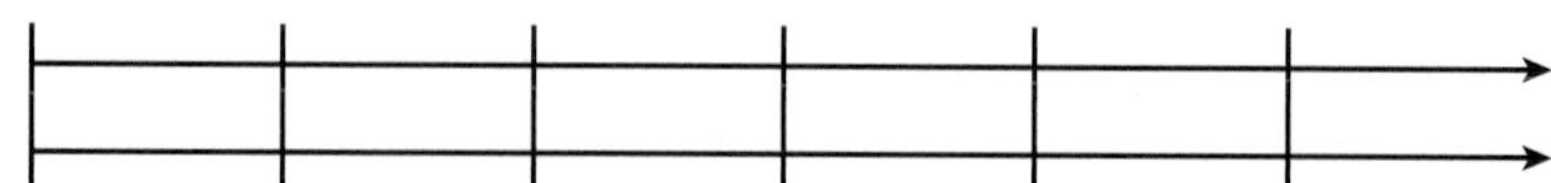

Write your answers
on Activity Workbook
page 111.

▶ Three Ways to Represent a Relationship

Mr. Prieto makes his own biodiesel fuel by mixing vegetable oil and ethanol in the ratio of 5 liters of vegetable oil to 1 liter of ethanol. The amount of vegetable oil and ethanol vary together.

8. Define the variable v for the amount of vegetable oil, and define the variable e for the amount of ethanol in Mr. Prieto's biodiesel fuel mixture.

   Let v be the number of ____?____.

   Let e be the number of ____?____.

9. Complete the table. Then discuss how the table, the diagram, and the equations are related.

Table

e	v

Diagram

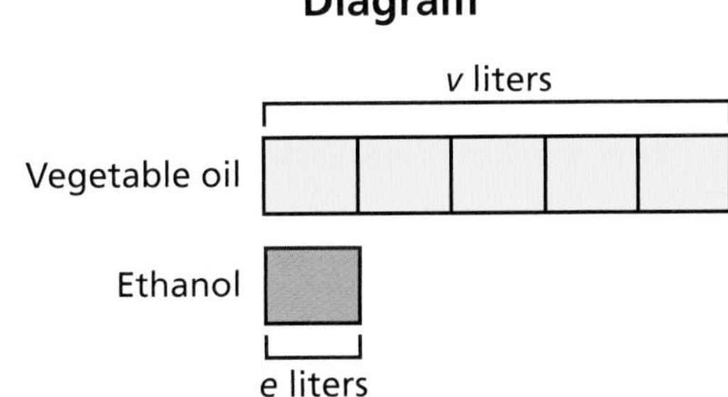

Equations

$v = e + e + e + e + e$

$v = 5e$

$e = v \div 5$

$e = \frac{1}{5}v$

▶ What's the Error?

Dear Math Students,

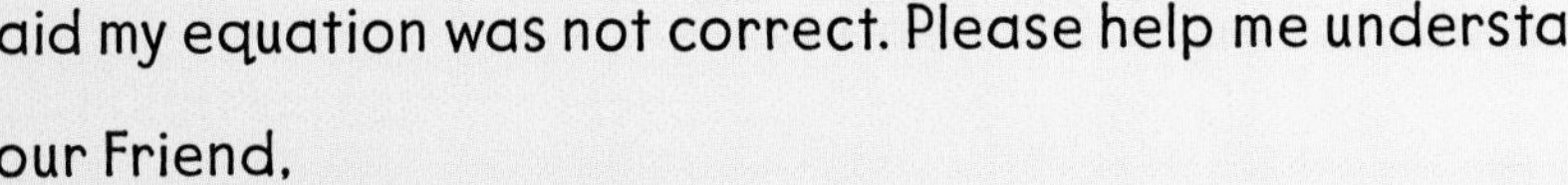

I thought that because Mr. Prieto's ratio of vegetable oil to ethanol was 5:1, I could write the equation $5v = e$. My teacher said my equation was not correct. Please help me understand why.

Your Friend,

Puzzled Penguin

10. Write a response to Puzzled Penguin.

5–10
Class Activity

Write your answers
on Activity Workbook
page 112.

▶ Write Equations for a Relationship

An electronics store offers a payment plan for purchases over $200. Customers can make a $100 down payment and then pay the remainder in three equal payments.

Let t be the total amount of a customer's purchase in dollars.

Let p be the amount of each of the three equal payments in dollars.

11. Write the missing amounts in the table. Use the diagram and the table to help you find equations that relate t and p.

Table

t	p
■	150
1,000	■
■	250
475	■

Diagram

t

100	p	p	p

Equations

$t =$ ■

$p =$ ■

In a bread dough recipe, the ratio of cups of flour to cups of water is 2 to 1.

f	w
■	1
4	■
■	5
16	■

12. Define variables for the amounts of flour and water.

Let f represent ______?______.

Let w represent ______?______.

13. Complete the table of values at the right for f and w.

14. Make a diagram for f and w.

15. Write equations relating f and w.

$f =$ ■ $w =$ ■

Vocabulary

dependent variable
independent variable

▶ Walking Rates

Student 1 walks at a constant rate of 3 feet per second.

Student 2 walks at a constant rate of 5 feet per second.

The elapsed time and the distance walked for each student vary together.

Let t be the number of seconds elapsed since a student started walking.

Let d be the number of feet a student has walked.

The double number lines below show how the variables t and d vary together for the two students.

Student 1

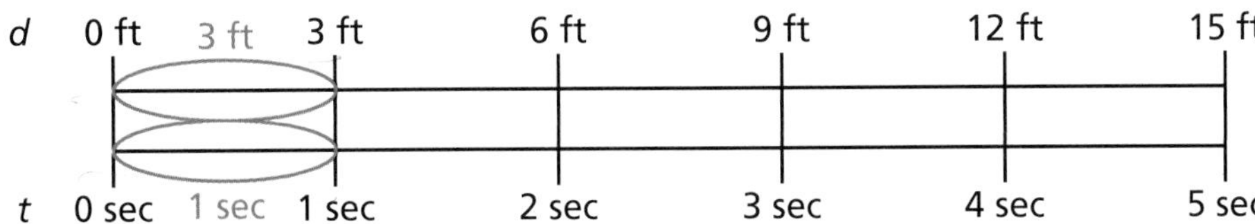

Student 2

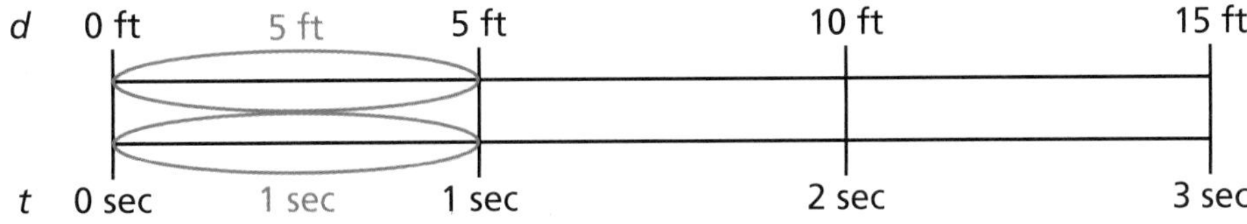

1. Can t and d be whole numbers? Can they be fractions or decimals?

When two variables are related, we can often think of one as the **dependent variable** and the other as the **independent variable**. The distance each student walks depends on the elapsed time. So d is the dependent variable, and t is the independent variable. In graphs and tables:

We use the x-axis and left column for the independent variable.

We use the y-axis and right column for the dependent variable.

Write your answers on Activity Workbook page 113.

▶ Tables and Equations for Constant Speed

2. Complete each table for the students mentioned on the previous page.

Student 1

Elapsed Time in Seconds (t)	Distance Walked in Feet (d)
0	
1	
2	
3	
4	
5	

Student 2

Elapsed Time in Seconds (t)	Distance Walked in Feet (d)
0	
1	
2	
3	
4	
5	

3. For each student, write an equation relating t and d.

   Student 1 equation:

   Student 2 equation:

4. How is each student's walking rate related to the equation?

▶ Graphs for Constant Speed

5. a. On the grids on the next page, graph the data in the tables from Exercise 2.

   b. Does it make sense to connect the points on the graphs? If so, connect them.

   c. Draw two unit rate triangles on each graph.

   d. How is each student's walking rate related to the graph?

▶ Graphs for Constant Speed (continued)

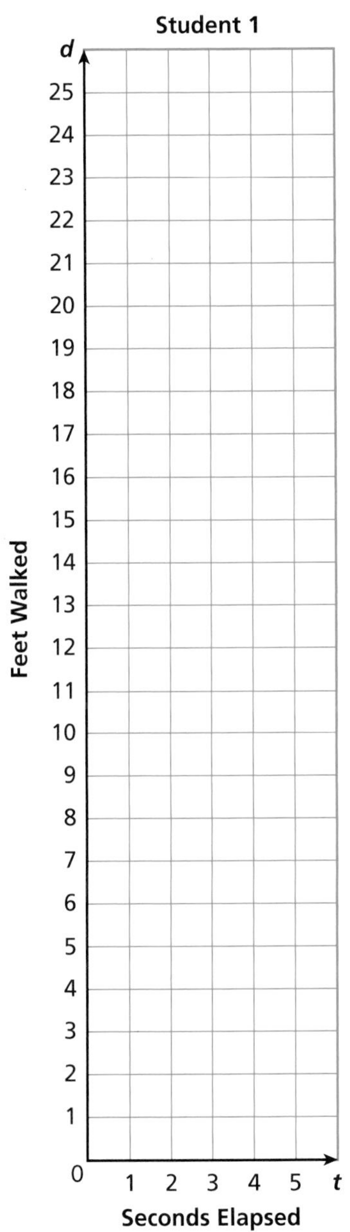

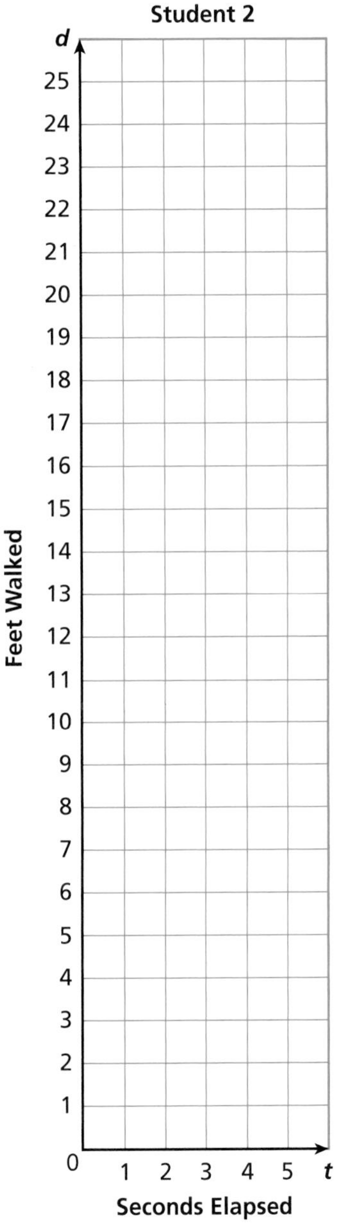

Write your answers on Activity Workbook page 115.

▶ Double Number Line for Constant Speed

Suppose Student 3 walks at a constant rate of 4 feet per second.

6. Label this double number line for Student 3.

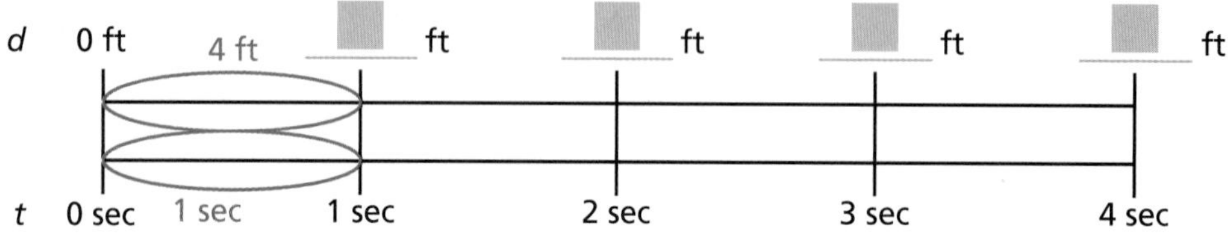

7. Complete the table at the right for Student 3.

8. Write an equation relating *d* and *t* for Student 3.

9. Seth and Kinsey want to know how far Student 3 will have walked after $2\frac{1}{2}$ seconds.

   a. Seth says he can use the double number line to find the distance. Explain how he might do this.

   b. Kinsey says she can use the equation to find the distance. Explain how she might do this.

Student 3

Elapsed Time in Seconds (*t*)	Distance Walked in Feet (*d*)
0	
1	
2	
3	
4	
5	

Calculate how far Student 3 walks in the given length of time.

10. $3\frac{1}{4}$ seconds

11. $2\frac{5}{8}$ seconds

▶ Find the Unit Rate

Suppose Student 4 walks at a constant rate of 7 feet every 2 seconds.

12. Label this double line graph for Student 4.

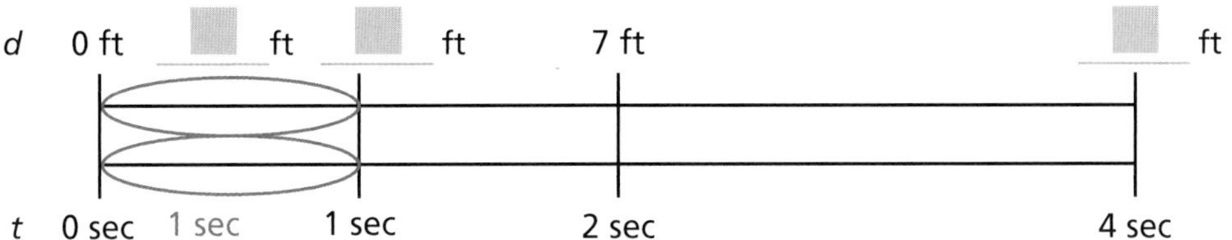

13. Complete the table below for Student 4.

Student 4

Elapsed Time in Seconds (t)	Distance Walked in Feet (d)
0	
1	
2	
3	
4	
5	

14. What is the unit rate for Student 4?

15. Write an equation relating d and t for Student 4.

Calculate how far Student 4 walks in the given length of time.

16. 3 seconds

17. $2\frac{1}{2}$ seconds

▶ Find the Unit Rate (continued)

Suppose Student 5 walks at a constant rate of 11 feet every 3 seconds.

18. Write an equation relating d and t for Student 5.

Calculate how far Student 5 walks in the given length of time. Show your work.

19. 6 seconds

20. $7\frac{1}{2}$ seconds

▶ Summarize Walking at a Constant Speed

21. Suppose a student walks at a constant rate of r feet per second. Label the double number line below for the student, and discuss why the equation $d = rt$ relates the distance, rate, and elapsed time for this situation.

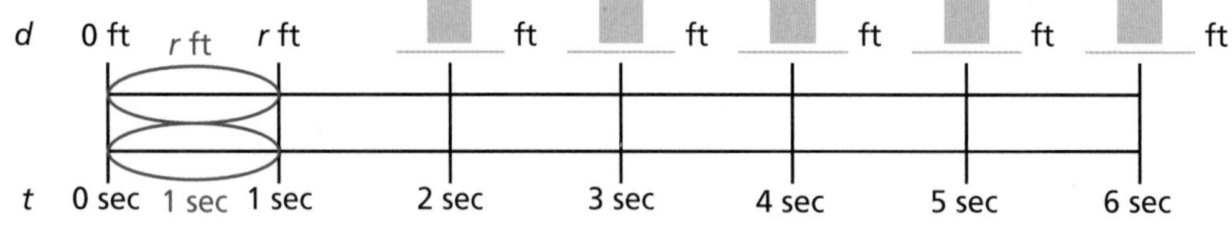

22. Summarize what you learned today about how distance, rate, and elapsed time are related for motion at a constant rate.

▶ Three Ways to Represent Motion at a Constant Speed

Suppose a high-speed train travels at a constant rate between Greenville and Orange Lake.

Let t be the number of minutes elapsed.

Let d be the number of miles the train has traveled.

The variables d and t vary together. Their relationship is represented by the equation $d = 2.5t$.

Let t be the independent variable. Let d be the dependent variable.

1. Complete the table.

Minutes Elapsed (t)	Miles Traveled (d)
0	
1	
2	
3	
4	
5	
6	

2. Graph the points from the table.

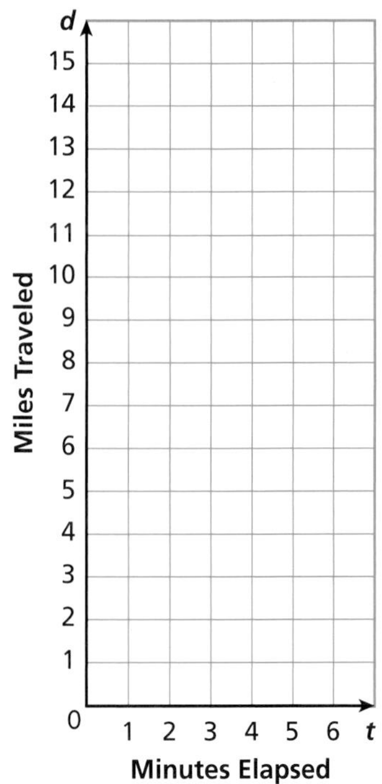

3. Does it make sense to connect the points on the graph? If so, connect them.

4. Draw a unit rate triangle on your graph.

5. What is the speed of the train in miles per minute (that is, what is the unit rate)?

6. With your class, discuss how t and d are related in the equation, in the table, and on the graph.

▶ Is the Change Constant?

SuperHero Supplies, Inc. produces different Superpower Soups. In the factory, each type of soup flows into a different vat.

Let t be the number of seconds elapsed.

Let v be the number of liters of soup in the vat.

For each vat, v and t vary together and are related by an equation.

Vat 1
(Super Strength)
$v = t^2$

Vat 2
(x-ray Vision)
$v = 5t$

Vat 3
(Flying)
$v = 5t + 3$

Vat 4
(Lightning Speed)
$v = 2t + 10$

Vat 5
(Invisibility)
$v = 3t + 10$

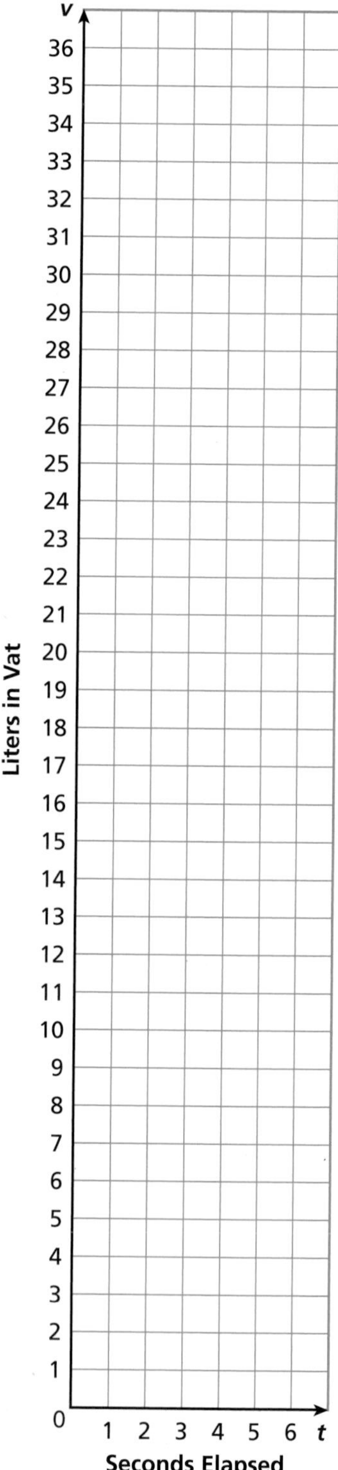

7. Complete the table for Vat 1.

Vat 1: $v = t^2$

Seconds Elapsed (t)	Liters in Vat (v)
0	
1	
2	
3	
4	
5	
6	

8. Plot the points for Vat 1. Connect the points if it makes sense to.

9. Is the soup flowing into Vat 1 at a constant rate?

▶ Compare Change

10. Complete the tables for Vats 2 and 3.

Vat 2: $v = 5t$

Seconds Elapsed (t)	Liters in Vat (v)
0	
1	
2	
3	
4	
5	
6	

Vat 3: $v = 5t + 3$

Seconds Elapsed (t)	Liters in Vat (v)
0	
1	
2	
3	
4	
5	
6	

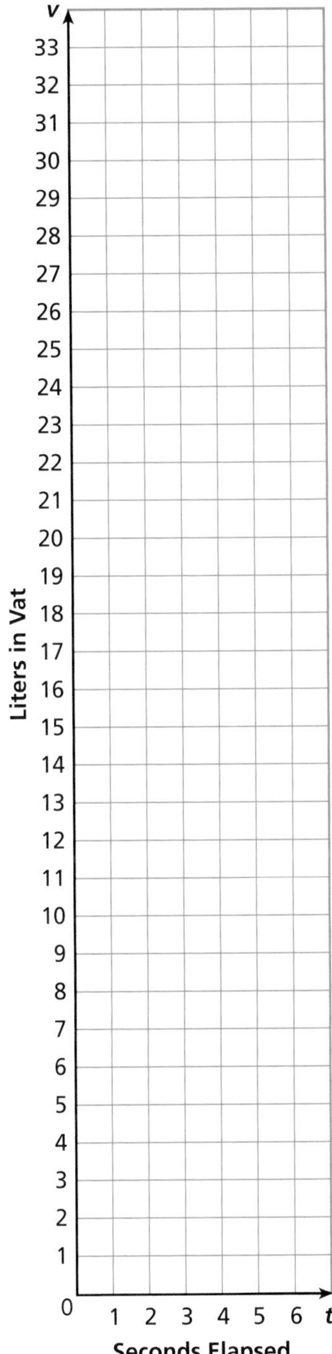

11. Plot the points for Vat 2 on the grid. Connect the points if it makes sense to.

12. Use a different color to plot the points for Vat 3 on the same grid. Connect the points if it makes sense to.

13. Tell whether soup is flowing into the vat at a constant rate.

Vat 2 ______ Vat 3 ______

14. What does the 5 in $v = 5t$ tell you?

15. What does the 5 in $v = 5t + 3$ tell you? What does the 3 tell you?

Use Activity Workbook page 121.

▶ Compare Change (continued)

16. Complete the tables for Vats 4 and 5.

Vat 4: $v = 2t + 10$

Seconds Elapsed (t)	Liters in Vat (v)
0	
1	
2	
3	
4	
5	
6	

Vat 5: $v = 3t + 10$

Seconds Elapsed (t)	Liters in Vat (v)
0	
1	
2	
3	
4	
5	
6	

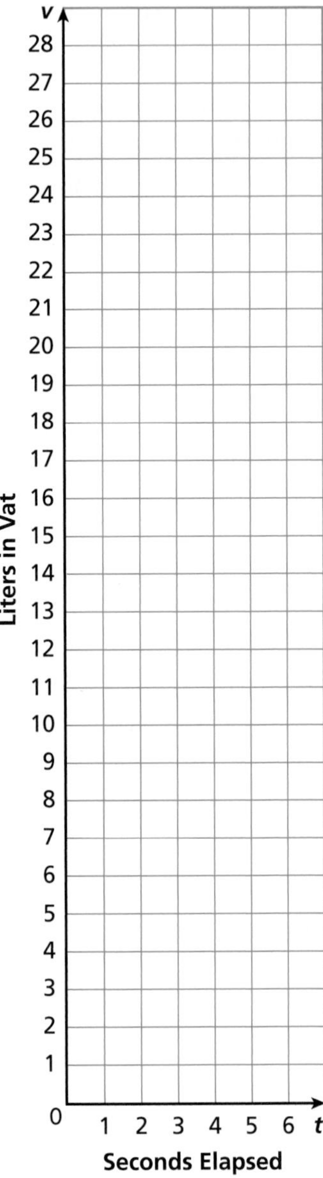

17. Plot the points for Vat 4 on the grid. Connect the points if it makes sense to.

18. Use a different color to plot the points for Vat 5 on the same grid. Connect the points if it makes sense to.

19. Tell whether soup is flowing into the vat at a constant rate.

Vat 4 __________ Vat 5 __________

20. What do the 2 in $v = 2t + 10$ and the 3 in $v = 3t + 10$ tell you?

21. What does the 10 in $v = 2t + 10$ and in $v = 3t + 10$ tell you?

Write your answers on Activity Workbook page 122.

▶ Compare Costs

Seward Elementary School plans to sell friendship bracelets. The bracelets can be purchased from three companies.

Company A charges \$30 for 24 bracelets, plus a flat rate of \$4 for shipping any number of bracelets.

Company B charges \$13 for 10 bracelets and does not charge for shipping.

Company C charges \$18 for 15 bracelets, plus a flat rate of \$10 for shipping any number of bracelets.

Let n be a number of bracelets, and let t be the total cost in dollars.

1. Complete this table for Company A. In the shaded cells, write expressions, rather than the final values.

Number of Bracelets (n)	Cost in Dollars	Shipping Cost in Dollars	Total Cost (t) in Dollars
24	30	4	34
12			
6			
2			
1	1.25	4	1 • 1.25 + 4
5			
17			
33			
n			

2. Write an equation that describes the total cost t of purchasing n friendship bracelets from Company A.

Company A: $t =$ ▭

3. Tell what the numbers in your equation represent.

5–13
Class Activity

Write your answers
on Activity Workbook
page 123.

▶ Compare Costs (continued)

4. Now consider Company B. Write an equation for the total cost in dollars t in terms of the number of friendship bracelets n. Show your work.

   Company B: $t = \square$

5. For Company C, write an equation for the total cost in dollars t in terms of the number of friendship bracelets n. Show your work.

   Company C: $t = \square$

6. In the first row of the table below, write your equations from Exercises 2, 4, and 5. Then complete the table to find the costs of buying different quantities of bracelets from each company.

Number of Bracelets (n)	Company A Cost $t = \square$	Company B Cost $t = \square$	Company C Cost $t = \square$	Lowest Total Cost?
25				
100				
150				
250				

Vocabulary

inequality

▶ Inequality Symbols

An **inequality** is a statement that compares two expressions using one of these symbols.

$>$ greater than $\geq$ greater than or equal to $\neq$ not equal to

$<$ less than $\leq$ less than or equal to

Example	How to Read It
$x > 7$	x is greater than 7.
$7 < 5 + 4$	7 is less than 5 plus 4.
$b - 1 \geq 12$	b minus 1 is greater than or equal to 12.
$10 \leq 2 \bullet w$	10 is less than or equal to 2 times w.
$6 \div 3 \neq 1$	6 divided by 3 is not equal to 1.

Write each statement as an inequality.

1. 3 is greater than or equal to t.
2. 60 is less than 8 times 8.
3. x is not equal to 0.
4. 10 plus b is greater than 4.
5. 9 is less than or equal to c.

Write each inequality using words.

6. $4 \bullet m \leq 16$
7. $7 \bullet 7 > 7 + 7$
8. $10 - 3 < z$
9. $14 \geq s$
10. $20 \neq 6 \bullet 5$

▶ Real World Inequalities (> and <)

Many real world situations can be represented by inequalities with the symbols < and >.

Example 1	**Example 2**
Situation: Children younger than 3 years old are admitted to the amusement park for free.	**Situation:** Everyone in the class got more than 7 points on the quiz.
What it means: Any child whose age in years is *less than* 3 is admitted free.	**What it means:** The quiz score of each student in the class is *greater than* 7.
Using an inequality: If a represents a child's age in years, then the child is admitted free if $a < 3$.	**Using an inequality:** If q is a quiz score of a student in the class, then $q > 7$.

11. The students in an elementary school go outside for recess on days when the temperature is above 20°F.

    a. Write *less than* or *greater than* in the blank below to make the statement true.

    When the temperature is ______?______ 20°F, students go outside for recess.

    b. Let t represent the temperature in degrees Fahrenheit. Write < or > in the circle to make the statement true.

    Students go outside for recess when t ◯ 20.

12. Fewer than 20 students arrived late to school on Wednesday even though there was a snowstorm on Tuesday night.

    Let s represent the number of students who arrived late. Write an inequality for the possible values of s.

▶ Real World Inequalities (≥ and ≤)

Many real world situations can be represented by inequalities with the symbols ≤ and ≥.

Example 1	Example 2
Situation: You must be at least 50 inches tall to ride the roller coaster.	**Situation:** Children 3 years old or younger can ride the train for free.
What it means: Your height must be *greater than or equal to* 50 inches to ride the roller coaster.	**What it means:** Any child whose age in years is *less than or equal to* 3 can ride for free.
Using an inequality: If h is your height in inches, then you can ride the roller coaster if $h \geq 50$.	**Using an inequality:** If a represents a child's age in years, then the child rides for free if $a \leq 3$.

13. A middle school has at most 15 students in each class.

 a. Write *less than or equal to* or *greater than or equal to* in the blank below to make the statement true.

 The number of students in each class is
 ______?______ 15.

 b. Write an inequality to represent the number of students in each class. Let s represent the number of students in a class, and include a ≤ or ≥ symbol in your inequality.

14. Employees at a company earn a minimum of $10 per hour.

 Let w represent the hourly wage in dollars of an employee at the company. Write an inequality for the possible values of w.

15. The maximum height for a NASA astronaut is 75 inches. Let h represent the height of a NASA astronaut. Write an inequality for the possible values of h.

Vocabulary

solution of an inequality

▶ Solutions of Inequalities

If an inequality has a variable, then a **solution of the inequality** is a value that can be substituted for the variable to make the inequality true.

16. One solution of $x < 15$ is $x = 9$ because $9 < 15$ is a true statement. Find two more solutions of $x < 15$.

17. One solution of $b + 4 > 6$ is $b = 2.2$ because $2.2 + 4 > 6$ is a true statement. Find two more solutions of $b + 4 > 6$.

18. Is $n = 5$ a solution of $n \geq 5$? Explain.

19. Is $n = 5$ a solution of $n > 5$? Explain.

20. One solution of $t - 3 \geq 10$ is $t = 13$ because $13 - 3 \geq 10$ is a true statement. Find two more solutions of $t - 3 \geq 10$.

21. One solution of $2r \leq 20$ is $r = 0.5$ because $2(0.5) \leq 20$ is a true statement. Find two more solutions of $2r \leq 20$.

22. Is $p = \frac{3}{2}$ a solution of $4p > 6$? Explain.

23. Is $y = 5$ a solution of $3y \leq 15$? Explain.

▶ Graphing Solutions (> and <)

Vocabulary
infinite
solution set

Most inequalities have an **infinite** number of solutions. This means it is not possible to show all of the solutions in a list. However, it is possible to show all of the solutions in a graph on a number line.

A **solution set** of an inequality is the set of all of its solutions. The graph of a solution set of an inequality is often a ray. When you graph the ray, you graph an open dot if the endpoint *is not* a solution. You graph a filled-in dot if the endpoint *is* a solution.

Example 1

This graph shows the solutions of $x > 3$.

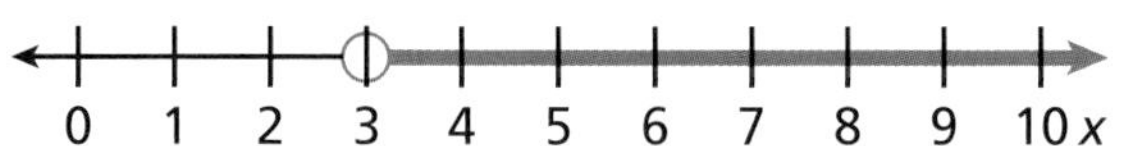

The open dot at 3 shows that 3 is *not* a solution. The blue arrow shows that all the numbers to the right of 3 (greater than 3) are solutions.

Example 2

This graph shows the solutions of $x < 6$.

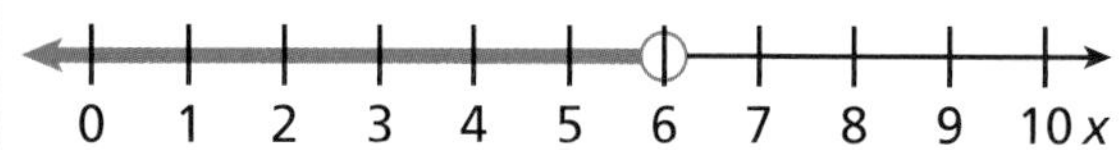

The open dot at 6 shows that 6 is *not* a solution. The blue arrow shows that all the numbers to the left of 6 (less than 6) are solutions.

Graph all the solutions of the inequality.

24. $m > 7$

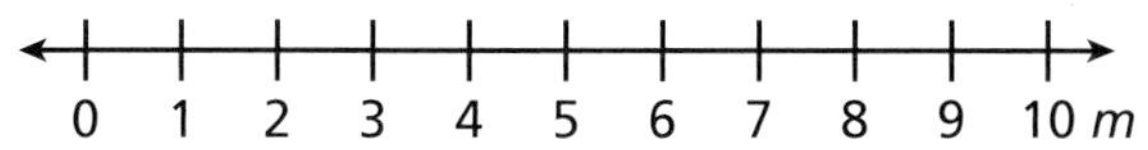

25. $t < 5$

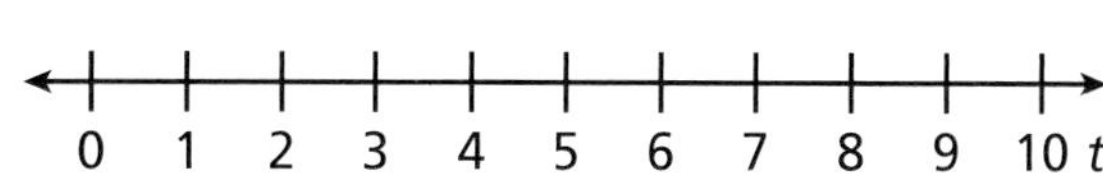

26. A shipping company charges an extra fee for boxes that weigh more than 200 pounds. Let *w* represent the weight in pounds of box for which an extra fee was charged. Write an inequality for the possible values of *w*.

Graph the inequality.

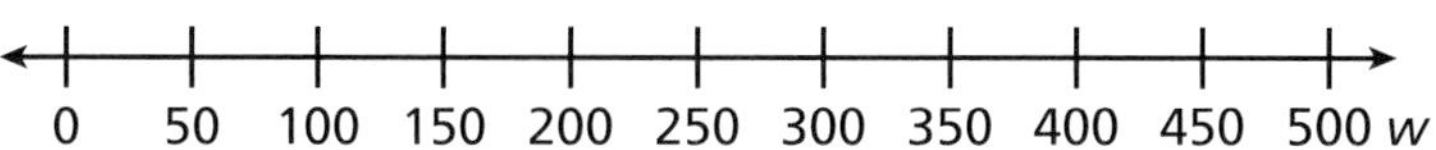

▶ Graphing Solutions (≥ and ≤)

When you graph a solution set on a number line, you use a filled-in dot to show that the endpoint is included in the set of solutions.

Example 1	Example 2
This graph shows the solutions of $x \geq 3$.	This graph shows the solutions of $x \leq 6$.
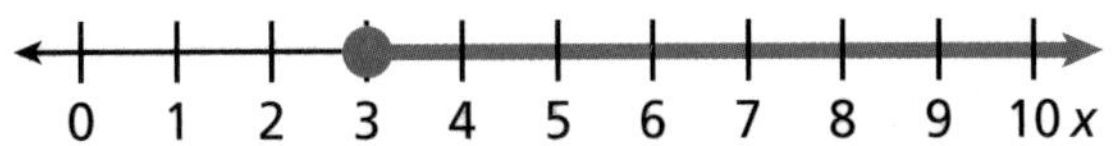	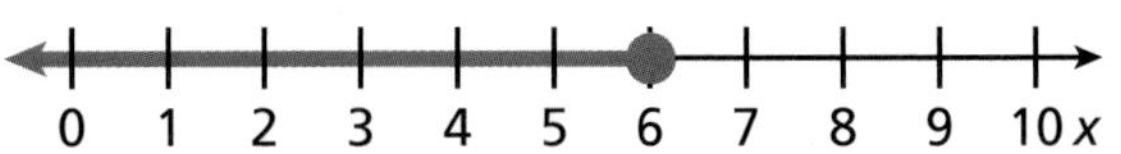
The filled-in dot at 3 shows that 3 is a solution. The blue arrow shows that all the numbers to the right of 3 are also solutions.	The filled-in dot at 6 shows that 6 is a solution. The blue arrow shows that all the numbers to the left of 6 are also solutions.

Graph all the solutions of the inequality.

27. $m \geq 7$

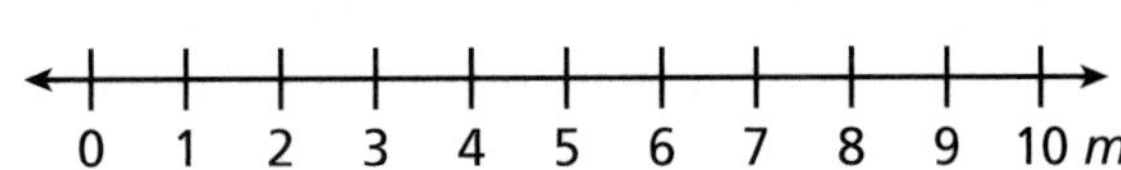

28. $t \leq 5$

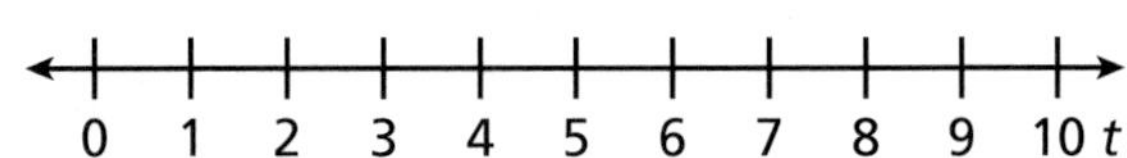

29. The weather reporter said temperatures would not rise above 3°F all week. Let t represent the temperatures in degrees Fahrenheit for the week. Write an inequality to represent the possible values of t.

Graph the inequality.

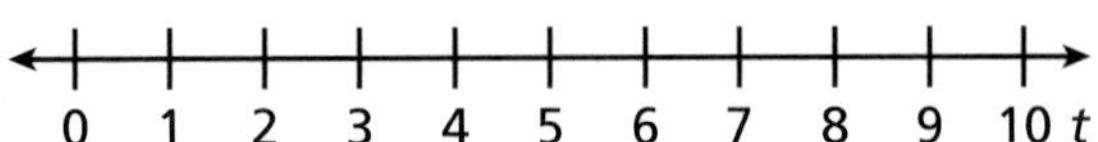

30. Describe a real world situation that can be represented by an inequality. Write an inequality to represent the situation, and then graph it on a number line.

Vocabulary

solution

▶ Check for Solutions

A **solution** of an equation or inequality with one variable is a number that can be substituted for the variable to make a true statement.

Example 1

$x = 4$ is a solution of $5x - 3 = 17$ because when 4 is substituted for x, the resulting statement, $5(4) - 3 = 17$, is true.

$$\begin{aligned} 5x - 3 &= 17 \\ 5(4) - 3 &= 17 \\ 20 - 3 &= 17 \\ 17 &= 17 \quad \text{true} \end{aligned}$$

Example 2

$x = 9$ is a solution of $1 + 4x > 3x + 1$ because when 9 is substituted for each x, the resulting statement, $1 + 4(9) > 3(9) + 1$, is true.

$$\begin{aligned} 1 + 4x &> 3x + 1 \\ 1 + 4(9) &> 3(9) + 1 \\ 1 + 36 &> 27 + 1 \\ 37 &> 28 \quad \text{true} \end{aligned}$$

Consider the following equation and inequalities.

$7x - 1 = 83 \qquad 7x - 1 < 83 \qquad 7x - 1 > 83$

1. Evaluate $7x - 1$ for $x = 11$.

   Is $x = 11$ a solution of

   $7x - 1 = 83$?

   $7x - 1 < 83$?

   $7x - 1 > 83$?

2. Evaluate $7x - 1$ for $x = 12$.

   Is $x = 12$ a solution of

   $7x - 1 = 83$?

   $7x - 1 < 83$?

   $7x - 1 > 83$?

3. Evaluate $7x - 1$ for $x = 13$.

   Is $x = 13$ a solution of

   $7x - 1 = 83$?

   $7x - 1 < 83$?

   $7x - 1 > 83$?

▶ Variable on Both Sides

Consider the following equation and inequalities.

$3x + 6 = 7x + 4$ $3x + 6 < 7x + 4$ $3x + 6 > 7x + 4$

4. Evaluate $3x + 6$ for $x = 0$.

   Evaluate $7x + 4$ for $x = 0$.

   Is $x = 0$ a solution of

   $3x + 6 = 7x + 4$?

   $3x + 6 < 7x + 4$?

   $3x + 6 > 7x + 4$?

5. Evaluate $3x + 6$ for $x = \frac{1}{2}$.

   Evaluate $7x + 4$ for $x = \frac{1}{2}$.

   Is $x = \frac{1}{2}$ a solution of

   $3x + 6 = 7x + 4$?

   $3x + 6 < 7x + 4$?

   $3x + 6 > 7x + 4$?

6. Evaluate $3x + 6$ for $x = 1$.

   Evaluate $7x + 4$ for $x = 1$.

   Is $x = 1$ a solution of

   $3x + 6 = 7x + 4$?

   $3x + 6 < 7x + 4$?

   $3x + 6 > 7x + 4$?

7. Evaluate $3x + 6$ for $x = 0.2$.

   Evaluate $7x + 4$ for $x = 0.2$.

   Is $x = 0.2$ a solution of

   $3x + 6 = 7x + 4$?

   $3x + 6 < 7x + 4$?

   $3x + 6 > 7x + 4$?

Vocabulary

solve

▶ Solve by Making the Sides Equal

Solving an equation or inequality means finding its solutions.

You can solve some equations by thinking about the value that will make the sides of the equation equal.

Example

To solve $2x + 6 = 8 + 6$, you might reason like this:

Both sides have two terms. On both sides, one of the terms is 6. For the sides to be equal, the other terms must be equal. So, $2x$ must be equal to 8, which means $x = 4$.

You can use substitution to check the solution.

$$\begin{aligned} 2x + 6 &= 8 + 6 \\ 2(4) + 6 &= 8 + 6 \\ 8 + 6 &= 8 + 6 \\ 14 &= 14 \end{aligned}$$

The sides of the equation are equal, so $x = 4$ is the solution.

Solve the equation by thinking about what value of x will make the sides of the equation equal.

8. $13 - 6 = x + 3$

   $x =$ ▢

9. $8 = x - 8$

   $x =$ ▢

10. $14 + 22 = 22 + x$

    $x =$ ▢

11. $24 \div 6 = (27 - x) \div 6$

    $x =$ ▢

12. $5x + 2x = 70$

    $x =$ ▢

13. $7x = 7 \bullet 2^3$

    $x =$ ▢

14. $6x + 0.3 = 6 + 0.3$

    $x =$ ▢

15. $2x + \frac{7}{8} = \frac{7}{8} + \frac{1}{2}$

    $x =$ ▢

▶ What's the Error?

Dear Math Students,

On my homework, I am supposed to find a solution of the inequality shown at the right.

I think $x = 7$ is a solution because when x is 7, both sides of the inequality are equal to 10.

Is my thinking correct?

Your Friend,

Puzzled Penguin

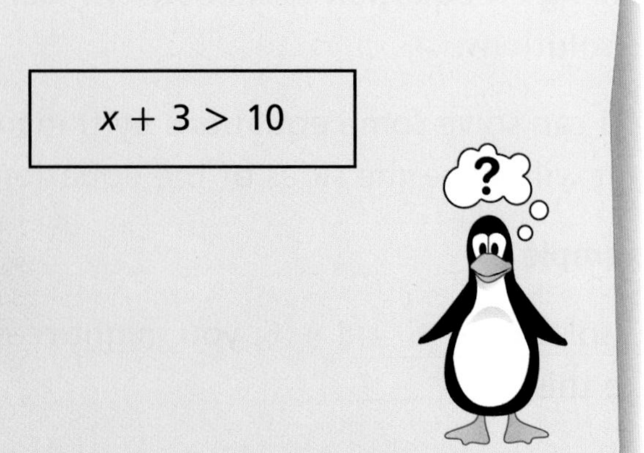

16. Write a response to Puzzled Penguin.

Dear Math Students,

Another problem on my homework asks me to find the solution to the equation shown at the right.

I know that both sides of any equation represent the same number. So, since 2^5 on the right side of the equation is $2 \cdot 5$ or 10, I think x should be 11.

Is $x = 11$ the solution to the equation $x - 1 = 2^5$?

Your Friend,

Puzzled Penguin

17. Write a response to Puzzled Penguin.

Write your answers on Activity Workbook page 126.

Vocabulary

inverse operations

▶ Use Inverse Operations

Use an inverse operation to write a related equation. Then solve the equation for *x*.

1. $x + 9 = 20$
2. $x - 3 = 2$
3. $x - 7 = 10$
4. $x + 12 = 25$
5. $x + 32 = 40$
6. $x - 14 = 34$

▶ Solve with Algebra Tiles

Write and solve the equation each model represents. Circle the tiles you remove from both sides.

7.

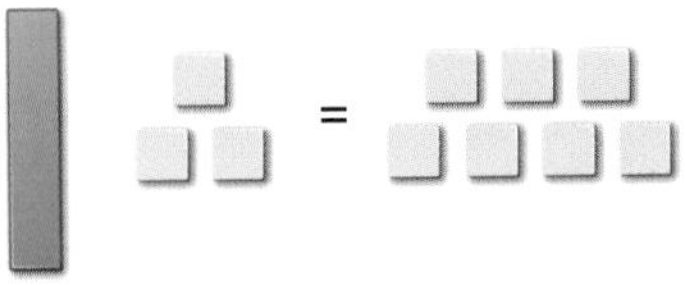

8.

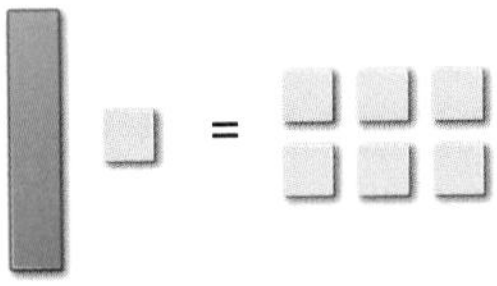

9.

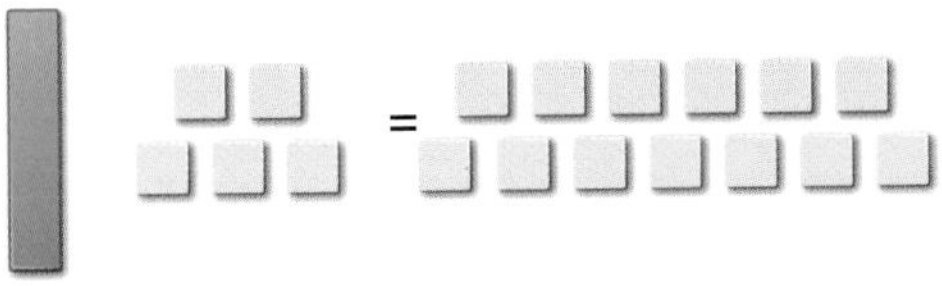

10.

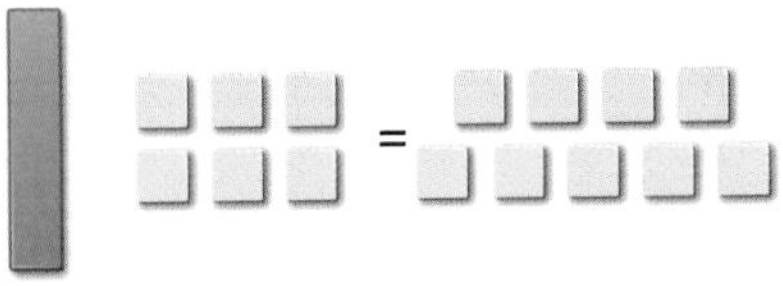

Use your algebra tiles to model each equation. Make a quick drawing of your model. Then solve the equation and check your answer using substitution.

11. $x + 2 = 6$ $x =$ ▢
12. $x + 5 = 16$ $x =$ ▢
13. $x + 8 = 10$ $x =$ ▢
14. $x + 3 = 12$ $x =$ ▢

▶ Maintain Equivalent Expressions

Write and solve the equation each balance represents.

15. $x - 1$ | 5

16. $x + \frac{1}{2}$ | 4

17. $x - 3$ | 7

18. $x + 74$ | 102

▶ Solve Addition and Subtraction Equations

Solve each equation using any method you choose. Use substitution to check your answer.

19. $x - 3 = 3$ $x =$ ▢

20. $x + 2 = 9$ $x =$ ▢

21. $x + 1.5 = 4$ $x =$ ▢

22. $x - 7.4 = 10.06$ $x =$ ▢

23. $x - \frac{3}{4} = 5\frac{1}{2}$ $x =$ ▢

24. $x + 1\frac{1}{3} = 7$ $x =$ ▢

▶ Write and Solve Addition and Subtraction Equations

Write an addition or subtraction equation to represent each problem. Then use the equation to solve the problem.

Show your work on your paper or in your journal.

25. Tyrell has saved \$62 to buy a new phone. How many more dollars must Tyrell save if the cost of the phone is \$89? Let *d* be the number of dollars Tyrell must still save.

26. When a mixed number is decreased by $6\frac{1}{4}$, the result is $9\frac{3}{8}$. What is the mixed number? Let *m* be the mixed number that is being decreased.

27. When a decimal number is increased by fifty-six hundredths, the result is eight tenths. What is the number? Let *d* be the decimal number that is being increased.

28. During May, 118 fewer students checked out books from the school library than during April. The number of students who checked out books during April was 208. How many students checked out books during May? Let *s* be the number of students who checked out books during May.

29. An odometer measures distance. The odometer on Jaylen's bicycle shows 105 miles, which is 57 more miles than the odometer on Lara's bicycle. How many miles are shown on the odometer of Lara's bicycle? Let *m* be the number of miles shown on Lara's odometer.

▶ What's the Error?

Dear Math Students,

The problem shown below was part of my homework assignment.

> To get ready for a social studies test, Vera studied for 35 more minutes than she studied for a language arts test. If Vera studied 45 minutes for her social studies test, how many minutes did she study for her language arts test?

Here are the steps I followed to solve the problem:

Step 1 I read the problem twice, like I always do. Then I chose *m* to represent the number of minutes Vera studied for her language arts test.

Step 2 I decided that the phrase *more minutes* suggests addition.

Step 3 The numbers in the problem are 35 minutes and 45 minutes, so I wrote the equation shown below.

$$45 + 35 = m$$

Step 4 I solved the equation by adding 45 and 35. For my answer, I wrote that Vera studied 80 minutes, or 1 hour and 20 minutes, for her language arts test.

When my homework assignment was graded, my answer was marked wrong! Can you help me understand what I did wrong, and explain how to find the correct answer?

Your Friend,

Puzzled Penguin

30. Write a response to the Puzzled Penguin.

▶ Use Inverse Operations

Use an inverse operation to write a related equation. Then solve the equation for *x*.

1. $2x = 18$
2. $x \div 5 = 5$
3. $x \div 3 = 9$
4. $6x = 42$
5. $10x = 50$
6. $x \div 2 = 12$

▶ Use Algebra Tiles to Model Multiplication Equations

Write and solve the equation each model represents.

7. 

8. 

9. 

10. 

Use algebra tiles to model and solve each equation for *x*. Check your work using substitution.

11. $2x = 10$ $x =$ ▒
12. $4x = 16$ $x =$ ▒
13. $3x = 18$ $x =$ ▒
14. $5x = 15$ $x =$ ▒

Vocabulary
multiplicative inverse

▶ The Multiplicative Inverse

A number is the **multiplicative inverse** of another number if the product of the numbers is 1. The multiplicative inverse of a number is the same as the reciprocal of the number.

Write the multiplicative inverse of each term.

15. 9

16. $\frac{3}{4}$

17. $\frac{1}{5}$

18. 10

Solving equations involves isolating the variable. In some equations, the coefficient of the variable is a fraction. One way to solve such an equation is to multiply *both sides* of the equation by the multiplicative inverse of the coefficient.

Use a multiplicative inverse to solve each equation.

19. $\frac{2}{3}x = 10$

    $x =$ ▢

20. $\frac{1}{5}x = 4$

    $x =$ ▢

21. $\frac{3}{4}x = 18$

    $x =$ ▢

▶ Solve Equations

Solve each equation using any method. Use substitution to check your answer.

22. $x + 39 = 101$

    $x =$ ▢

23. $6x = 18$

    $x =$ ▢

24. $x - 17 = 24$

    $x =$ ▢

25. $\frac{1}{3}x = 2$

    $x =$ ▢

26. $x \div 2 = 12$

    $x =$ ▢

27. $\frac{x}{9} = 8$

    $x =$ ▢

▶ Write and Solve Multiplication and Division Equations

Write a multiplication or division equation to represent each problem. Then use the equation to solve the problem.

Show your work on your paper or in your journal.

28. Two hundred seventy-six people are seated in 12 identical rows for a performance of a school play. How many people are in each row? Let p be the number of people in each row.

29. A \$20 T-shirt is on sale for $\frac{1}{10}$ off. How much money will Sierra save if she buys the shirt on sale? Let d be the number of dollars saved.

30. A land surveyor must partition a distance of 2,600 feet into 40 identical parts. Each part will represent what number of feet? Let f be the number of feet in each part.

31. A spring is 6 centimeters long, which is $\frac{3}{8}$ as long as it can be stretched. How far can the spring be stretched? Let d be the distance in centimeters the spring can be stretched.

32. For a school assembly, 304 students are to be seated in rows with 16 students in each row. How many rows of students will be seated for the assembly? Let r be the number of rows.

33. A rectangle has a length (l) of 5.2 centimeters and an area (A) of 18.2 square centimeters. Use the formula $A = lw$ to find w, the width of the rectangle in centimeters.

▶ What's the Error?

Dear Math Students,

An exercise on my homework assignment asked me to solve the equation shown below.

$$\frac{1}{2}x = 62$$

I know that one way to solve the equation is to use the multiplicative inverse of the coefficient.

The coefficient is $\frac{1}{2}$, and its multiplicative inverse is $\frac{2}{1}$. So, I multiplied the coefficient by $\frac{2}{1}$.

$$\frac{2}{1} \cdot \frac{1}{2}x = 62$$

The left side of the equation simplified to x.

$$\frac{\overset{1}{\cancel{2}}}{1} \cdot \frac{1}{\underset{1}{\cancel{2}}}x = 62$$

So, I concluded that $x = 62$, but my answer was marked wrong. Can you help me identify my error, and explain how to solve the equation correctly?

Your Friend,

Puzzled Penguin

34. Write a response to Puzzled Penguin.

▶ Math and Transportation

The rate you are charged to ride in a taxi cab varies from city to city. Most rates include a fixed initial charge, and a fixed cost for every fraction of a mile traveled.

The table below illustrates the cost of a taxi ride for various distances. The total cost includes a fixed $3 fee upon entry, and a cost for every one-fifth of a mile traveled.

Cost of a Taxi Ride

Distance in Miles (d)	Mileage Cost in Dollars	Initial Charge in Dollars	Total cost in Dollars (t)
$\frac{1}{5}$	2	3	5
$\frac{3}{5}$		3	
1			
$1\frac{2}{5}$		3	
2		3	

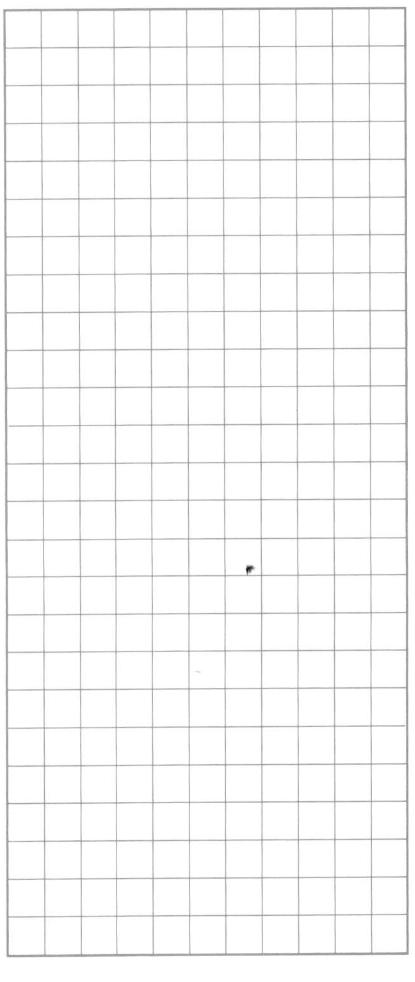

1. Complete the table.
2. Which three quantities vary, and which two quantities are constant?
3. Graph the data for distance and total cost. Describe your graph.
4. Write an equation that can be used to find the total cost in dollars (t) of a ride for any distance in miles (d).
5. Use your graph to predict the cost of a $1\frac{4}{5}$ mile ride. Use your equation to check your prediction.

Use Activity Workbook page 128.

▶ Broken-Line Graphs

Have you ever had a ride in a hot air balloon, or wondered what riding in one would be like?

The table below shows some flight data about the first few minutes of a hot air balloon ride.

Flight Data of a Hot Air Balloon

Elapsed Time in Minutes	Height above Ground in Feet
1	100
2	300
3	650
4	700
5	550

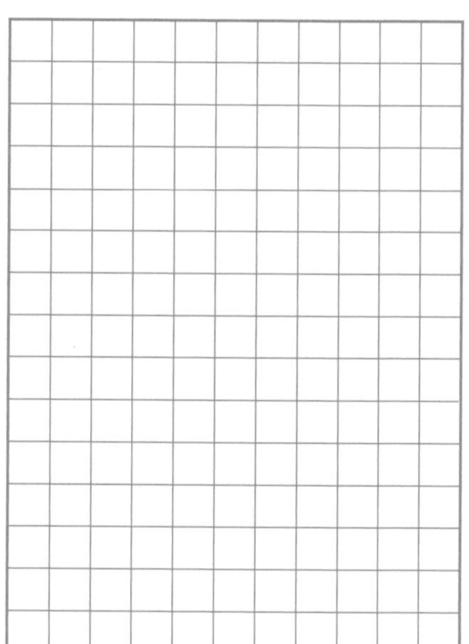

6. Graph the data.
7. **Discuss** Compare your graph with the taxi-ride graph on the previous page. How are the graphs alike and how are they different?
8. **Discuss** Why is one of the graphs a straight line and the other graph a broken line?
9. Which type of graph can be extended and used to make a precise prediction? Give an example to support your answer.

Use the Activity Workbook Unit Test on pages 129–132.

▶ Vocabulary

Choose the best term from the box.

Vocabulary
power coefficient exponent

1. In the expression 5^3, the number 3 is the ___?___. (Lesson 5-2)

2. The expression x^5 is a(n) ___?___. (Lesson 5-2)

▶ Concepts and Skills

Complete.

3. Explain how the diagram at the right shows that $2(x + 5) = 2x + 10$. (Lesson 5-8)

x 5
2

4. Circle the terms in the expression. Explain how you know they are terms. (Lesson 5-3)

$10a + a^2 - 9 \div 2$

5. If $x - 2 = 7$, how do you know that $x - 2 + 2 = 7 + 2$? (Lesson 5-16)

Simplify. Follow the Order of Operations. (Lessons 5-1, 5-2)

6. $32 \div 4(12 - 8) =$ ▒

7. $40 - 2 \bullet 10 + 2^2 =$ ▒

Evaluate the expression for $a = 3$ and $b = 5$. (Lessons 5-1, 5-2)

8. $7 + b^2 - 3a$

9. $10 + a(5 + b)$

10. Circle all the expressions the model represents. (Lessons 5-4, 5-6, 5-7, 5-8)

x	4	x	4

$x + 4 + x + 4$ $\quad$ $4x + 4x$ $\quad$ $2x + 4$

$2(x + 4)$ $\quad$ $2x + 8$ $\quad$ $8x$

11. Circle all the expressions that represent the surface area of the cube. (Lessons 5-5, 5-6, 5-7)

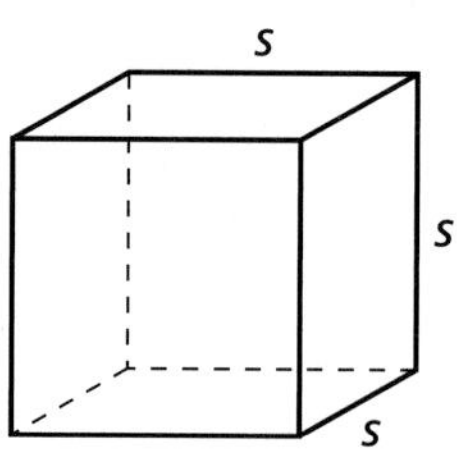

s^3 $\quad$ $6s$ $\quad$ $4s^2$

$6s^2$ $\quad$ $s^2 + s^2 + s^2 + s^2 + s^2 + s^2$

12. Apply the Distributive Property to part of the expression to write an equivalent expression. (Lessons 5-7, 5-8)

$x + 4(x + 3) =$ ▭

13. Simplify the expression. (Lessons 5-2, 5-6, 5-7)

$8x - 6^2 + 2(3x) + 36 =$ ▭

Write each sum as a product by using the Distributive Property to pull out the greatest common factor (GCF). (Lesson 5-8, 5-9)

Example: $24 + 32 = 8 \bullet 3 + 8 \bullet 4 = 8(3 + 4) = 8 \bullet 7$

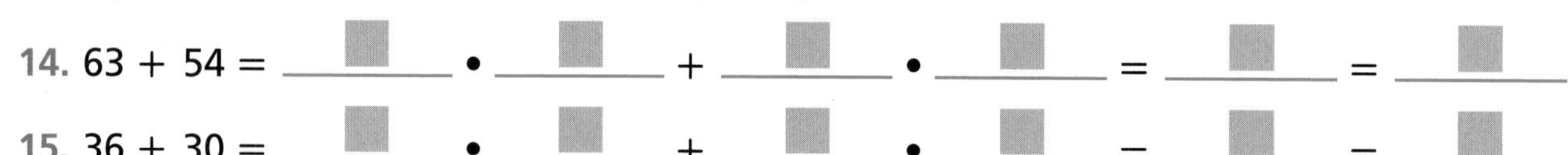

14. $63 + 54 =$ ▭ $\bullet$ ▭ $+$ ▭ $\bullet$ ▭ $=$ ▭ $=$ ▭

15. $36 + 30 =$ ▭ $\bullet$ ▭ $+$ ▭ $\bullet$ ▭ $=$ ▭ $=$ ▭

Circle the solution(s) to the equation or inequality. (Lesson 5-14, 5-15)

16. $6x - 5 \geq 13$ $\quad$ $x = 1$ $\quad$ $x = 3$ $\quad$ $x = 5$

17. $10 + x = 3x$ $\quad$ $x = 3$ $\quad$ $x = 5$ $\quad$ $x = 7$

18. $x + 7 < 25$ $\quad$ $x = 10$ $\quad$ $x = 18$ $\quad$ $x = 25$

Solve using any method. Use substitution to check your answer. (Lesson 5-16, 5-17)

19. $x + 49 = 65$ $x =$ ▒

20. $15x = 135$ $x =$ ▒

▶ Problem Solving

In Problems 21 and 22, write an equation to represent the problem. Then use the equation to solve the problem.

21. Twelve of the students in science club went on a trip to the planetarium. If this is $\frac{3}{4}$ of the students in the club, what is the total number of students in the club? (Lesson 5-17)

22. After Janelle deposited $72.50 in her savings account, her balance was $323. What was her balance before she made the deposit? (Lesson 5-16)

23. Bennett's phone plan charges extra if he talks more than 300 minutes in a month. He was charged extra in May. (Lesson 5-14)

    Let *m* be the number of minutes Bennett talked on his phone in May. Write an inequality for the possible values of *m*.

    Graph the inequality on the number line.

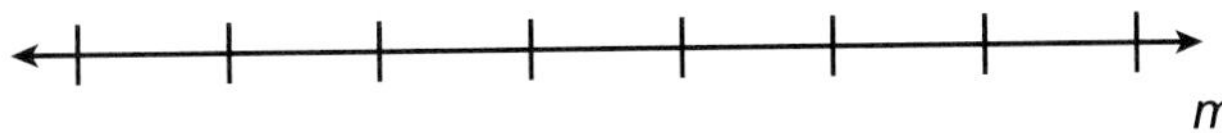

24. When the temperature is 20°F or less, Jenn wears her full-length parka. (Lesson 5-14)

Let t be the temperatures for which Jenn wears her parka. Write an inequality for the possible values of t.

Graph the inequality on the number line.

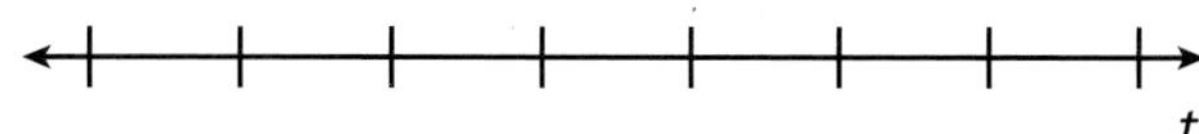

25. **Extended Response** An online sock store charges $3 per pair of socks. They charge $1 for delivery, no matter how many pairs you buy. (Lessons 5-10, 5-11, 5-12, 5-13)

a. Complete this table.

Pairs Bought, n	Cost of Socks ($)	Shipping Charge ($)	Total cost ($), c
1		1	
2	6	1	7
3		1	
4		1	
5		1	

b. Plot the values for pairs bought, n, and total cost, c, from the table. Draw a dashed line through the points.

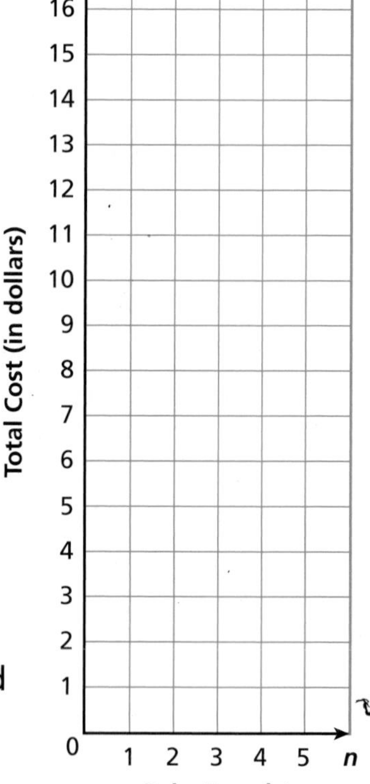

c. Write an equation for the total cost c for n pairs.

$c =$

d. Explain how the cost for each pair of socks is represented in the graph and in the equation.

e. Explain how the shipping charge is represented in the graph and in the equation.

Share with your family the Family Letter on Activity Workbook page 133.

Dear Family,

In this unit, we are reviewing the volume of rectangular prisms with whole number edge lengths and analyzing the difference between surface area and volume and the units used to measure them.

The **surface area** of a solid figure is the total area of all its faces. **Volume** is the measure of the space that a three-dimensional figure occupies.

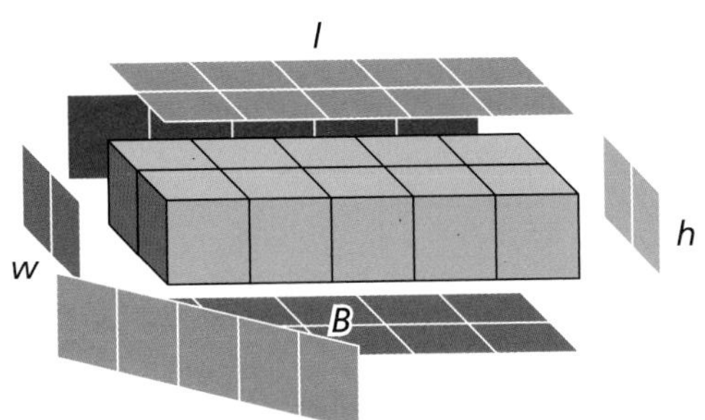

l is the length.
w is the width.
h is the height.
B is the area of the base.

Surface Area

SA = (2 × 10) + (2 × 2) + (2 × 5) = 34

Surface Area = 34 cm²

Volume

V = lwh or V = Bh

V = 5 × 2 × 1 **or** V = 10 × 1

Volume = 10 cm³

Surface area is measured in **square units**.
Volume is measured in **cubic units**.

This unit also introduces the volume of rectangular prisms with fractional edge lengths.

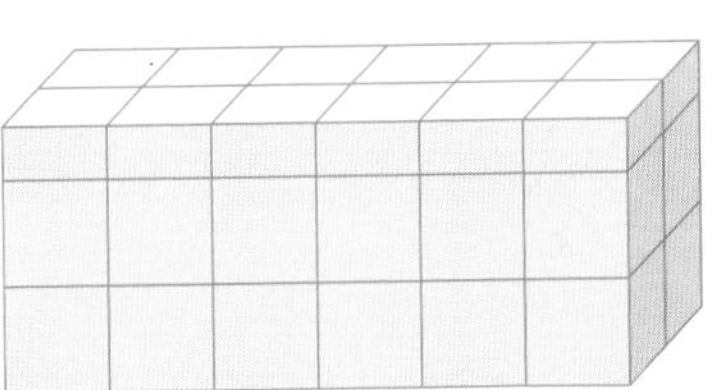

$V = Bh = 12 \bullet 2\frac{1}{2} = 30$,
30 unit³

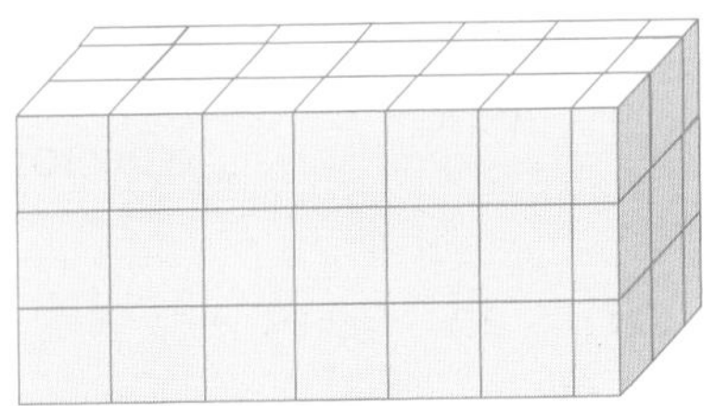

$V = lwh = 6\frac{1}{2} \bullet 2\frac{1}{2} \bullet 3 = 48\frac{3}{4}$,
$48\frac{3}{4}$ unit³

If you need practice materials or if you have any questions, please call or write to me.

Sincerely,
Your child's teacher

This unit includes the Common Core Standards for Mathematical Content for Geometry and Algebra, 6.G.1, 6.G.2, 6.G.4, 6.EE.2, 6.EE.2c and all Mathematical Practices.

Muestra a tu familia la Carta a la familia de la página 134 del Cuaderno de actividades y trabajo.

Estimada familia:

En esta unidad, repasaremos cómo obtener el volumen de prismas rectangulares cuyos lados tienen longitudes expresadas en números enteros. También analizaremos la diferencia entre el área total y el volumen y examinaremos las unidades de medida usadas.

El **área total** de un cuerpo geométrico es la suma del área de todas sus caras. El **volumen** es la medida del espacio que ocupa una figura tridimensional.

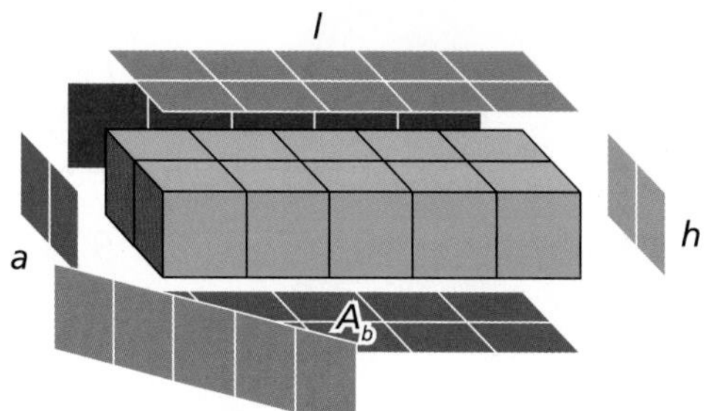

l es el largo
a es el ancho
h es la altura
A_b es el área de la base

Área total

$A_t = (2 \times 10) + (2 \times 2) + (2 \times 5) = 34$

Área total = 34 cm^2

Volumen

V = lah **ó** $V = A_bh$

$V = 5 \times 2 \times 1$ **ó** $V = 10 \times 1$

Volumen = 10 cm^3

El área total se mide en **unidades cuadradas**.
El volumen se mide en **unidades cúbicas**.

En esta unidad también se presenta el volumen de prismas rectangulares cuyos lados tienen longitudes expresadas en fracciones.

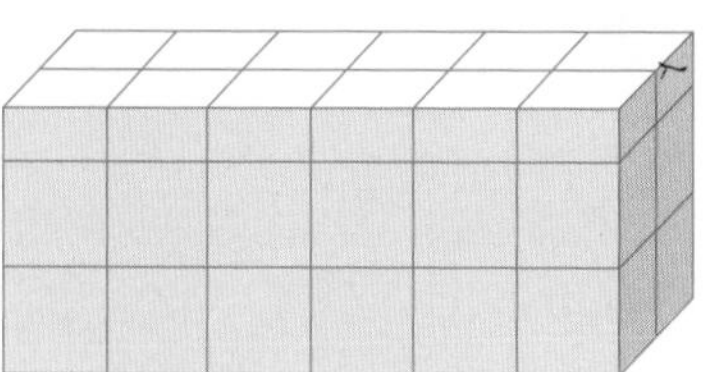

$V = A_bh = 12 \bullet 2\frac{1}{2} = 30$,
30 unidades^3

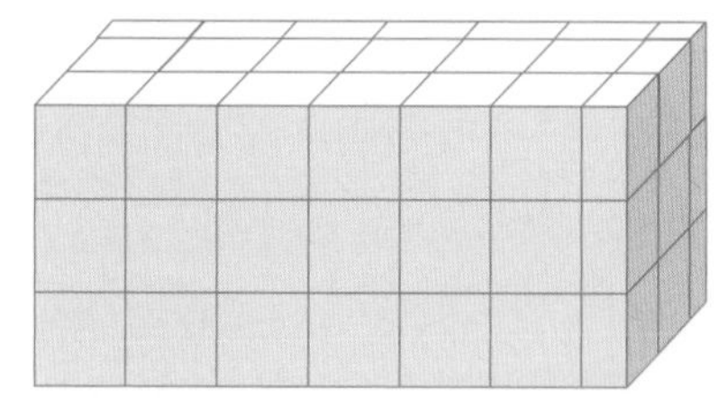

$V = lah = 6\frac{1}{2} \bullet 2\frac{1}{2} \bullet 3 = 48\frac{3}{4}$,
$48\frac{3}{4}$ unidades^3

Si necesita material para practicar o si tiene preguntas, por favor comuníquese conmigo.

Atentamente,
El maestro de su hijo

Esta unidad incluye los Common Core Standards for Mathematical Content for Ratios and Proportional Relationships, 6.G.1, 6.G.2, 6.G.4, 6.EE.2, 6.EE.2c and all Mathematical Practices.

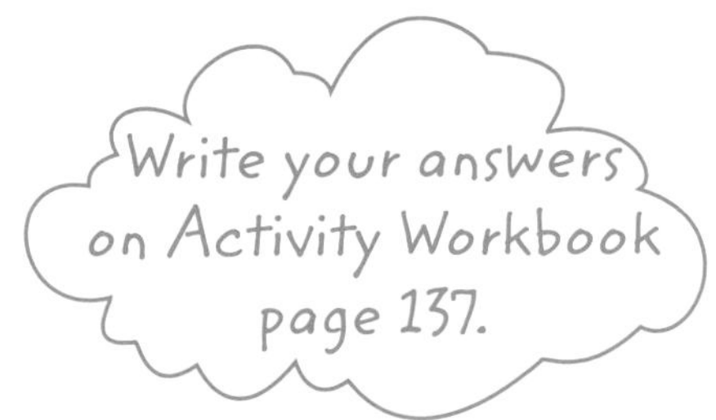

Write your answers on Activity Workbook page 137.

▶ Cubic Units

The volume of a solid figure is the amount of space occupied by the figure. Volume is measured in cubic units.

Vocabulary

volume
unit cube
centimeter cube
inch cube
cubic unit (unit³)
cubic centimeter (cm³)
cubic inch (in.³)

1. How can you measure the amount of space each of these rectangular prisms takes up? How much space is inside each of the rectangular prisms? How many unit cubes does it take to fill the rectangular prism?

A **unit cube** is a cube with each edge 1 unit long. The volume of a unit cube is 1 cubic unit. It can be written 1 cubic unit or 1 unit³.

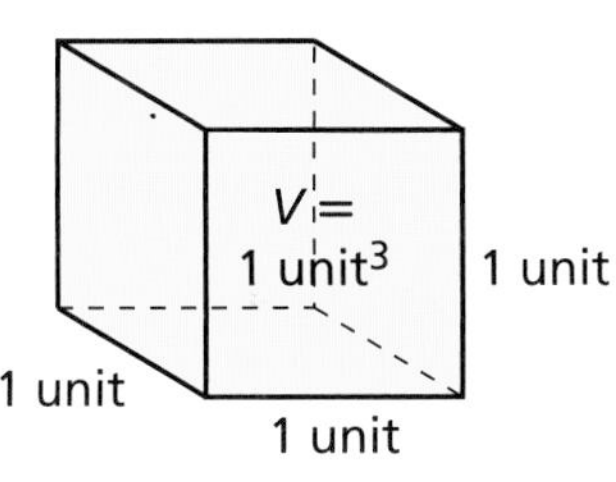

2. Label the length, width, and height of the centimeter cube on the right. Write the volume of a centimeter cube in two ways.

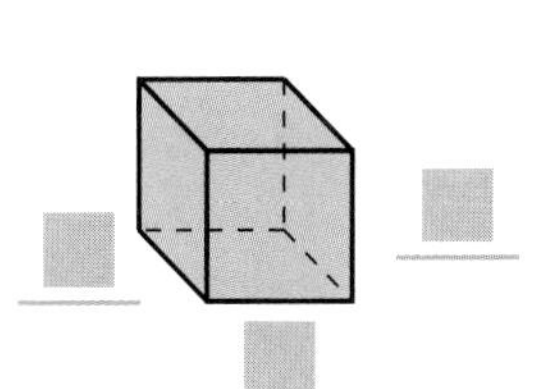

Write the volume of the cube in two ways.

3. inch cube
4. meter cube
5. foot cube
6. yard cube

▶ How Are Surface Area and Volume Different?

Complete.

7. What is the surface area of the unit cube you made?

8. What is the surface area of an inch cube?

9. How is volume different than surface area?

10. How is the unit used to measure surface area different from the unit used to measure volume?

11. What is the surface area and volume of the prism you made?

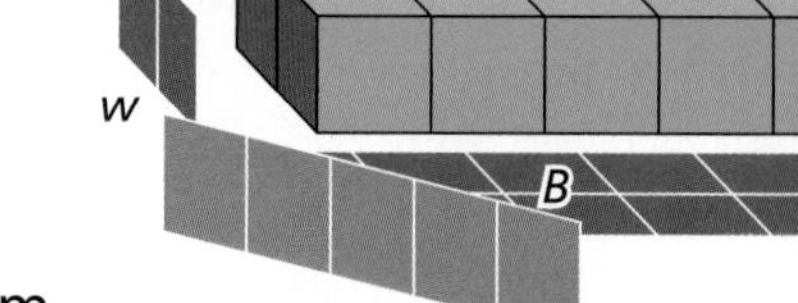

$SA =$ ▢

$V =$ ▢

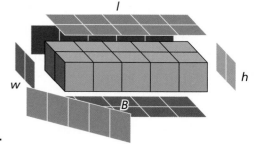

12. Write a formula for the surface area of the prism.

$SA =$ ▢

13. Write two formulas for the volume of a rectangular prism.

$V =$ ▢ $V =$ ▢

Find the surface area and volume of the prisms.

14.

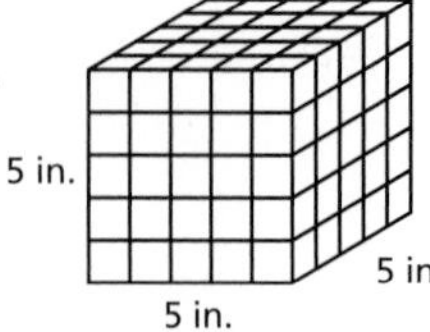

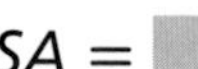

$SA =$ ▢

$V =$ ▢

15.

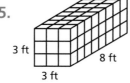

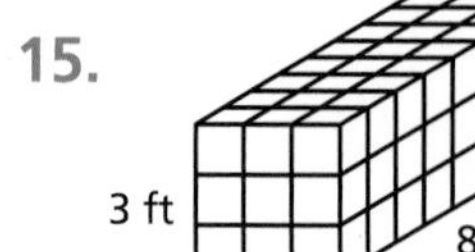

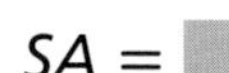

$SA =$ ▢

$V =$ ▢

16.

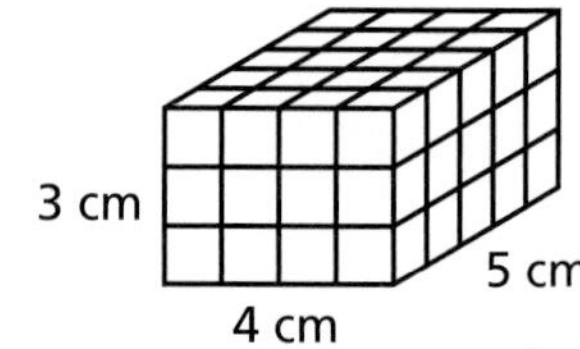

$SA =$ ▢

$V =$ ▢

▶ What's the Error?

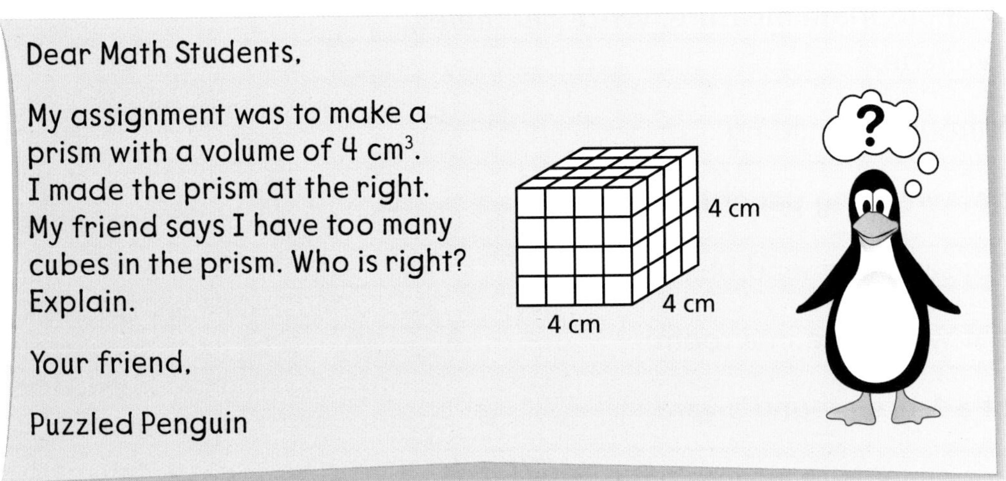

Dear Math Students,
My assignment was to make a prism with a volume of 4 cm³. I made the prism at the right. My friend says I have too many cubes in the prism. Who is right? Explain.
Your friend,
Puzzled Penguin
4 cm
4 cm
4 cm
?

17. Write a response to the Puzzled Penguin.

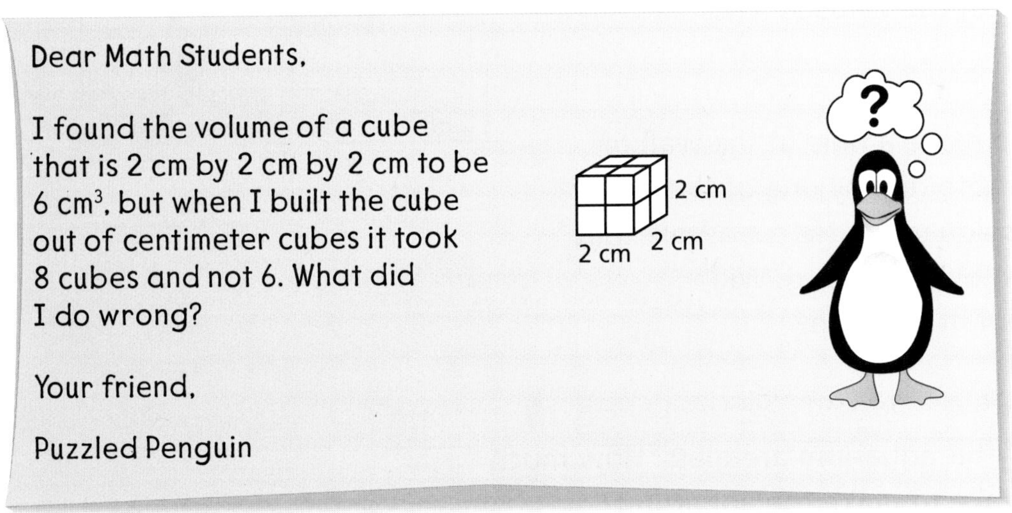

Dear Math Students,
I found the volume of a cube that is 2 cm by 2 cm by 2 cm to be 6 cm³, but when I built the cube out of centimeter cubes it took 8 cubes and not 6. What did I do wrong?
Your friend,
Puzzled Penguin
2 cm
2 cm
2 cm
?

18. Write a response to the Puzzled Penguin.

▶ Choose a Measure

Choose the most appropriate measure. Write *perimeter*, *surface area*, or *volume*.

19. the distance around a building

20. the amount of wrapping paper on a gift box

21. the amount of sand in a sand box

22. the amount of wall space in a room

23. the length of a fence around a yard

24. the amount of peanuts in a container

▶ Solve Real World Problems

Solve.

25. How many cubic feet of water will it take to fill this aquarium? What is the open surface area of the water?

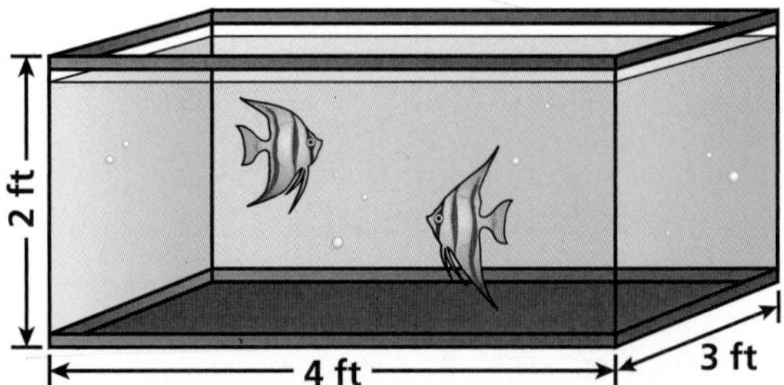

26. Hal wants to make a hole in the wall of his restaurant to display one of the larger faces of this aquarium. He cut a hole that is 25 in. high by 27 in. long. Will the aquarium fit? Explain.

27. The sides of this aquarium are glass. How much glass did it take to make the aquarium?

28. What is the greatest number of rectangular fish food boxes that are 2 in. × 2 in. × 4 in. that will fit in a carton with a volume of 3,456 $in.^3$ and a 12 in. × 24 in. rectangular base?

▶ Rectangular Prisms with Volumes Less Than 1 Cubic Unit

Place the cubes on your desk in order from greatest volume to least volume as shown below.

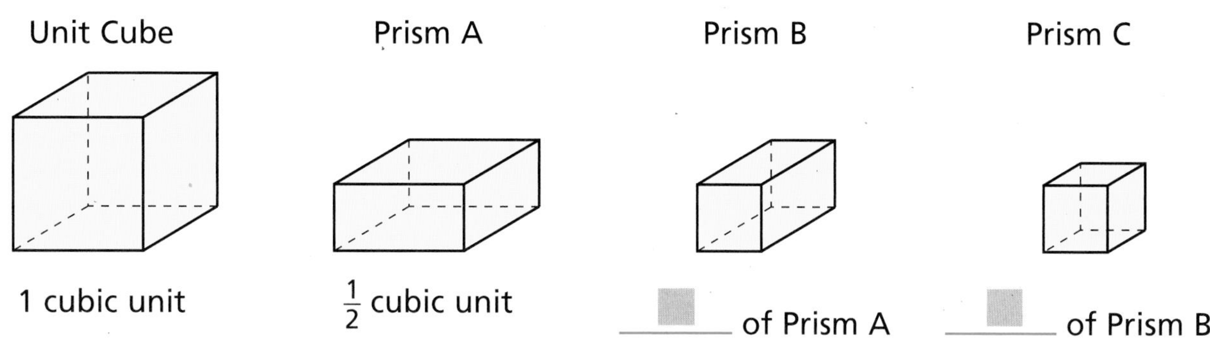

1 cubic unit | $\frac{1}{2}$ cubic unit | ____ of Prism A | ____ of Prism B

1. How many of each of these prisms does it take to make the Unit Cube?

   Prism A: ____ Prism B: ____ Prism C: ____

2. What is the volume of each prism?

   Prism A: V = ____

   Prism B: V = ____

   Prism C: V = ____

Some students found the volume of prism B by multiplying.

	Volume of Prism B	Volume of Prism C
Terence	$\frac{1}{2}$ of $\frac{1}{2}$ of a unit cube or $\frac{1}{4}$ unit^3.	
Serena	$\frac{1}{2} \bullet \frac{1}{2}$ of a cubic unit or $\frac{1}{4}$ unit^3.	
Emma	It takes $\frac{1}{4}$ of a unit cube or $\frac{1}{4}$ unit^3 to make prism B.	

3. Why are all 3 descriptions correct?

4. Complete the chart to show how Terrence, Serena, and Emma would describe the volume of Prism C.

▶ Calculate Volume Less Than 1 Cubic Unit

Complete the table.

	Prism	length (l)	width (w)	height (h)	length × width × height (lwh)	lwh = V
5.	1 unit, 1 unit, 1 unit	1 unit	1 unit	1 unit	1 • 1 • 1	1 • 1 • 1 = 1 or 1 unit^3
6.	$\frac{1}{2}$ unit, 1 unit, 1 unit					
7.	1 unit, 1 unit, $\frac{1}{2}$ unit					
8.	$\frac{1}{2}$ unit, 1 unit, $\frac{1}{2}$ unit					
9.	1 unit, $\frac{1}{2}$ unit, $\frac{1}{2}$ unit					
10.	$\frac{1}{2}$ unit, $\frac{1}{2}$ unit, $\frac{1}{2}$ unit					

11. How is the volume of a prism related to the length, width, and height of the prism?

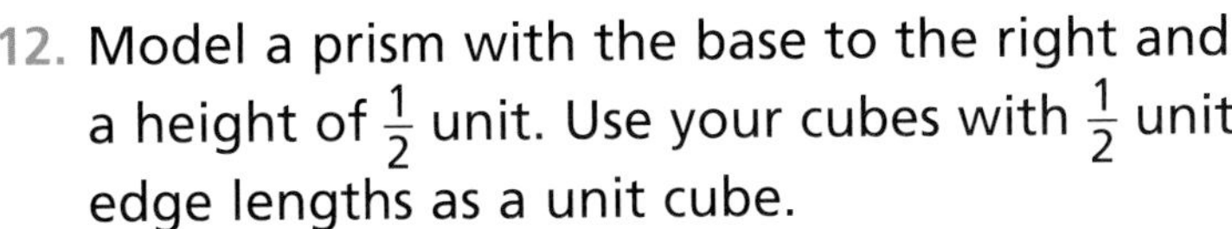

▶ Find Volume by Packing with Unit Cubes

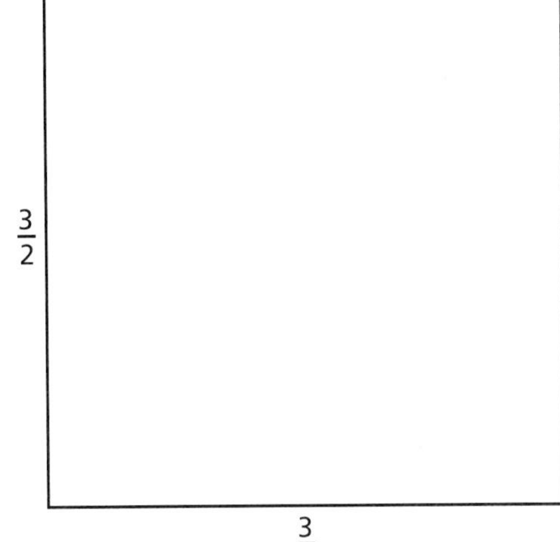

12. Model a prism with the base to the right and a height of $\frac{1}{2}$ unit. Use your cubes with $\frac{1}{2}$ unit edge lengths as a unit cube.

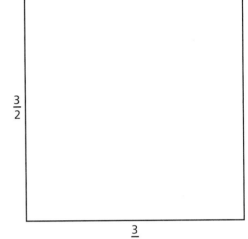

13. How many cubes with $\frac{1}{2}$ unit edge lengths did it take to make the prism?

14. What equation can you write to show the volume of 9 of these cubes?

15. What other equation can you write to describe the volume of the $\frac{3}{2}$ unit by $\frac{3}{2}$ unit by $\frac{1}{2}$ unit prism?

16. Suppose you built a prism on a square base of $\frac{4}{3}$ unit by $\frac{4}{3}$ unit with a height of $\frac{1}{3}$ unit. If you use a cube with $\frac{1}{3}$ unit edge lengths as a unit cube, how many cubes would it take to form the prism?

17. What two equations could you write to show the volume of the $\frac{4}{3}$ unit by $\frac{4}{3}$ unit by $\frac{1}{3}$ unit prism?

18. What equation could you write to show the volume of a $\frac{1}{n}$ by $\frac{1}{n}$ by $\frac{1}{n}$ cube?

▶ Volumes of Prisms with Fractional Edge Lengths

Find the volume.

19. 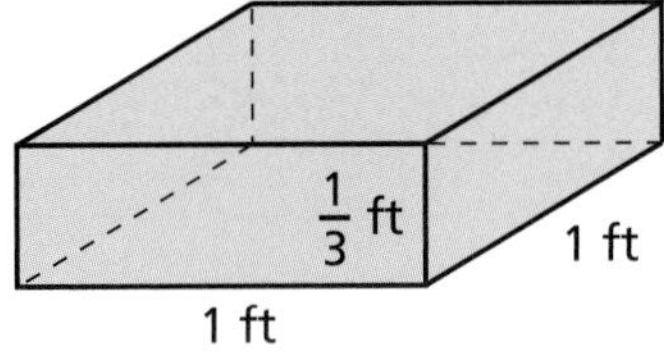

$V =$ ▒

20. 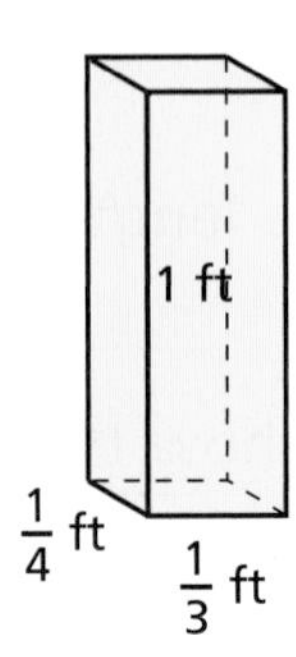

$V =$ ▒

21. 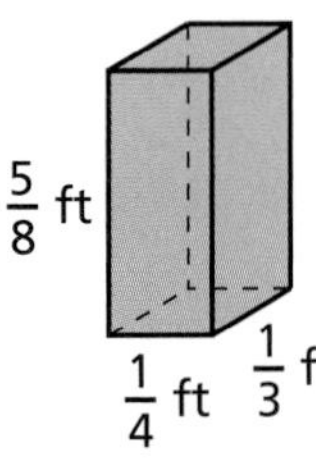

$V =$ ▒

22. 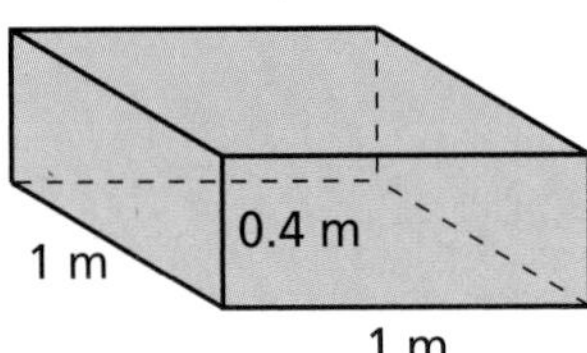

$V =$ ▒

23. 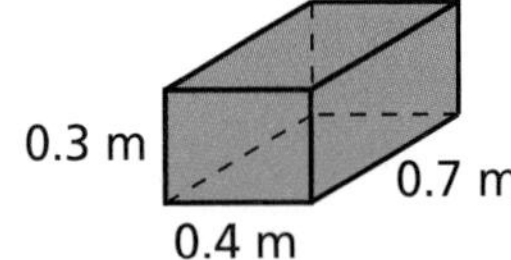

$V =$ ▒

24. 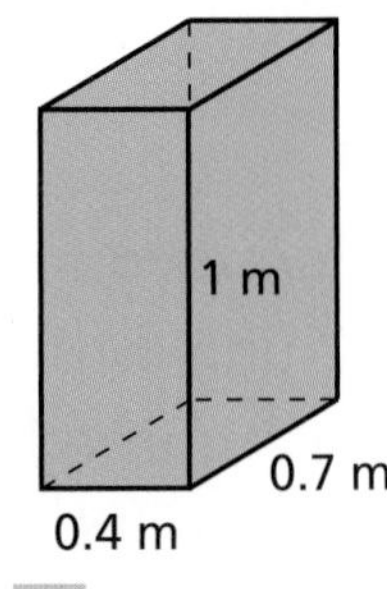

$V =$ ▒

25. Describe two different rectangular prisms that each have a volume of $\frac{6}{175}$ in.^{3}

a. What three factors will result in a product of 6?

b. What three factors will result in a product of 175?

c. What fractions can you make with these factors that could be the dimensions of one rectangular prism?

d. What different fractions can you make with these factors that could be the dimensions of a different rectangular prism?

26. Describe two different rectangular prisms that each have a volume of 0.125 m^3.

▶ Build a Prism with Whole and Half Layers

Here is how to build a prism that has a length of 5 cm, a width of 2 cm, and a height of $2\frac{1}{2}$ cm using whole and half layers.

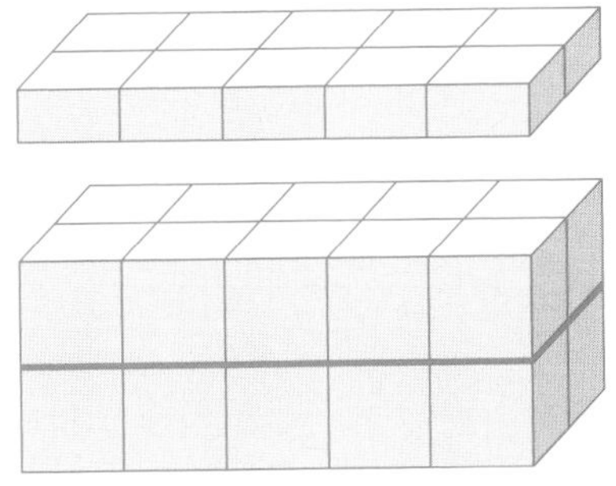

- Stack two layers of a prism that has a 5 cm by 2 cm base and is 1 cm tall.
- Next stack one layer of a prism that has a 5 cm by 2 cm base and is $\frac{1}{2}$ cm tall.

Build prisms with whole and half layers to complete the table below.

	length (l) (in cm)	width (w) (in cm)	length × width (lw)	Area of Base (B)	height (h)	$V = Bh$
1.	5	2	5 • 2	10 10 cm^2	$\frac{1}{2}$ cm	
2.	5	2			1 cm	
3.	5	2			$1\frac{1}{2}$ cm	
4.	5	2			2 cm	
5.	5	2			$3\frac{1}{2}$ cm	
6.	5	2			4 cm	
7.	5	2			$4\frac{1}{2}$ cm	
8.	5	2			5 cm	
9.	5	2			$5\frac{1}{2}$ cm	

10. Explain the expression you wrote for the volume of the prism with the $3\frac{1}{2}$ cm height in terms of layers of cubes.

▶ Build a Prism with Fractional Base Dimensions

Here is how to build a prism that has a length of $4\frac{1}{2}$ cm and a width of $2\frac{1}{2}$ cm and a height of $5\frac{1}{2}$ cm using whole and half layers.

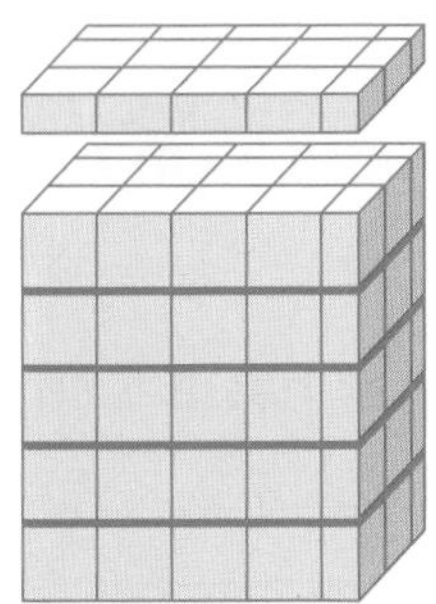

- Stack five layers of a prism that has a $4\frac{1}{2}$ cm by $2\frac{1}{2}$ cm base and is 1 cm tall.
- Next stack one layer of a prism that has a $4\frac{1}{2}$ cm by $2\frac{1}{2}$ cm base and is $\frac{1}{2}$ cm tall.

Use this table to record the volumes of the prisms you build.

	length (l) (in cm)	width (w) (in cm)	Area of Base (B)	height (h)	V = Bh
11.	$4\frac{1}{2}$	$2\frac{1}{2}$	$11\frac{1}{4}$ $11\frac{1}{4}$ cm^2	1cm	$V = 11\frac{1}{4} \bullet 1 = 11\frac{1}{4}$ $V = 11\frac{1}{4}$ cm^3
12.	$4\frac{1}{2}$	$2\frac{1}{2}$		$\frac{1}{2}$ cm	
13.	$4\frac{1}{2}$	$2\frac{1}{2}$		$1\frac{1}{2}$ cm	
14.	$4\frac{1}{2}$	$2\frac{1}{2}$		$2\frac{1}{2}$ cm	
15.	$4\frac{1}{2}$	$2\frac{1}{2}$		$3\frac{1}{2}$ cm	
16.	$4\frac{1}{2}$	$2\frac{1}{2}$		4 cm	
17.	$4\frac{1}{2}$	$2\frac{1}{2}$		$4\frac{1}{2}$ cm	

18. Explain the expression you wrote for the volume of the prism with a $2\frac{1}{2}$ cm height in terms of layers of cubes.

▶ Use Formulas

Find the volume. Each cube represents 1 cm^3.

19.

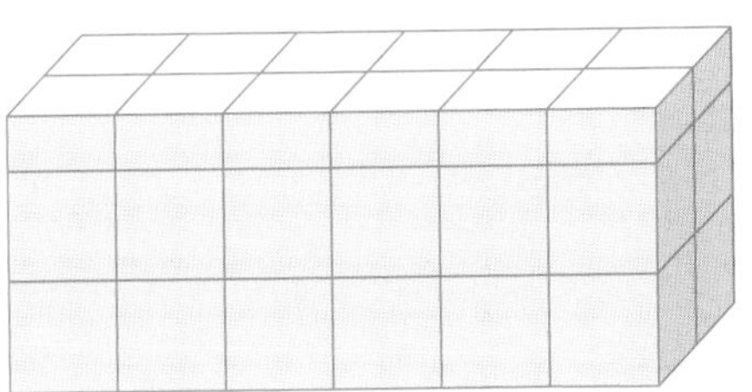

V = ▒

20.

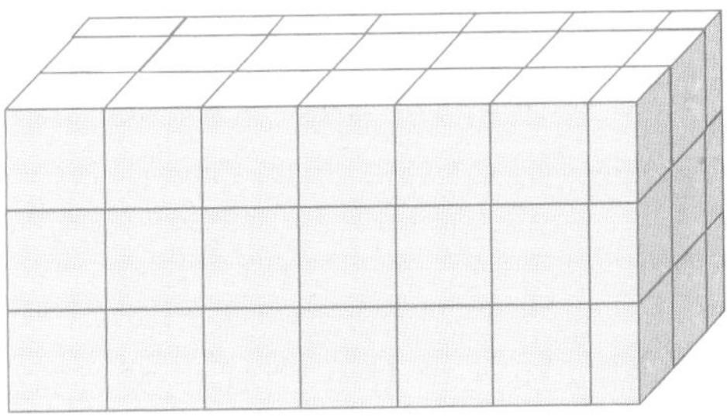

V = ▒

21.

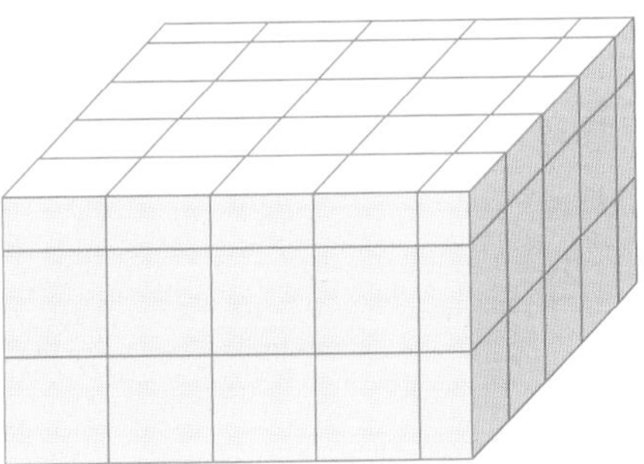

V = ▒

22.

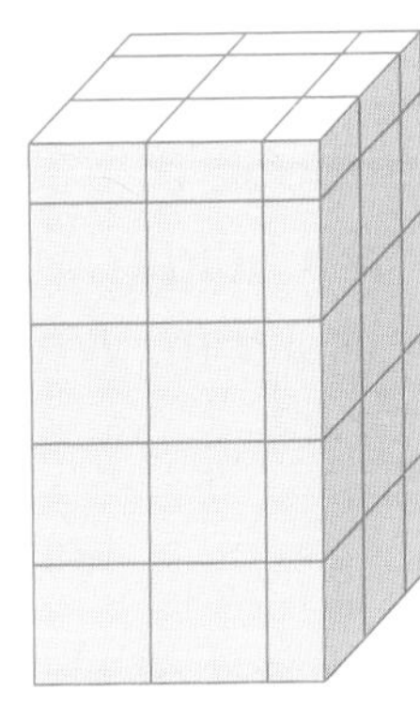

V = ▒

23. Explain why we can use the two formulas below for the volume of a prism. V stands for the volume of the rectangular prism. l and w stand for the length and width of the base, h stands for the height, and B stands for the area of the base.

$V = lwh$

$V = Bh$

▶ Find the Unknown Dimension or Volume

Write and solve an equation.

Show your work on your paper or in your journal.

24. A ring box in the shape of a rectangular prism has a volume of 25 cm^3 and is $2\frac{1}{2}$ cm tall. What is the area of the base (B) of the ring box?

25. A jewelry box in the shape of a rectangular prism has a volume of 90 $in.^3$ and a height of $2\frac{1}{2}$ in. What are possible dimensions for the length and width of the base?

26. A storage tank in the shape of a rectangular prism has a volume of 35 m^3 and a height of 2.5 m. The length of the base of the prism is 3.5 m. What is the width of the base of the storage tank?

27. A shipping box in the shape of a rectangular prism has a volume of $1\frac{1}{2}$ ft^3. The area of the base is $\frac{2}{3}$ ft^2. What is the height of the shipping box?

28. A small trunk in the shape of a rectangular prism has a volume of 0.15 m^3. The area of the base is 0.25 m^2. What is the height of the small trunk?

29. A stack of sticky notes in the shape of a rectangular prism has a base with an area of $1\frac{1}{8}$ $in.^2$ and a height that is $1\frac{1}{3}$ in. What is the volume of the stack of sticky notes?

30. An eraser in the shape of a rectangular prism has a length of 3.5 cm, a width of 2.8 cm and a height 1.4 cm. What is the volume of the eraser?

▶ Volumes of Prisms with Fractional Edge Lengths

Write a numerical expression for the volume. Then calculate the volume.

1.

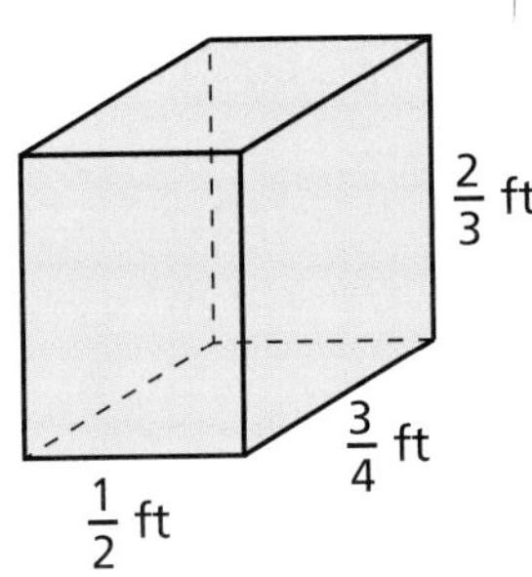

$V =$ ▢

2.

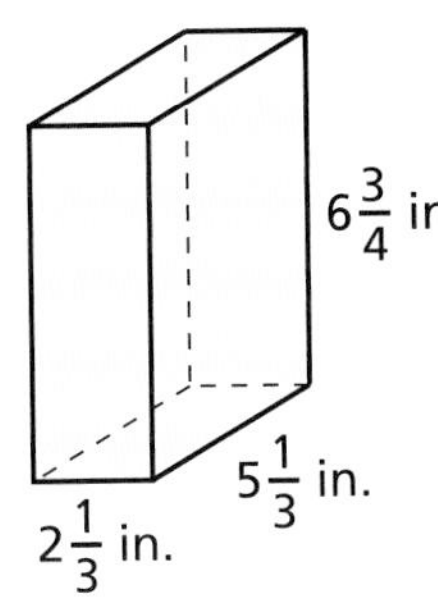

$V =$ ▢

3.

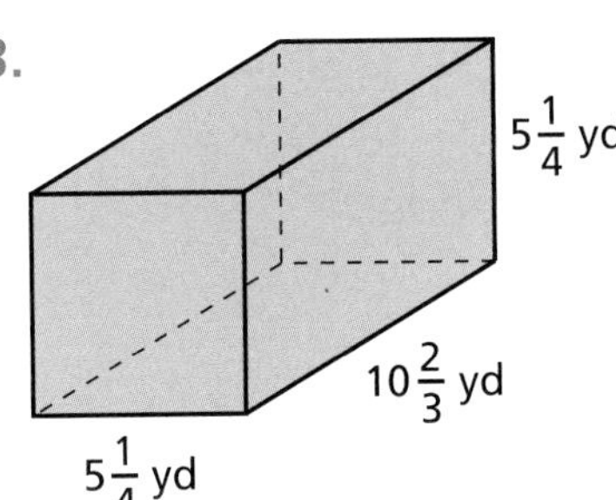

$V =$ ▢

4.

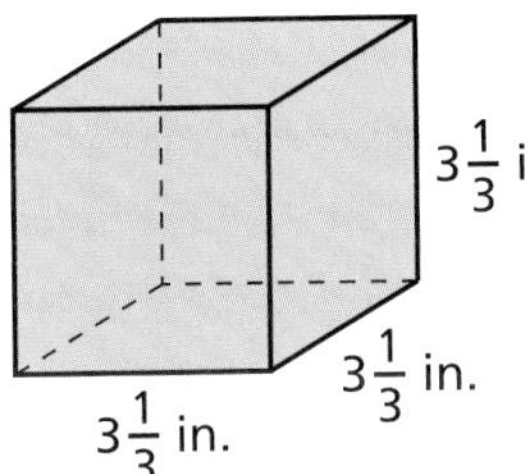

$V =$ ▢

5.

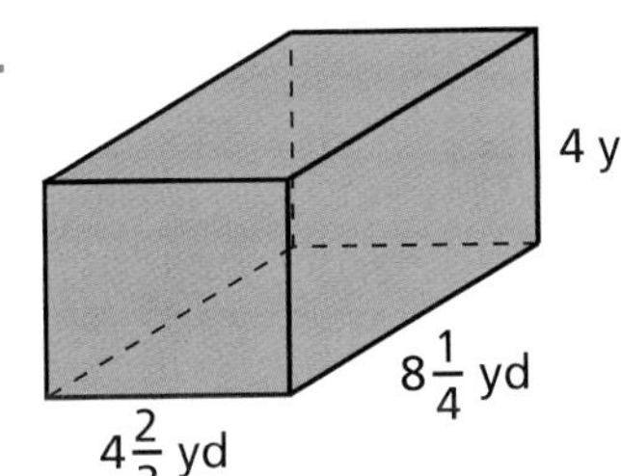

$V =$ ▢

6.

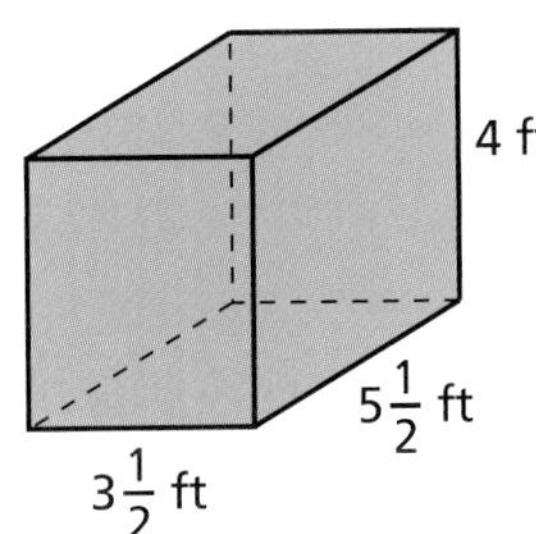

$V =$ ▢

Find the unknown dimension or volume of each rectangular prism.

7. $l = 4.5$ cm

   $w = 2.7$ cm

   $h = 3.2$ cm

   $V =$ ▢

8. $V = 156$ ft^3

   $l = 4\frac{4}{5}$ ft

   $w = 6\frac{1}{2}$ ft

   $h =$ ▢

9. $V = 209.3$ m^3

   $l = 7$ m

   $h = 4.6$ m

   $w =$ ▢

10. $V = 279$ in.^{3}

    $w = 6\frac{1}{5}$ in.

    $h = 7\frac{1}{2}$ in.

    $l =$ ▢

▶ Solve Real World Problems

Solve.

Show your work on your paper or in your journal.

11. A 20 ft by 20 ft square garden is being covered with 3 in. of mulch. How many cubic feet of mulch will be needed?

12. A rectangular cargo container is 2.5 m wide, 3.1 m tall, and 10 m long. What is the volume of the container in cubic meters?

13. Sue's collection of baseball cards forms a stack that is 3 in. high. If the cards are $2\frac{1}{4}$ in. wide and $5\frac{1}{2}$ in. long. What is the volume of the stack of cards?

14. Sue bought a box to hold her baseball cards. The box is $2\frac{1}{2}$ in. wide and $5\frac{1}{2}$ in. long and has a volume of 55 in.^{3} How tall a stack of cards can fit in the box?

15. A rectangular shipping box has a bottom that is 1 ft by 2 ft. The height of the box is 9 in. What is the volume of the box in cubic feet?

16. A tree ornament comes in a box that is $5\frac{1}{2}$ in. tall with a square top and bottom. The box has a volume of $49\frac{1}{2}$ in.^{3} How long is each side of the base?

17. A foam mattress measures $3\frac{1}{3}$ ft by $6\frac{2}{3}$ ft by 6 in. How many cubic feet of foam form the mattress?

▶ Units for l, w, h, B, and V

If V is the volume of the prism, then we can write these formulas.

$V = lwh$ $V = Bh$

These equations show how the volume of the prism is related to other dimensions of the prism.

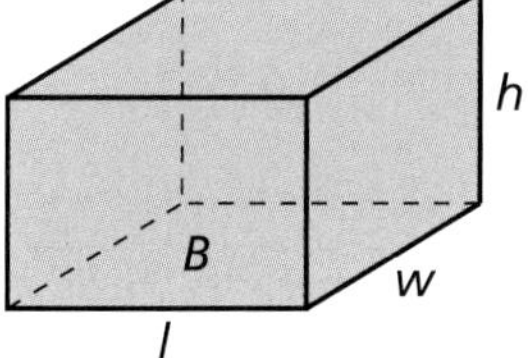

Complete.

1. If the value for h is given in centimeters , what unit should we use for l and w?
2. If the values for l, w, and h are given in centimeters, what unit should we use for B?
3. If the values for l, w, and h are given in centimeters, what unit should we use for V?

▶ What's the Error?

Dear Math Students,

Here is how I found the number of cubic feet of mulch needed on the garden pictured at the right.

$V = lwh$

$V = 10 \cdot 10 \cdot 3 = 300$

The volume is 300 ft^3.

My friend says this is not the correct answer. What did I do wrong?

Your friend,
Puzzled Penguin

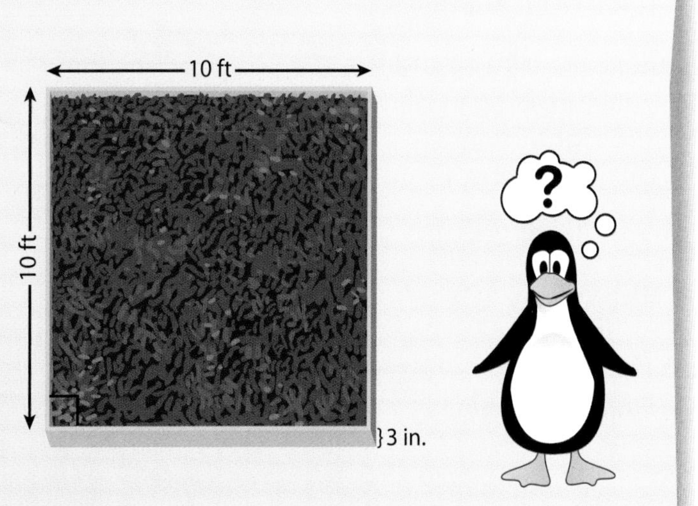

4. Write a response to the Puzzled Penguin.

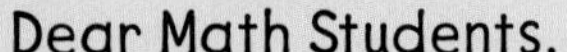

▶ What's the Error?

Dear Math Students,

I see in the formula $V = lwh$ that I need to multiply three edge lengths to find the volume. The prism has a lot more edges. Why don't we multiply all the edge lengths to find the volume?

Your friend,

Puzzled Penguin

5. Write a response to the Puzzled Penguin.

Dear Math Students,

Here is how I found the volume of the prism at the right. Is my answer correct?

$V = 4\frac{1}{2} \times 2 = 9$

The volume is 9 in.^{3}

Your friend,

Puzzled Penguin

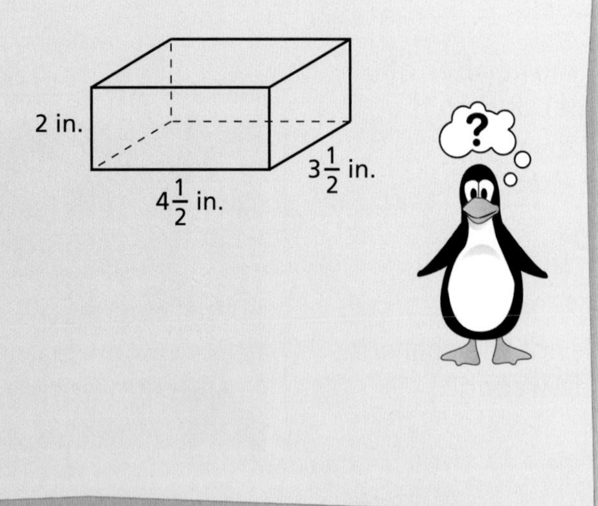

6. Write a response to the Puzzled Penguin.

▶ Write Equations for Volume

Write an equation for volume, V, using the variables given.

7. 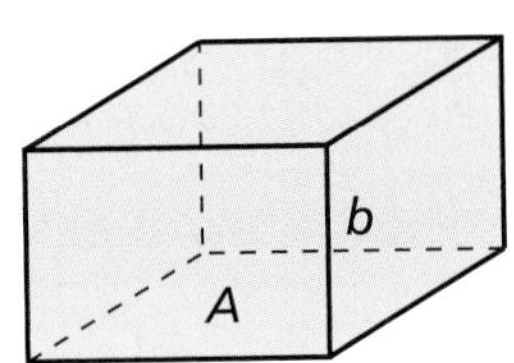

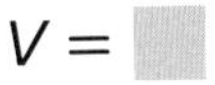

$V =$

8. 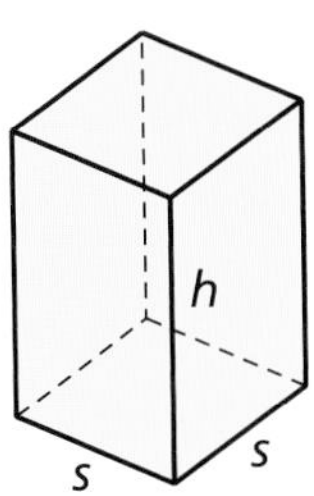

$V =$

9. 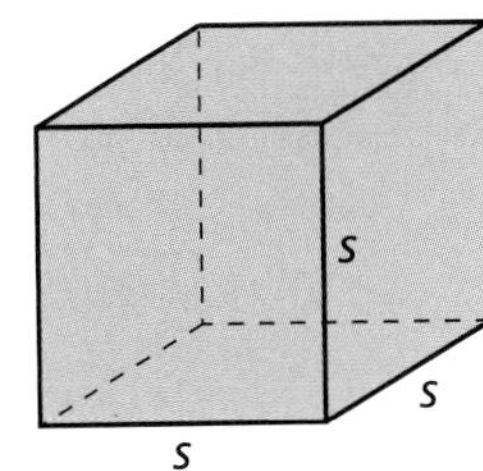

$V =$

10. A rectangular prism that is c units by d units by e units has a volume, V, cubic units. Write an equation relating c, d, e, and V.

11. A rectangular prism has base of area M square units and is t units tall. Write an equation relating M, t, and V.

12. A rectangular prism is 5 units tall and has a base of area W square units. Write an equation relating W and V.

▶ Surface Area and Volume of a Cube

Solve.

Each edge of a cube is $\frac{1}{2}$ in. long.

13. What is the surface area of the cube?

14. What is the volume of the cube?

A cube has a volume of 8 m^3.

15. What is the length of each edge?

16. What is the surface area of the cube?

One face of a cube has an area of 2.25 cm^2.

17. What is the length of each edge?

18. What is the volume of the cube?

▶ Solve Real World Problems

Solve.

Show your work on your paper or in your journal.

19. An aquarium is 18 in. by 16 in. by 12 in. Water fills $\frac{3}{4}$ of the aquarium. What is the volume of the water?

20. A sandbox is 5 ft by 6 ft by 1 ft. Sand fills half the sandbox. What is the volume of the sand?

21. Which holds more: two cube containers with $12\frac{1}{2}$ ft edges or one rectangular prism container with height $12\frac{1}{2}$ ft, width 11 ft, and length 25 ft? How much more?

22. Which has the greatest surface area: A cube gift box with $\frac{1}{2}$ ft edges or a rectangular prism gift box with a height of $\frac{1}{2}$ ft, width $\frac{1}{4}$ ft, and length 1 ft? How much more?

23. The length of a shipping box is twice its width. The width of the box is $7\frac{1}{2}$ in. The height is $2\frac{1}{2}$ in. less than the length. What is the volume of the box?

24. If a mailbox at a post office rents for one year for \$0.15 per in.^{3}, how much will it cost to rent a mailbox that is $4\frac{1}{2}$ in. by 12 in. by $5\frac{1}{2}$ in.?

25. A box of staples has length $4\frac{1}{2}$ in., width $2\frac{1}{4}$ in. and height $\frac{3}{4}$ in. What is the greatest number of boxes of staples that can be shipped in a box measuring 1 ft by 1 ft by 1 ft?

▶ Math and Construction

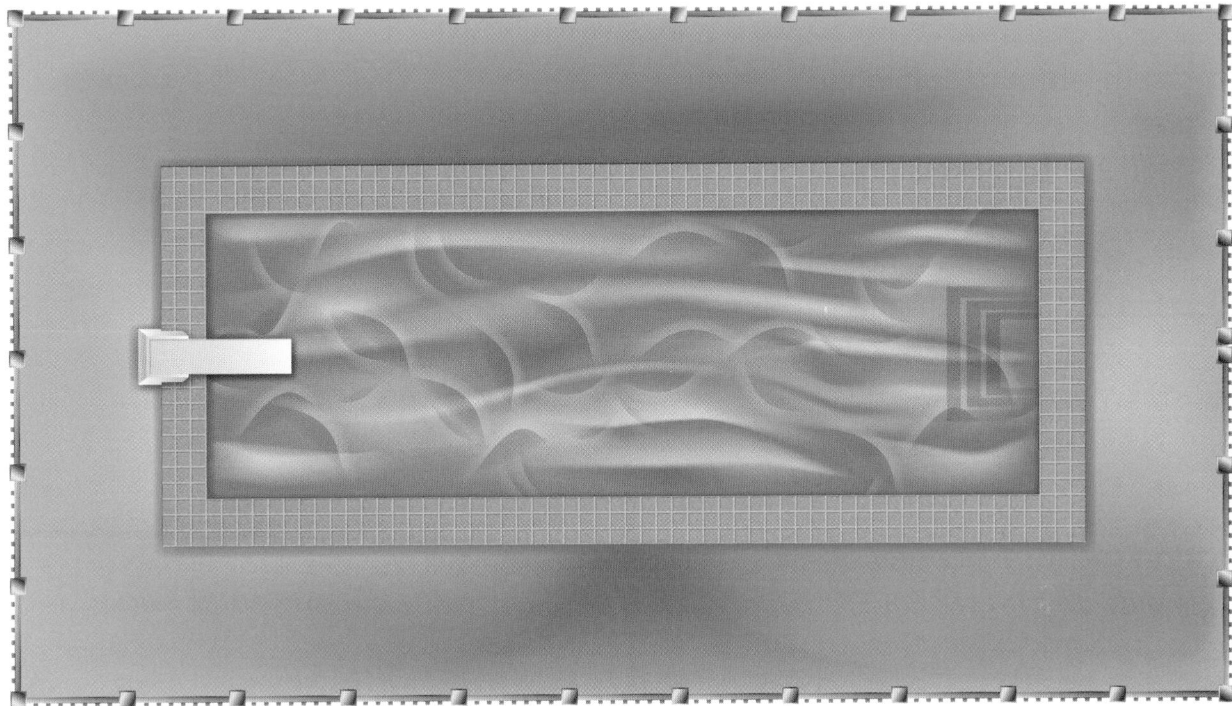

The Best Pool Construction Company is building a community swimming pool. The company has hired you and your associate to find how much tile and fencing needs to be ordered to finish the pool.

The pool is a rectangle 60 ft long and 20 ft wide. One third of the pool is 4 ft deep and the remaining part has a depth of 7 ft. There is to be a 3-ft wide tile deck around the entire pool and a safety fence around the entire area 11 ft from the edge of the tile deck.

1. What strategy will you use to find how much fence and tile is needed?

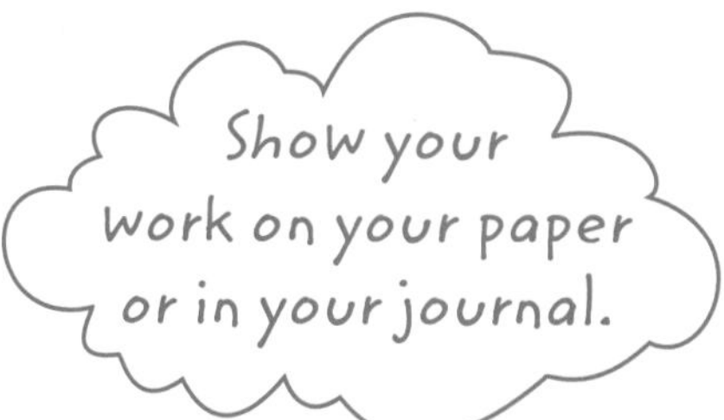

Show your work on your paper or in your journal.

▶ Make a Drawing

Complete.

2. Use the information in the problem on Student Book page 263 to make a drawing at the right of a top view of the pool, tile, and fence. Label all the dimensions.

3. How many square feet of tile should be ordered for tile deck?

4. Safety fence is sold in 8-ft sections. How many sections should be ordered?

5. How many cubic feet of water will it take to fill the pool up to 6 in. below the top?

Use the Activity Workbook Unit Test on pages 143–144.

▶ Vocabulary

Choose the best term from the box.

Vocabulary

cubic unit
surface area
unit cube
volume

1. ____?____ is the measure of the amount of space occupied by an object. **(Lesson 6-1)**

2. A ____?____ is a unit of volume made by a cube with all edges one unit long. **(Lessons 6-1, 6-2)**

3. ____?____ is the total area of the 2-dimensional surfaces of a 3-dimensional figure. **(Lesson 6-1)**

▶ Concepts and Skills

Complete.

4. Why is volume measured in cubic units? **(Lesson 6-1)**

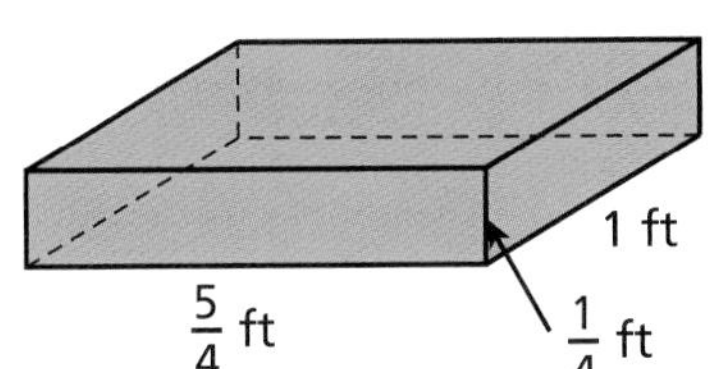

5. The volume of the prism at the right can be found buy packing it with unit cubes of the appropriate edge lengths. What edge lengths would be appropriate? Why? **(Lesson 6-2)**

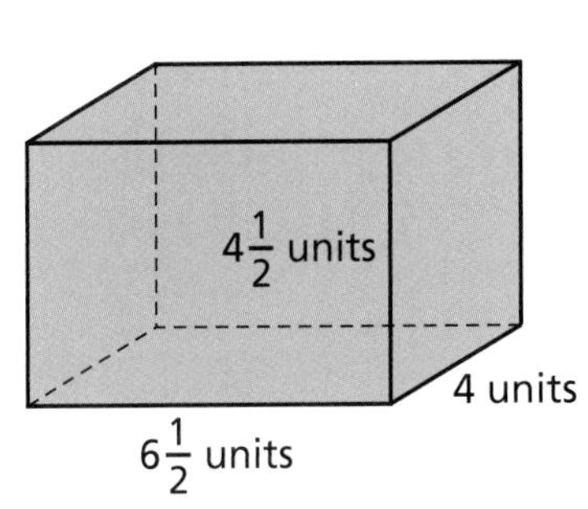

6. Why can you use the formulas $V = Bh$ and $V = lwh$ to find volume? **(Lesson 6-3, 6-4)**

7. Explain how to find the volume of the prism at the right using layers. **(Lesson 6-3)**

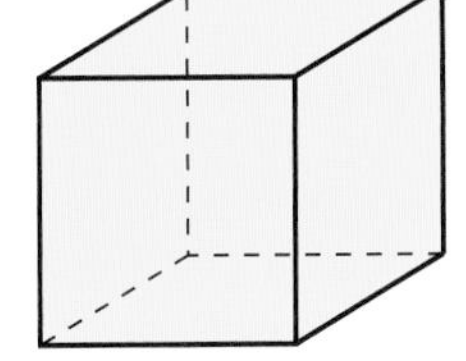

8. Label the prism at the right if the equation for the volume is $V = Mt$. **(Lesson 6-5)**

Find the volume. (Lessons 6-1, 6-2, 6-3, 6-4)

9. 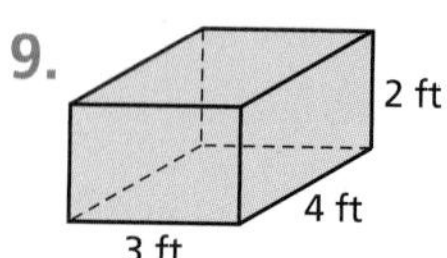

10. 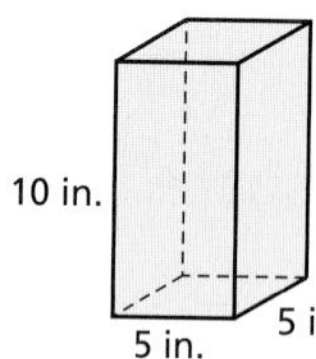

11. 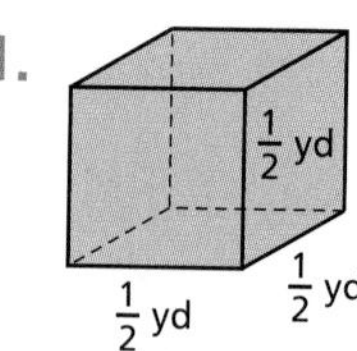

12. 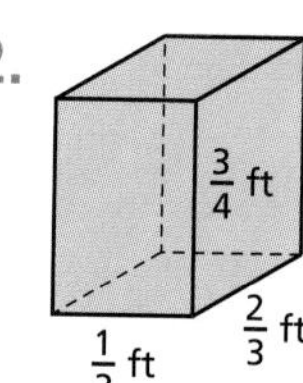

13. 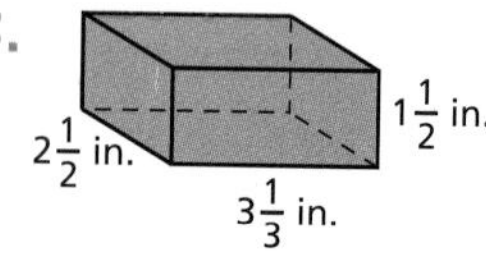

14. 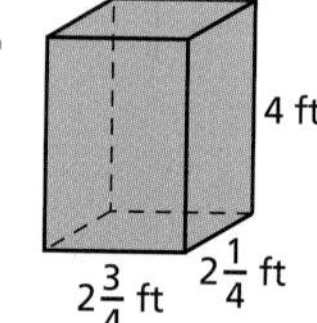

15. 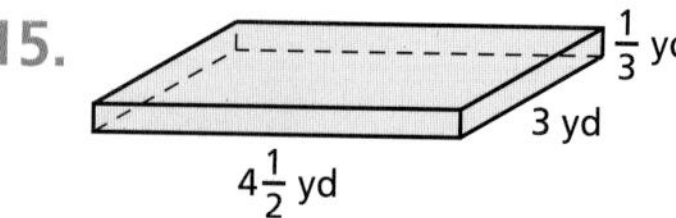

Write an equation for volume using the variables given. (Lesson 6-5)

16. 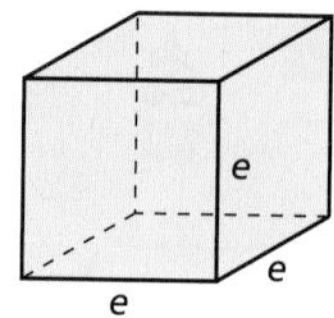

17. 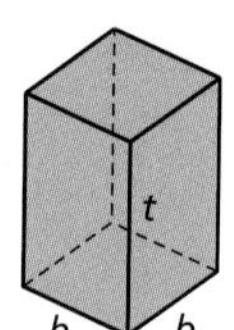

18. 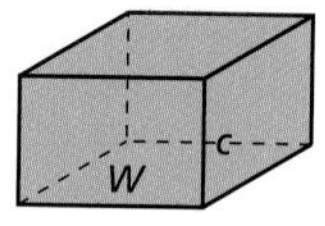

▶ Problem Solving

Solve.

19. A gift box has a volume 189 in.^{3} The area of the base of the gift box is $49\frac{3}{4}$ in.^{2} What is the height of the gift box? (Lesson 6-1, 6-2, 6-3, 6-4)

20. **Extended Response** A small pool in the shape of a rectangular prism has a length of $6\frac{1}{2}$ ft, a width of 5 ft and a height of 24 in. Jeb says the volume of the pool is 780 ft^3. Is he correct? If not, explain what he did wrong and give the correct volume. (Lessons 6-3, 6-4)

Family Letter

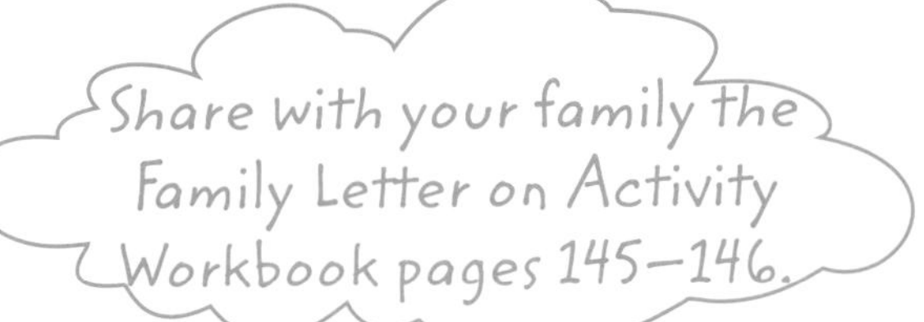
Share with your family the
Family Letter on Activity
Workbook pages 145–146.

Dear Family,

In our math class we are studying ratios, rates, and percent. We will work with tables, diagrams and equations. These will help your child to develop her or his understanding of ratios, rates, and percent as well as to learn methods for solving problems. You can help your child by asking him or her to explain the tables, diagrams and equations.

Here are some examples of the kinds of problems we will solve and the kinds of tables, diagrams, and equations we will use.

- Purple Berry juice is made from 2 cups of raspberry juice for every 3 cups of blueberry juice. How many cups of blueberry juice are needed for 11 cups of raspberry juice?

Table with Unit Rate

	B	R	
	3	2	
$\div 2$	$\frac{3}{2}$	1	$\div 2$
$\cdot 11$	$\frac{33}{2}$	11	$\cdot 11$

Equation

$$\frac{2}{3} = \frac{11}{x}$$

$$2x = 33$$

$$x = \frac{33}{2}$$

The answer is $\frac{33}{2}$ or $16\frac{1}{2}$ cups of blueberry juice.

- A juice company's KiwiBerry juice is made by mixing 2 parts kiwifruit juice with 3 parts strawberry juice. To make 20 liters of KiwiBerry juice, how much kiwifruit juice is needed?

Factor Puzzle

	k	KB
	2	5
1	2	5
4	8	20

Tape Diagram

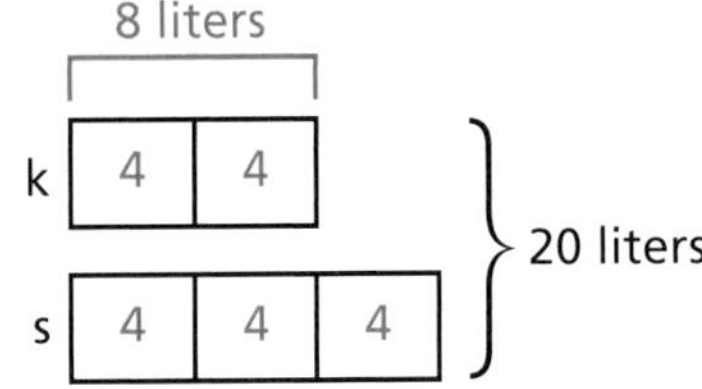
8 liters
k 4 4
s 4 4 4
20 liters

The answer is 8 liters of kiwifruit juice.

continued ▶

- If 12 milligrams of niacin is 60% of the recommended daily allowance for niacin, then what is the recommended daily allowance for niacin?

Double Number Line Diagram

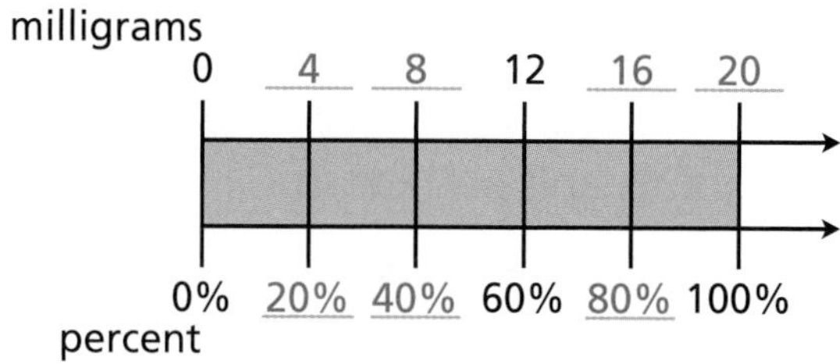

Equation

$$\frac{12}{x} = \frac{60}{100}$$
$$60x = 12 \cdot 100$$
$$x = \frac{12 \cdot 100}{60}$$
$$x = 20$$

The answer is 20 milligrams.

- A double number line can be used to convert between centimeters and millimeters. Complete the double number line to show how centimeters and millimeters are related.

Double Number Line Diagram

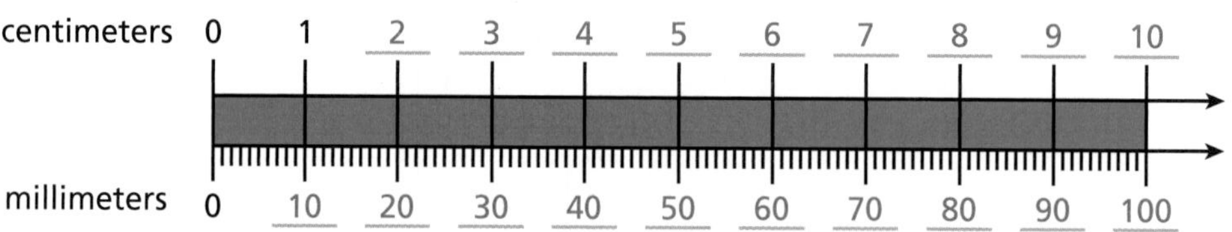

If you have any questions or comments, please call or write to me.

Sincerely,
Your child's teacher

This unit includes the Common Core Standards for Mathematical Content for Ratios and Proportional Relationships, 6.RP.1, 6.RP.2, 6.RP.3, 6.RP.3a, 6.RP.3b, 6.RP.3c, 6.RP.3d; Expressions and Equations, 6.EE.6, 6.EE.7, 6.EE.9; Geometry, 6.G.1, 6.G.4; and all Mathematical Practices.

Muestra a tu familia la Carta a la familia de las páginas 147 y 148 del Cuaderno de actividades y trabajo.

Estimada familia,

En la clase de matemáticas estamos estudiando razones, tasas y porcentajes. Para que su hijo logre una mejor comprensión de esos conceptos y aprenda métodos de resolución de problemas, trabajaremos con tablas, diagramas y ecuaciones. Usted puede ayudar, pidiéndole a su hijo o hija que le explique cómo usar las tablas, los diagramas y las ecuaciones.

Aquí tiene algunos ejemplos de los tipos de problemas que resolveremos y de los tipos de tablas, diagramas y ecuaciones que usaremos.

- Para hacer jugo azul se necesitan 2 tazas de jugo de frambuesa por cada 3 tazas de jugo de arándanos. ¿Cuántas tazas de jugo de arándanos se necesitan si se usan 11 tazas de jugo de frambuesa?

Tabla con tasa por unidad

	A	F	
	3	2	
$\div 2$	$\frac{3}{2}$	1	$\div 2$
$\bullet 11$	$\frac{33}{2}$	11	$\bullet 11$

Ecuación

$$\frac{2}{3} = \frac{11}{x}$$
$$2x = 33$$
$$x = \frac{33}{2}$$

La respuesta es $\frac{33}{2}$ o $16\frac{1}{2}$ tazas de jugo de arándanos.

- Una compañía hace jugo de kiwi con fresa mezclando 2 partes de jugo de kiwi con 3 partes de jugo de fresa. Para hacer 20 litros, ¿cuánto jugo de kiwi se necesita?

Rompecabezas de factores

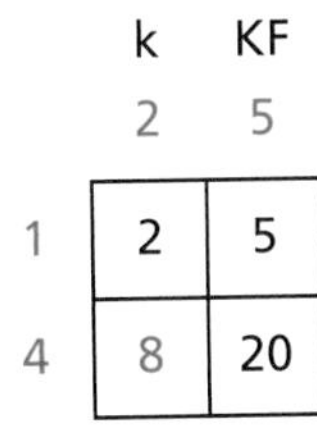

Diagrama en forma de cinta

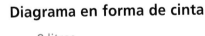

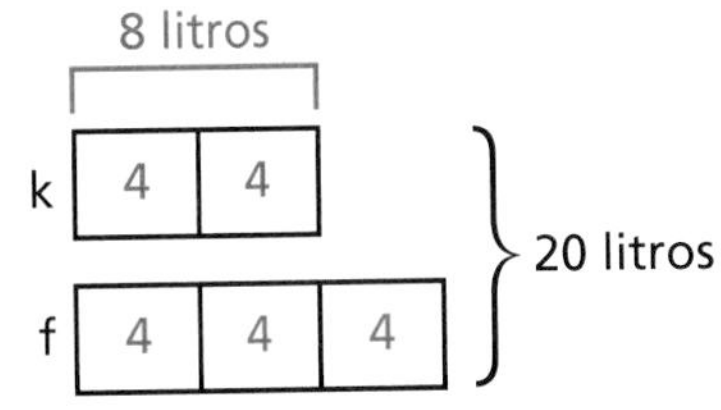

continúa ▶

- Si 12 miligramos de niacina equivalen al 60% del consumo diario que se recomienda, entonces, ¿cuál es el consumo diario total de niacina que se recomienda?

Diagrama de recta numérica doble

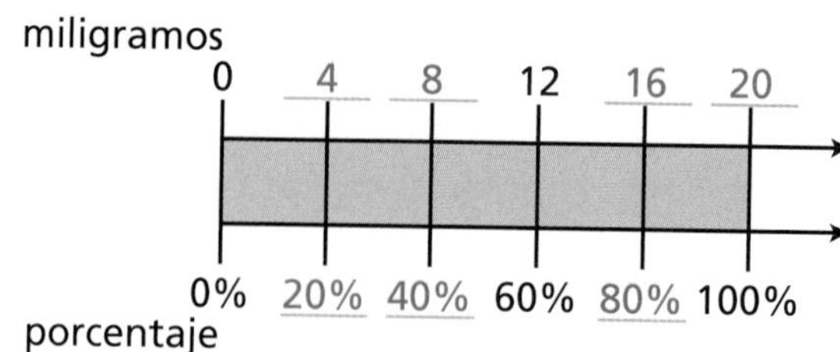

Ecuación

$$\frac{12}{x} = \frac{60}{100}$$

$$60x = 12 \bullet 100$$

$$x = \frac{12 \bullet 100}{60}$$

$$x = 20$$

La respuesta es 20 miligramos.

- Se puede usar una recta numérica doble para realizar conversiones entre centímetros y milímetros. Completen la recta numérica doble para mostrar cómo se relacionan los centímetros y los milímetros.

Diagrama de recta numérica doble

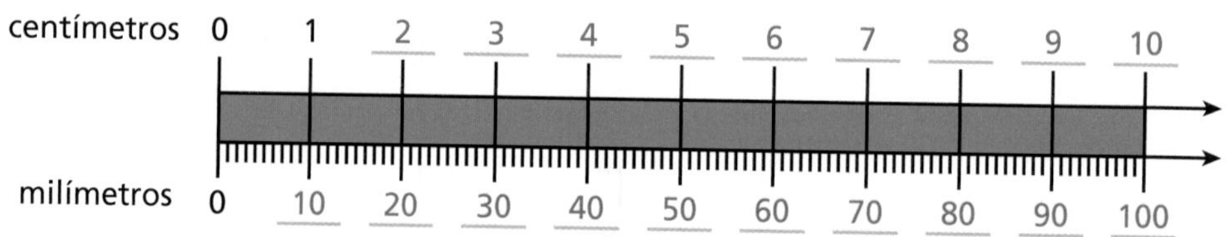

Si tiene comentarios o preguntas, por favor comuníquese conmigo.

Atentamente,
El maestro de su hijo

Esta unidad incluye los Common Core Standards for Mathematical Content for Ratios and Proportional Relationships, 6.RP.1, 6.RP.2, 6.RP.3, 6.RP.3a, 6.RP.3b, 6.RP.3c, 6.RP.3d; Expressions and Equations, 6.EE.6, 6.EE.7, 6.EE.9; Geometry, 6.G.1, 6.G.4; and all Mathematical Practices.

7–1
Class Activity

Write your answers on Activity Workbook page 149.

Vocabulary
compare ratios

▶ Compare Paint Ratios

Grasshopper Green paint has a blue:yellow paint ratio of 2:7. Gorgeous Green paint has a blue:yellow ratio of 4:5.

You can **compare ratios**. You can find out which ratio makes paint that is more blue and which ratio makes paint that is more yellow.

To find out which paint is more blue, make the values for yellow the same. One way to do this is to make the value for yellow be the product of the yellow values in the basic ratios.

1. What is the product of the yellow values in the basic ratios?

2. Complete these ratio tables.

Grasshopper Green	
Blue	**Yellow**
2	7
	35

Gorgeous Green	
Blue	**Yellow**
4	5
	35

3. Which paint is more blue? Why?

4. Which paint is less blue?

5. To find out which paint is more yellow, make the values for blue the same. Complete these ratio tables.

Grasshopper Green	
Blue	**Yellow**
2	7
4	14

Gorgeous Green	
Blue	**Yellow**
4	5

4:14
4:5

6. Which paint is more yellow?

7. Which paint is less yellow?

▶ Graph and Compare Paint Ratios

8. Look back at the tables in Exercises 2 and 5 on page 271. Write the three ratios for each paint color in these tables.

Grasshopper Green	
Blue	**Yellow**
2	7
4	14
6	21

Gorgeous Green	
Blue	**Yellow**
4	5
8	10
12	15

9. Graph two points from each table. Draw and label a line for *Grasshopper Green* and a line for *Gorgeous Green*.

y
30
25
20
Yellow 15
10
5
0 5 10 15 x
Blue

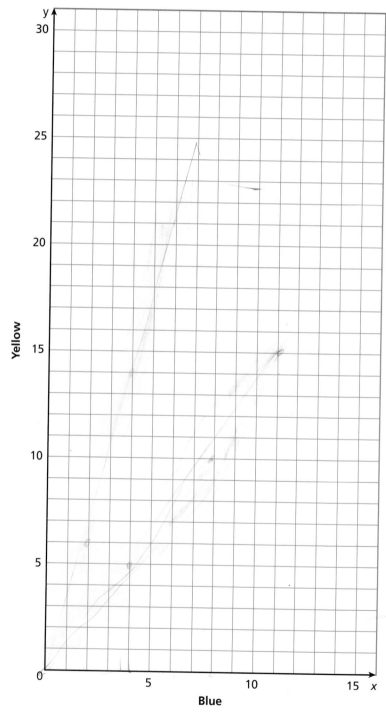

10. Discuss how the graphs can be used to decide which paint is more blue, less blue, more yellow, and less yellow.

Write your answers on Activity Workbook page 151.

▶ Ratio as a Quotient

You can use a unit rate to describe *any* ratio. A unit rate for a ratio tells the amount of the first attribute for 1 unit of the second attribute.

Look again at Sue's and Ben's drink recipes.

Sue's recipe has 5 cups cherry juice and 4 cups orange juice.

Ben's recipe has 6 cups cherry juice and 5 cups orange juice.

1. Find the amount of cherry juice in each drink for 1 cup of orange juice. Remember that when you divide both quantities in a ratio table by the same number, you get an equivalent ratio.

Sue's Recipe

Cherry	Orange
5	4
$\frac{5}{4}$	1

(÷ 4 on both columns)

$\frac{5}{4}$ is the quotient of 5 ÷ 4.

Sue has $\frac{5}{4}$ cups of cherry juice for every cup of orange juice.

The unit rate for the ratio 5:4 is $\frac{5}{4}$.

Ben's Recipe

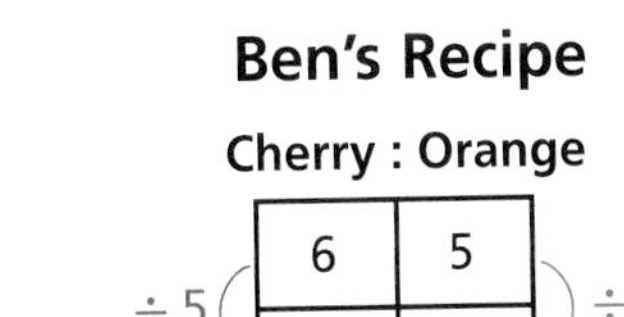

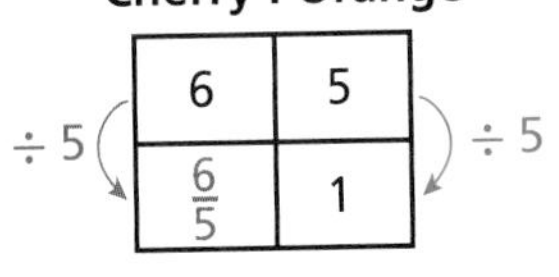

Cherry	Orange
6	5
$\frac{6}{5}$	1

(÷ 5 on both columns)

____ is the quotient of 6 ÷ 5.

Ben has ____ cups of cherry juice for every cup of orange juice.

The unit rate for the ratio ____ is ____.

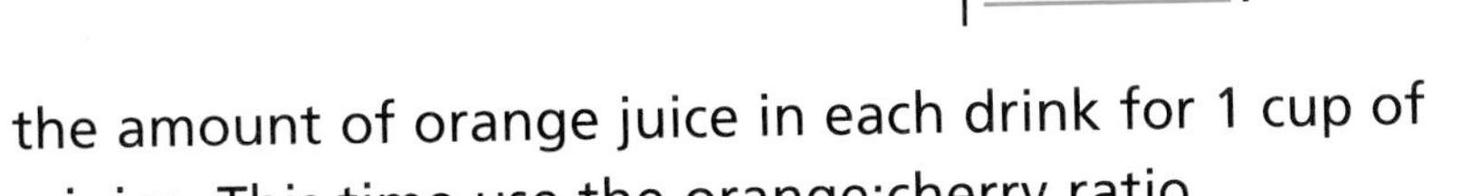

2. Find the amount of orange juice in each drink for 1 cup of cherry juice. This time use the orange:cherry ratio.

Sue's Recipe

Orange	Cherry
4	5
____	1

Sue has ____ cup of orange juice for every cup of cherry juice.

The unit rate for the ratio ____ is ____.

Ben's Recipe

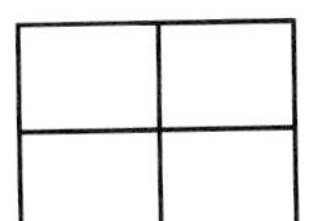

Ben has ____ cup of orange juice for every cup of cherry juice.

The unit rate for the ratio ____ is ____.

► Use Unit Rate Language to Describe Ratios

Complete each sentence using a fraction.

3. Pedro uses a ratio of 7 quarts of blue paint to 4 quarts of white paint, a ratio of 7 to 4.

   a. Pedro uses ______ quarts of blue paint for every quart of white paint.

   b. The unit rate for the ratio 7:4 is ______.

4. Grandpa's soup uses 3 cups of tomatoes to 8 cups of broth, a ratio of 3 to 8.

   a. Grandpa uses ______ cup of tomatoes for every cup of broth.

   b. The unit rate for the ratio 3:8 is ______.

5. The unit rate for the ratio a:b (b not equal to 0) is ______.

► Compare Ratios Using Unit Rates

Look back at the unit rates you found on page 273 to answer these questions.

6. Whose drink is more cherry-flavored, Sue's or Ben's? How can you use unit rates to decide?

7. Whose drink is more orange-flavored, Sue's or Ben's? How can you use unit rates to decide?

Vocabulary

unit rate strategy

▶ The Unit Rate Strategy

You can use the **unit rate strategy** to find the unknown in a proportion problem.

8. Maria's favorite juice recipe uses 4 cups of mango juice and 3 cups of strawberry juice. How many cups of strawberry juice should she mix with 5 cups of mango juice to make her favorite juice?

   Answer: ________ cups

Since the unknown is the number of cups of *strawberry* juice, use the unit rate for the ratio *strawberry*:mango.

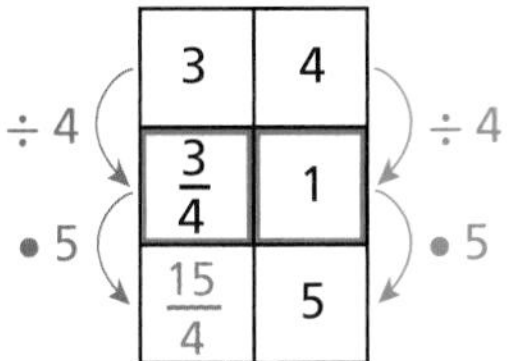

9. Adelina makes 2 drawings in her sketchbook while Jayden makes 5 drawings in his sketchbook. If both continue at their same constant rates, how many drawings will Adelina have made when Jayden has made 7 drawings?

   Answer: ________ drawings

Since the unknown is the number of *Adelina's* drawings, use the unit rate for the ratio *Adelina*:Jayden.

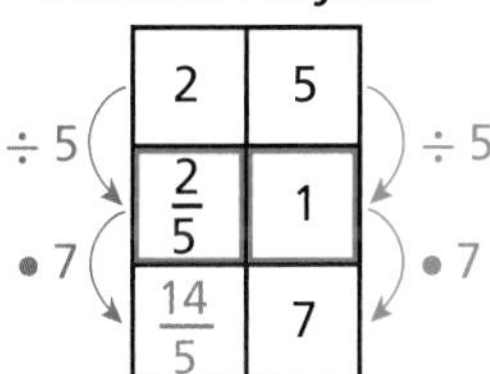

Solve. Use the unit rate strategy.

10. Diana can do 3 sit-ups in the time it takes Walter to do 2. How many sit-ups will Walter have done when Diana has done 12 sit-ups?

    Answer: ________ sit-ups

11. Grandfather paid $6 for 14 apples. If I buy the same kind of apples, how much will 35 apples cost?

    Answer: ________

▶ Variations on the Unit Rate Strategy

12. Gen, Claire, and Joey all use the unit rate strategy to solve this problem. But they record their thinking in different ways. Discuss how their methods are alike and how they are different.

> John can plant 7 tomato vines in the time it takes Joanna to plant 4 tomato vines. At that rate, when Joanna has planted 11 tomato vines, how many has John planted?

a. *Gen*: I use a ratio table. First I divide and then I multiply.

John : Joanna

	John	Joanna	
	7	4	
÷ 4	$\frac{7}{4}$	1	÷ 4
• 11	$\frac{77}{4}$	11	• 11

b. *Claire*: I make a Factor Puzzle and put the unit rate on top.

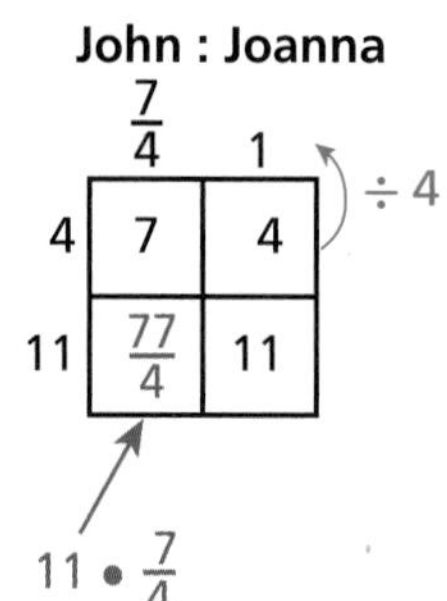

c. *Joey*: I "go through 1." I don't even write the unit rate.

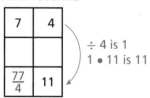

John : Joanna

John	Joanna
7	4
$\frac{77}{4}$	11

÷ 4 is 1
1 • 11 is 11

So I do the same for 7: 7 ÷ 4 • 11

$\frac{7}{4} \bullet 11 = \frac{77}{4}$

Answer: $\frac{77}{4}$ tomato vines

Solve using any variation of the unit rate strategy.

13. Shawn plants 6 tulip bulbs in the time it takes Martin to plant 7 tulip bulbs. How many tulip bulbs will Shawn have planted when Martin has planted 21 bulbs?

Answer:

14. Amanda buys 3 pounds of blueberries for $12. At the same price per pound, how much will 8 pounds of blueberries cost?

Answer:

Write your answers on Activity Workbook page 152.

▶ Horizontal Ratio Tables

1. Complete the ratio table.

Cups of Juice

Tangerine	◯	▒	1	8	▒	▒
Cherry	◯	1	▒	6	15	2

a. The basic ratio of $\frac{\text{tangerine}}{\text{cherry}}$ is ______.

b. There are ______ cups of tangerine juice for every cup of cherry juice.

c. The basic ratio of $\frac{\text{cherry}}{\text{tangerine}}$ is ______.

d. There is ______ cup of cherry juice for every cup of tangerine juice.

2. A flower mix has 21 tulips and 14 daffodils.

a. The basic ratio of $\frac{\text{tulips}}{\text{daffodils}}$ is ______.

b. There are ______ tulips for every daffodil.

c. The basic ratio for $\frac{\text{daffodils}}{\text{tulips}}$ is ______.

d. There is ______ daffodil for each tulip.

e. Using the basic ratio, how many tulips would be placed with 6 daffodils?

f. Using the basic ratio, how many daffodils would be placed with 6 tulips?

Solve.

3. At the farm the ratios of mothers to baby sheep in each field are equivalent. If there are 20 mothers and 24 babies in the small field, how many babies are with the 45 mothers in the large field?

Use Activity Workbook page 153.

▶ Equivalent Fractions and Equivalent Ratios

4. Show how the pattern of equivalent fractions continues.

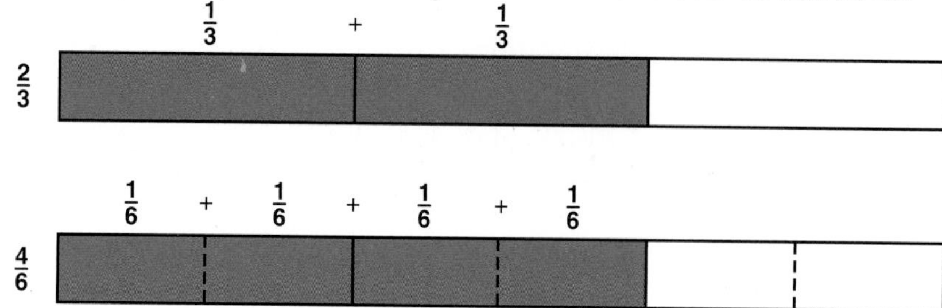

$\frac{2 \cdot 2}{2 \cdot 3} = \frac{4}{6}$

a. $\frac{6}{9}$

b. ______

c. $\frac{8}{12}$

d. ______

5. Show how the pattern of equivalent ratios continues.

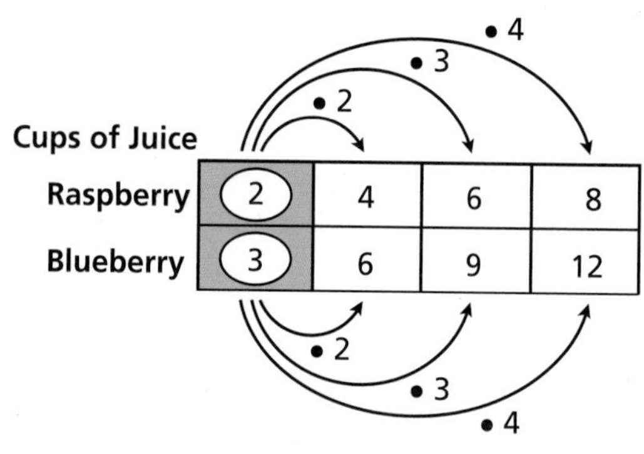

2 cups of raspberry:3 cups of blueberry

4 cups of raspberry:6 cups of blueberry

a. ______ cups of raspberry: ______ cups of blueberry

b. ______ cups of raspberry: ______ cups of blueberry

6. Draw to show the ratio pattern.

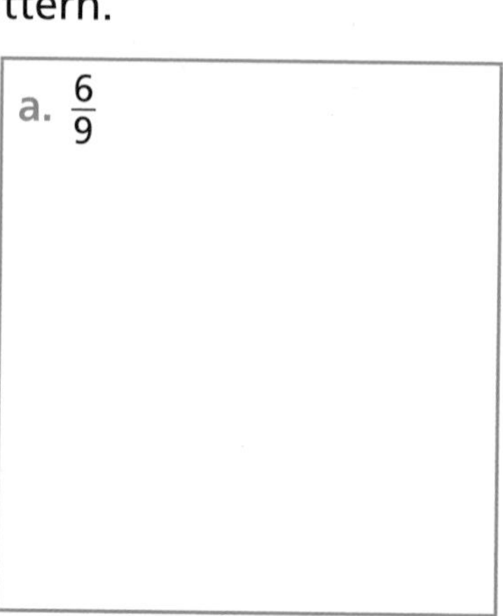

b. $\frac{8}{12}$

7. Discuss how equivalent fractions and equivalent ratios are alike and different.

Vocabulary

cross-multiplication

▶ Understanding Cross-Multiplication

When two equivalent ratios are written in a Factor Puzzle, the products of the numbers in opposite corners are equal. This results in a strategy for solving proportions called **cross-multiplication**.

$\frac{10}{15} = \frac{18}{27}$

Factor Puzzle

	5	9
2	10	18
3	15	27

Multiply opposite corners. Products are equal.

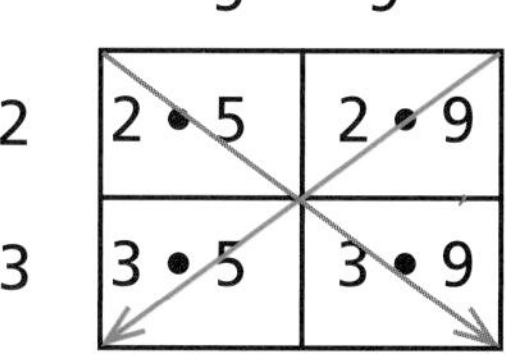

$(2 \cdot 9)(3 \cdot 5) = (2 \cdot 5)(3 \cdot 9)$

$18 \cdot 15 = 10 \cdot 27$

Cross-multiply. Products are equal.

$\frac{10}{15} = \frac{18}{27}$

$18 \cdot 15 = 10 \cdot 27$

Cross-multiply to write an equation. Then, solve for the unknown.

1. $\frac{10}{15} = \frac{18}{q}$

   $18 \cdot 15 = 10q$

   $q =$

2. $\frac{8}{p} = \frac{14}{21}$

   $p =$

3. $\frac{10}{25} = \frac{t}{15}$

   $t =$

4. $\frac{s}{40} = \frac{10}{16}$

   $s =$

Write the ratios in each proportion in fraction form. Then, solve by using cross-multiplication.

5. $16:20 = 12:a$

   $a =$

6. $18:b = 27:33$

   $b =$

7. $6:15 = c:20$

   $c =$

8. $d:9 = 4:6$

   $d =$

▶ Cross-Multiplication and Unit Rates

9. Zander paid $7 for 5 avocados. How much would 9 avocados cost?

Discuss how these solution strategies relate to each other.

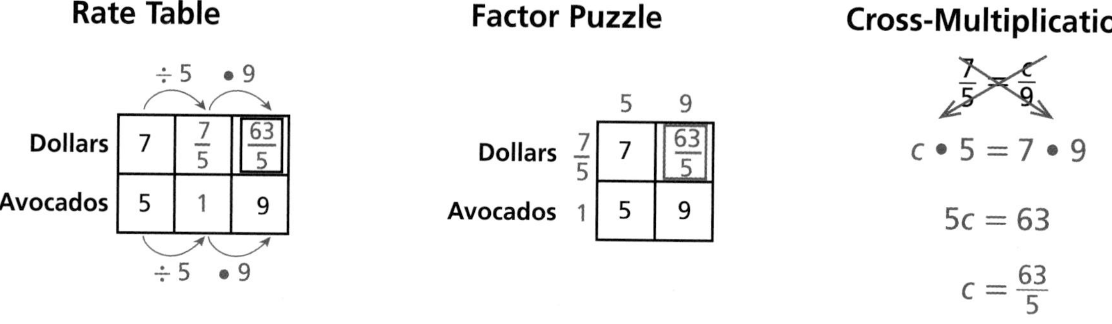

The price for 9 avocados is $\frac{63}{5}$ dollars, or $12.60.

▶ What's the Error?

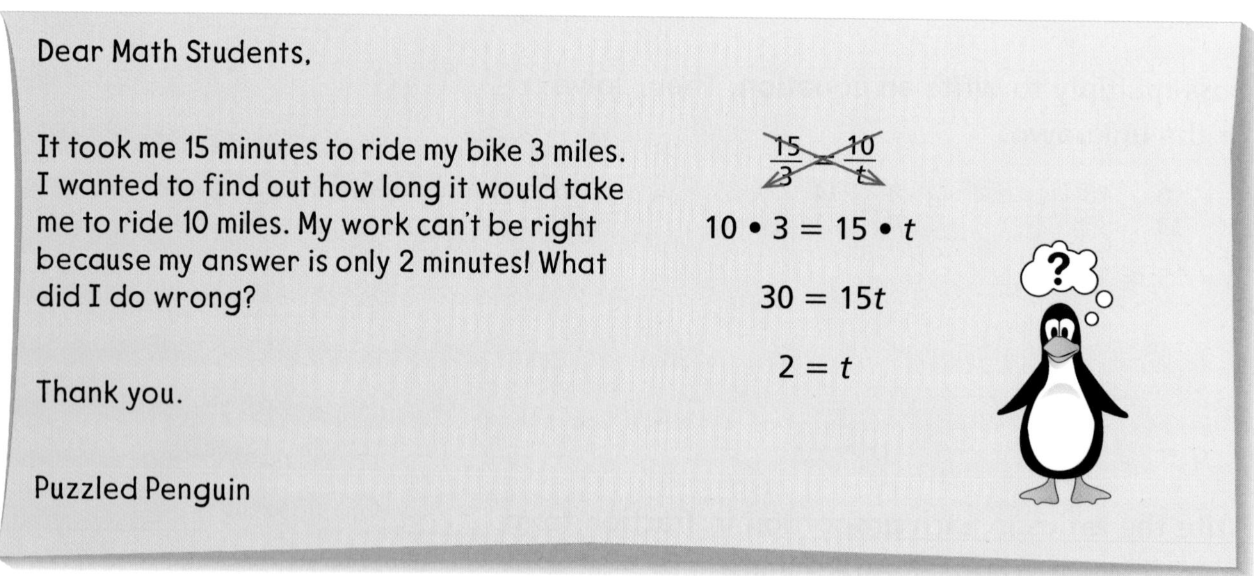
Dear Math Students,

It took me 15 minutes to ride my bike 3 miles. I wanted to find out how long it would take me to ride 10 miles. My work can't be right because my answer is only 2 minutes! What did I do wrong?

Thank you.

Puzzled Penguin

10. Write a response to the Puzzled Penguin.

Write your answers on Activity Workbook page 154.

Vocabulary

tape diagram

▶ Using Tape Diagrams to Model Ratios

A juice company's KiwiBerry juice is made by mixing 2 parts kiwifruit juice with 3 parts strawberry juice.

The ratio of parts of kiwifruit juice to parts of strawberry juice can be modeled by using a **tape diagram**.

KiwiBerry Juice

2 parts kiwifruit

3 parts strawberry

Solve each problem three ways: using the tape diagram, using a Factor Puzzle, and using cross-multiplication.

1. How many liters of kiwifruit juice should be mixed with 15 liters of strawberry juice to make KiwiBerry juice? ____ liters

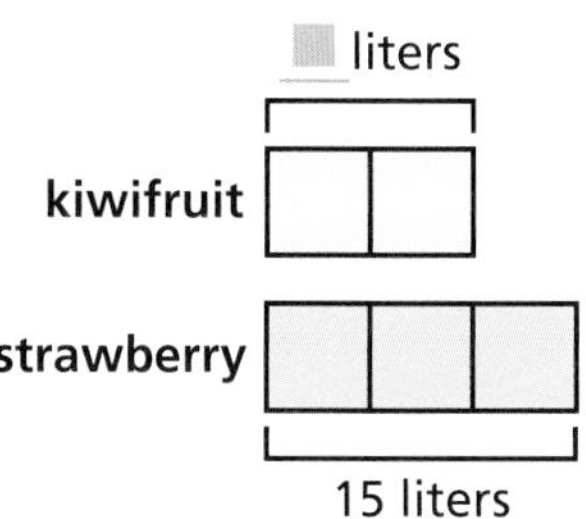

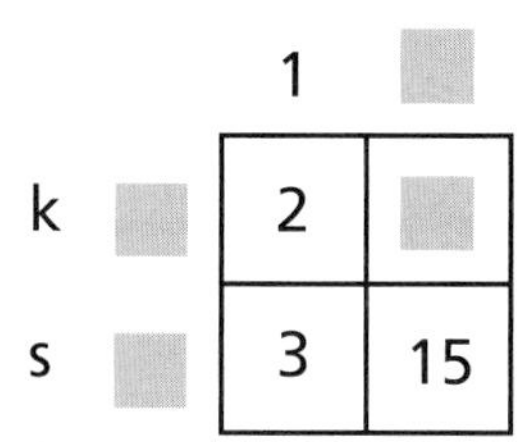

$\frac{2}{3} = \frac{x}{15}$

2. How many liters of strawberry juice should be mixed with 50 liters of kiwifruit juice to make KiwiBerry juice? ____ liters

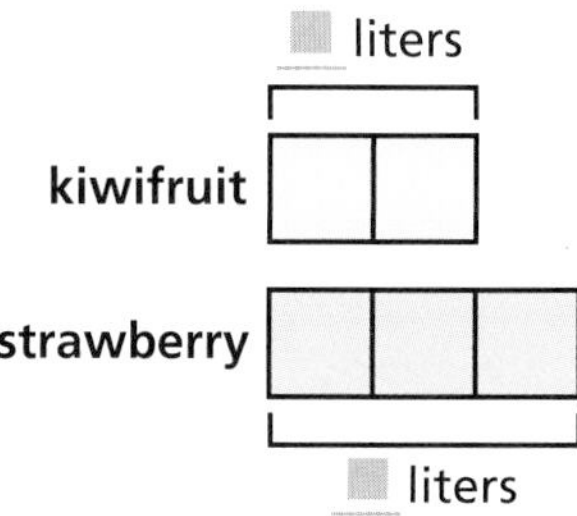

k

s

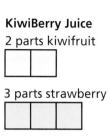

3. How many liters of kiwifruit juice should be mixed with 20 liters of strawberry juice to make KiwiBerry juice? ____ liters

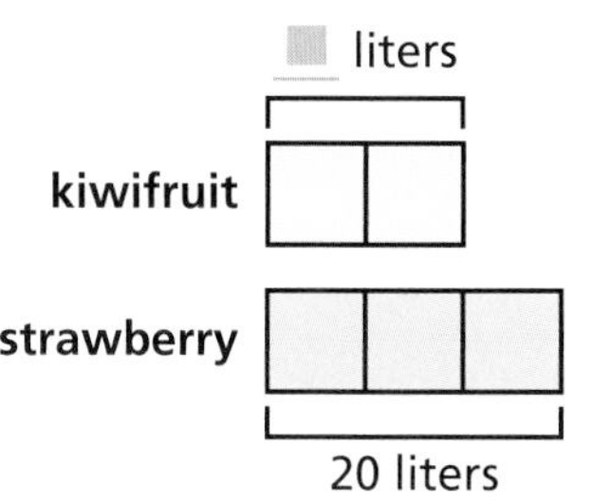

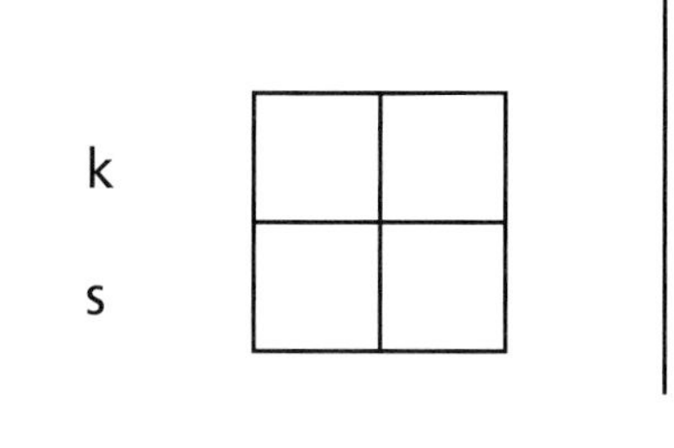

▶ Using Tape Diagrams to Model Ratios (continued)

To make Perfect Purple paint, blue paint and red paint are mixed in a ratio of 3 to 5.

Solve each problem three ways: using a tape diagram, using a Factor Puzzle, and using cross-multiplication.

4. How many liters of red paint should be mixed with 21 liters of blue paint to make Perfect Purple paint? _____ liters

5. How many liters of blue paint should be mixed with 23 liters of red paint to make Perfect Purple paint? _____ liters

Choose a method to solve.

6. To make bricks, you can mix clay and sand in a ratio of 2 to 3. How much clay do you need to mix with 10 cubic yards of sand? _____ cubic yards

Write your answers on Activity Workbook page 155.

▶ Part-to-Whole Ratios

Remember that KiwiBerry juice is made by mixing 2 parts kiwifruit juice with 3 parts strawberry juice.

We can solve problems involving the total amount of juice or the total number of parts.

Solve each problem three ways: using the tape diagram, using a Factor Puzzle, and using cross-multiplication.

7. How many liters of kiwifruit juice should be used to make 50 liters of KiwiBerry juice?

____ liters

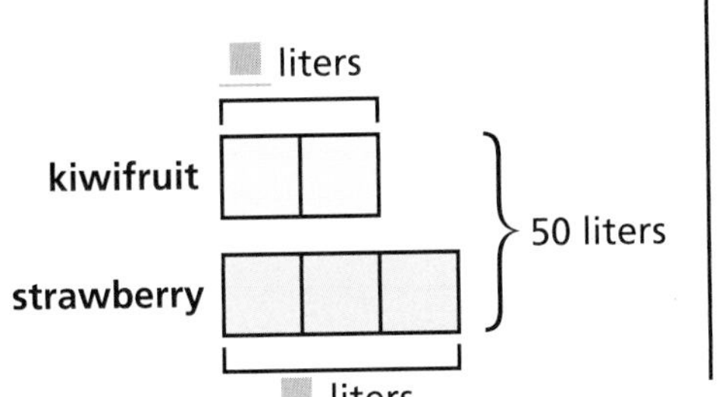

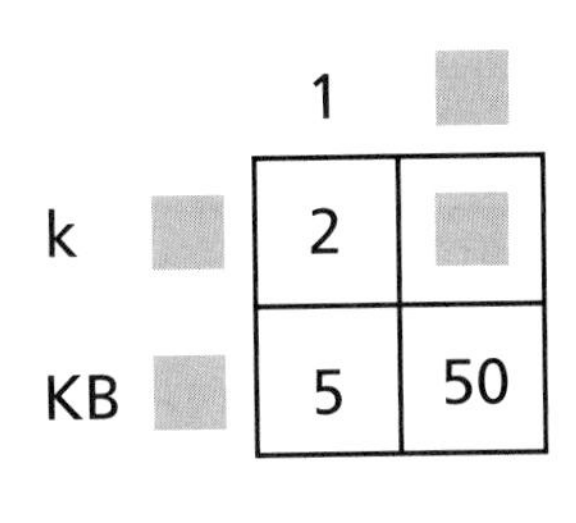

$\frac{2}{5} = \frac{x}{50}$

8. How many liters of strawberry juice should be used to make 20 liters of KiwiBerry juice?

____ liters

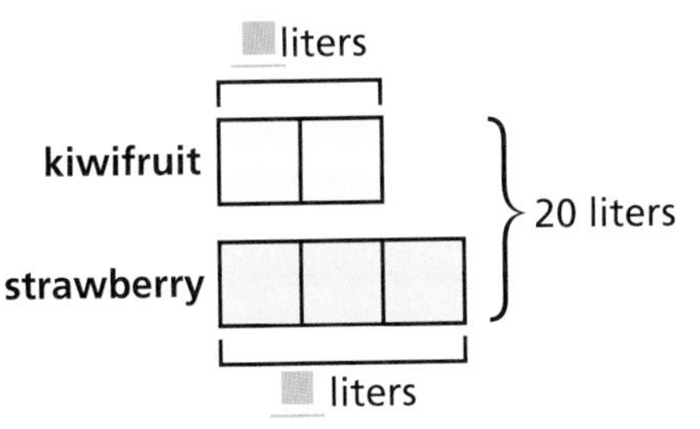

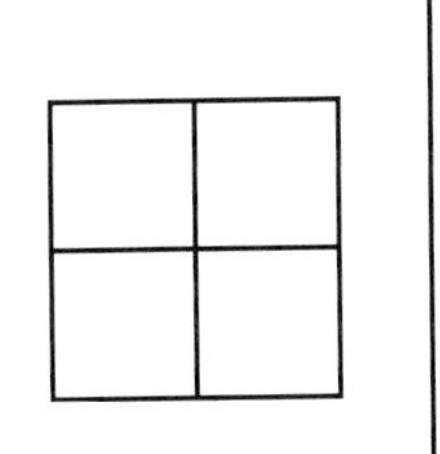

9. If 7 liters of kiwifruit juice are used, how many liters of KiwiBerry juice can be made?

____ liters

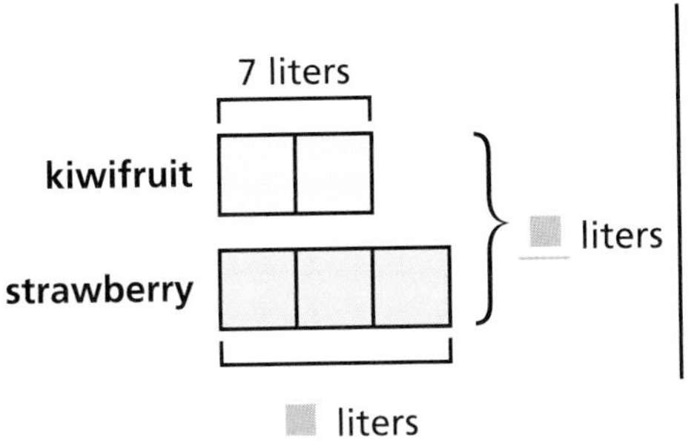

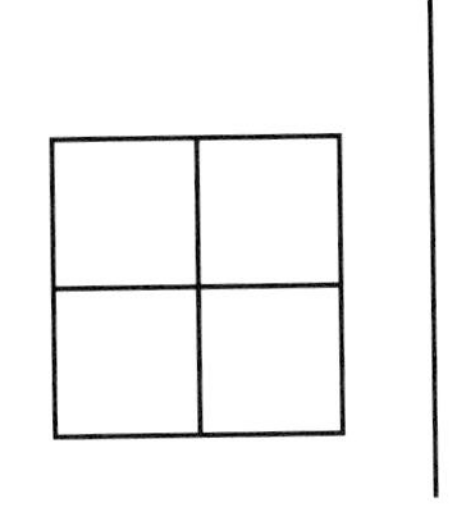

▶ Part-to-Whole Ratios (continued)

To make Perfect Purple paint, blue paint and red paint are mixed in a ratio of 3 to 5.

Solve each problem three ways: using a tape diagram, using a Factor Puzzle, and using cross-multiplication.

10. How much red paint is needed to make 20 liters of Perfect Purple paint?

_____ liters

11. If 10 liters of blue paint are used, how many liters of Perfect Purple paint can be made?

_____ liters

Choose a method to solve.

12. To make bricks, you can mix clay and sand in a ratio of 2 to 3. To make 55 cubic feet of the mixture, how much sand do you need to use? How much clay do you need to use?

_____ cubic yards of clay

_____ cubic yards of sand

▶ Different Ways to Describe Ratios

Seth made a sand mixture by mixing 4 parts green sand with 3 parts yellow sand.

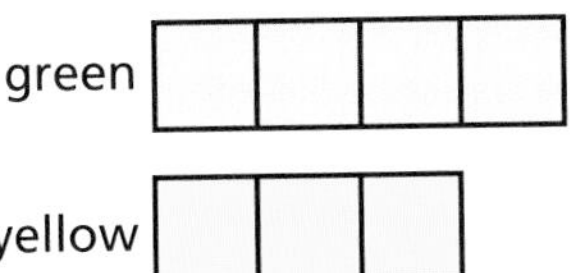

Complete each sentence to describe the green sand to yellow sand ratio.

1. The mixture is ______ parts green sand and ______ parts yellow sand.
2. Green sand and yellow sand are mixed in a ratio of ______ to ______ or ______ : ______.
3. For every ______ cups of green sand, there are ______ cups of yellow sand in the mixture.

Complete each sentence to describe the green sand to total ratio.

4. There are ______ parts green sand in ______ parts total mixture.
5. Green sand and total mixture are in a ratio of ______ to ______ or ______ : ______.
6. For every ______ cups of green sand, there are ______ cups of mixture.

Describe the yellow sand to total ratio in three ways.

7.
8.
9.

Write your answers on Activity Workbook page 156.

Vocabulary
multiplicative comparison

▶ Different Portions Can Be One Whole

10. Complete each tape diagram.

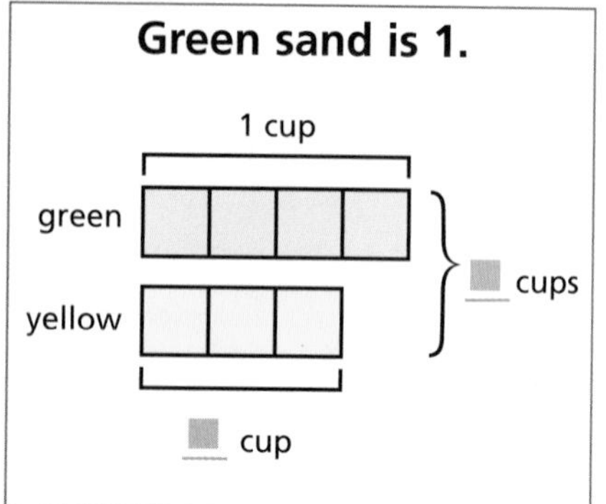

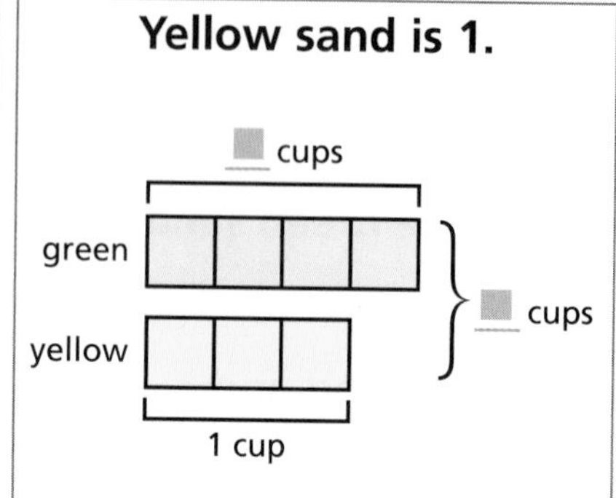

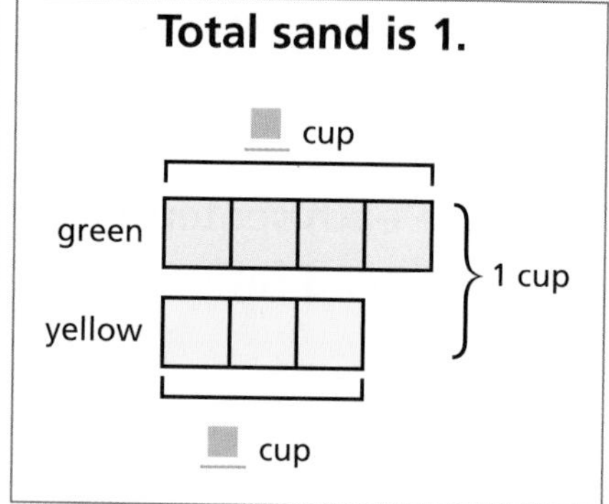

▶ Unit Rates

Write a fraction to complete each unit rate.

11. ______ cup of yellow sand for every 1 cup of green sand in the mixture

12. ______ cups of green sand for every 1 cup of yellow sand in the mixture

13 ______ cup of green sand and ______ cup of yellow sand for every 1 cup of mixture

14. ______ cups of mixture for every 1 cup of green sand

15. ______ cups of mixture for every 1 cup of yellow sand

▶ Multiplicative Comparisons

Write a fraction to complete each multiplicative comparison.

16. The amount of yellow sand is ______ times the amount of green sand.

17. The amount of green sand is ______ times the amount of yellow sand.

18. The total amount of mixture is ______ times the amount of green sand.

19. The total amount of mixture is ______ times the amount of yellow sand.

▶ What's the Error?

Dear Math Students,

I made my own sand mixture. I mixed 2 parts purple and 5 parts orange.

purple ☐☐

orange ☐☐☐☐☐

Then I wrote this multiplicative comparison.

- The amount of purple sand is $\frac{2}{5}$ times the amount of the total mixture.

My friend says that I made a mistake. Did I? If I did, can you tell me what mistake I made and help me correct it?

Your friend,

Puzzled Penguin

20. Write a response to Puzzled Penguin.

▶ Use Equations to Relate Quantities

21. Let g be the number of cups of green sand in Seth's ratio.
Let y be the number of cups of yellow sand in Seth's ratio.

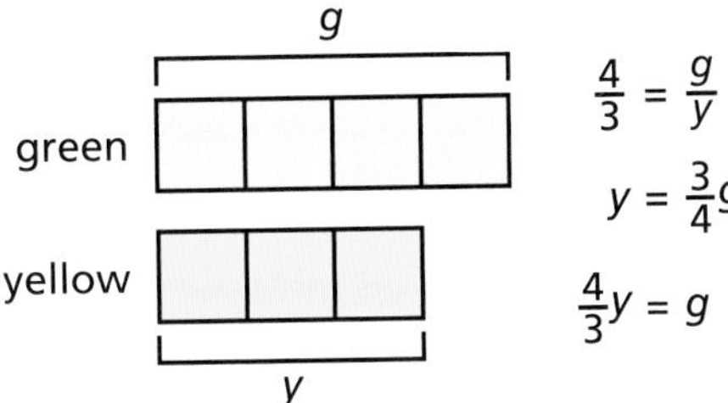

$\frac{4}{3} = \frac{g}{y}$

$y = \frac{3}{4}g$

$\frac{4}{3}y = g$

Discuss why these three equations can all be used to relate g and y.

▶ Blue-and-Red Mixtures

22. Make up your own blue-and-red sand mixture. Your mixture should have a total of 5 parts. Draw a tape diagram to show the ratio of blue to red.

23. Describe the ratio of blue sand to red sand in three ways.

24. Describe the ratio of blue sand to the total mixture in three ways.

25. Write two sentences that use a fraction to compare the amounts of the two colors. Use the words *times as much*.

26. Suppose you make a large batch of your blue-and-red sand mixture. Let b be the number of cups of blue sand that you use, and let r be the number of cups of red sand that you use. Write three equations relating b and r.

27. How is your mixture different from a mixture with the same colors mixed in a different ratio?

▶ Practice Solving Rate and Ratio Problems

Solve. Use different methods including tables, Factor Puzzles, cross-multiplication, and tape diagrams. Look for the problems that cannot be solved with any of these!

Show your work on your paper or in your journal.

1. In a lab, Chemical 1 and Chemical 2 are mixed in a ratio of 4 to 5. How much of Chemical 1 is needed to mix with 35 liters of Chemical 2?

2. In a lab, Chemical 1 and Chemical 2 are mixed in a ratio of 4 to 5. How much of each chemical is needed to make 35 liters of the mixture?

   Chemical 1:  Chemical 2:

3. Pokey the snail travels 25 centimeters every 2 minutes. How far will Pokey go in 15 minutes?

4. When Gary the snail travels at a steady rate of 15 centimeters per minute, it takes him 6 minutes to get from the pineapple to the rock. How long will it take Gary to get from the pineapple to the rock if he travels at a steady rate of 30 centimeters per minute?

5. At a factory, an assembly line produces 100 cans every 3 minutes. How long will it take the assembly line to produce 250 cans?

6. At a factory, an assembly line produces 100 cans every 3 minutes. How many cans will the factory produce in 8 hours?

▶ Practice Solving Rate and Ratio Problems (continued)

Show your work on your paper or in your journal.

7. At a factory, each assembly line produces 100 cans every 3 minutes. If two assembly lines are working, how many cans will they produce in 15 minutes?

8. It takes Brittany 2 hours to mow 5 acres of grass. At that rate, how long would it take Brittany to mow 8 acres?

9. It takes Brittany 2 hours to mow 5 acres of grass. If Austin mows grass at the same rate as Brittany, how long will it take the two of them working together to mow 15 acres of grass?

10. Jorge and Ryan are running laps around the track. Jorge runs 5 laps for every 4 laps that Ryan runs. When Ryan has run 15 laps, how many laps will Jorge have run?

11. At a perfume factory, fragrance designers are mixing musk oil and spice cologne in different ratios. Mixture 1 is 2 parts musk oil to 5 parts spice cologne. Mixture 2 is 3 parts musk oil to 7 parts spice cologne. Which will have more of a spice fragrance? Explain.

12. Fragrance designers make Roselily perfume by mixing rose and lily perfumes. In Roselily perfume, the amount of rose is $\frac{2}{5}$ times as much as the amount of lily. What is the ratio of rose to lily in Roselily? Draw a tape diagram to show the ratio.

7–8
Class Activity

Use Activity Workbook page 157.

Vocabulary

percent

▶ Define Percent

Percent means "out of 100" or "for each 100." The symbol for percent is %.

> 37% is read "37 percent."
>
> It can mean the fraction $\frac{37}{100}$, the ratio 37:100, or the rate 37 *per* 100.

The fans at a sold-out concert are in 100 equal sections of seats. Each small rectangle in the diagram represents one section of fans.

1. Color one section blue.

   What fraction of the fans is this?

   What percent of the fans is this?

2. Color three sections red.

   What fraction of the fans is this?

   What percent of the fans is this?

3. Color 23% of the sections green.

   What fraction of the fans is this?

4. Color 37% of the sections yellow.

   What fraction of the fans is that?

5. Shade some sections in purple. What percent did you shade?

▶ Percents of Bar Diagrams

The bars in Exercises 6–9 are divided into 100 equal parts.

6. Shade 5% of the bar.

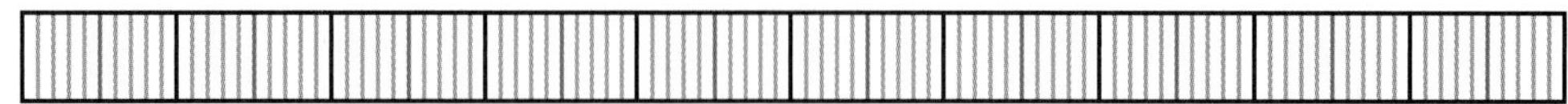

7. Shade 15% of the bar.

8. Shade 45% of the bar.

9. Shade 85% of the bar.

10. Label each section with the percent of the whole bar it represents. Under the section, write the fraction it represents.

Bar A

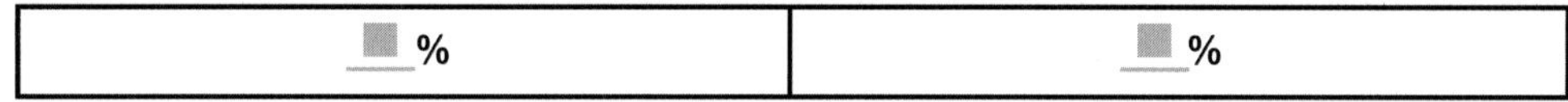

Bar B

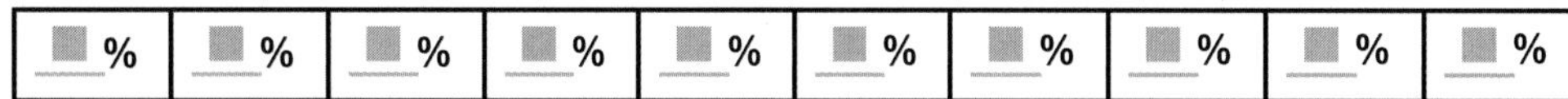

Bar C

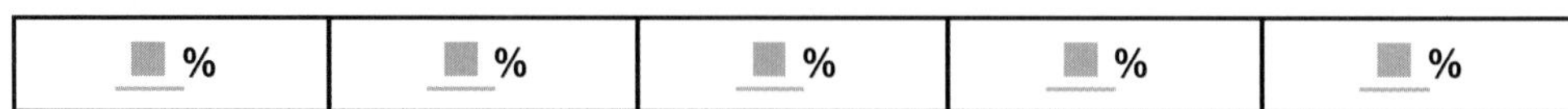

Bar D

11. Shade 70% of Bar B.
12. Shade 60% of Bar C.
13. Shade 75% of Bar D.

▶ Relating Percents, Decimals, and Fractions

14. Label each long tick mark with a decimal, a percent, and a fraction with a denominator of 10. If the fraction can be simplified, write the simplified form as well.

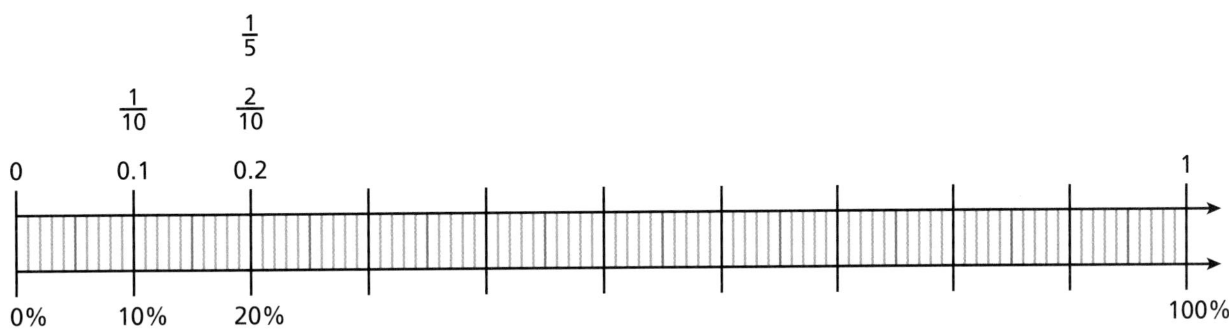

15. Write each percent as a fraction with denominator 100 and as a decimal. Then place the percents and decimals on the number lines.

Percent	83%	51%	46%	6%	60%	27%	127%	3%	30%	130%
Fraction	$\frac{83}{100}$	■	■	■	■	■	$\frac{127}{100}$	■	■	■
Decimal	0.83	■	■	■	■	■	1.27	■	■	■

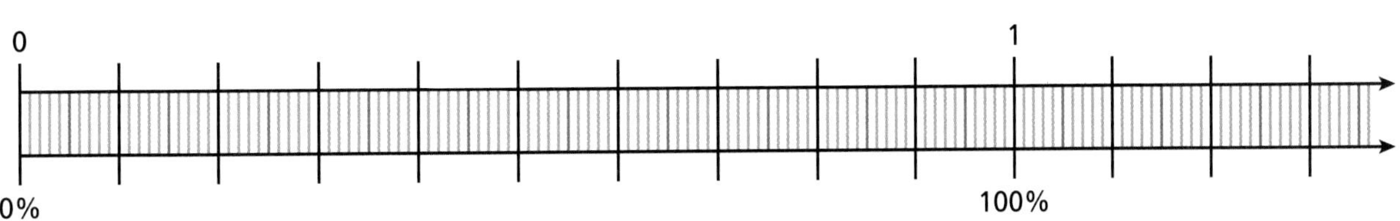

▶ What's the Error?

Dear Math Students,

I said that 7% is 0.7, but my friend said that I am not right. Why not? Please help me understand how percents and decimals are related.

Thank you.

Puzzled Penguin

16. Write a response to Puzzled Penguin.

▶ Percents and Area

What percent of the figure is shaded?

17. ______

Katie's reasoning:
This part is half, so it is 50%.
These 5 parts make 50%.
So, they are 10% each.

18. ______

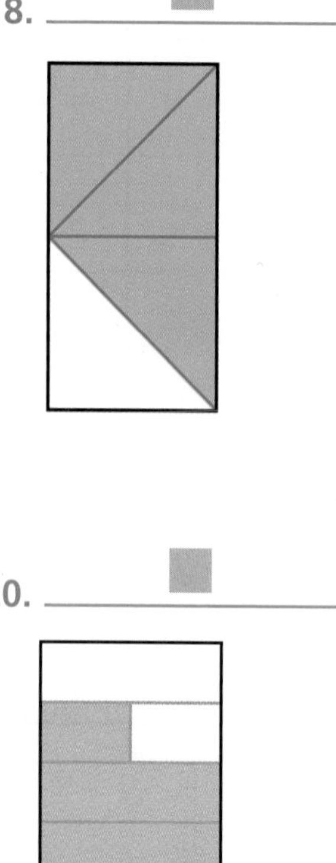

19. ______

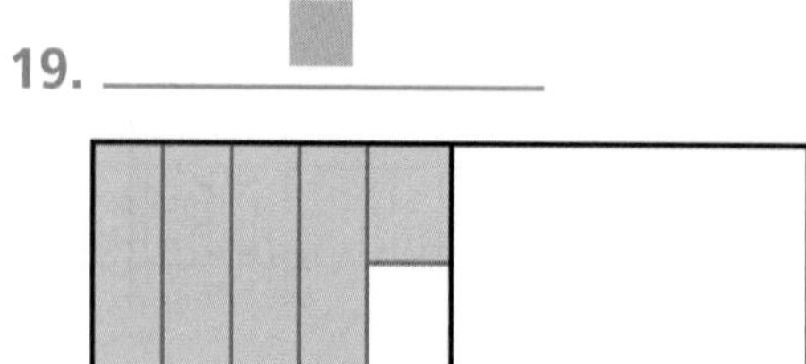

20. ______

7–9
Class Activity

Use Activity Workbook page 160.

▶ Model Finding a Percent of a Number

The 300 students at a school are in 100 groups of 3.

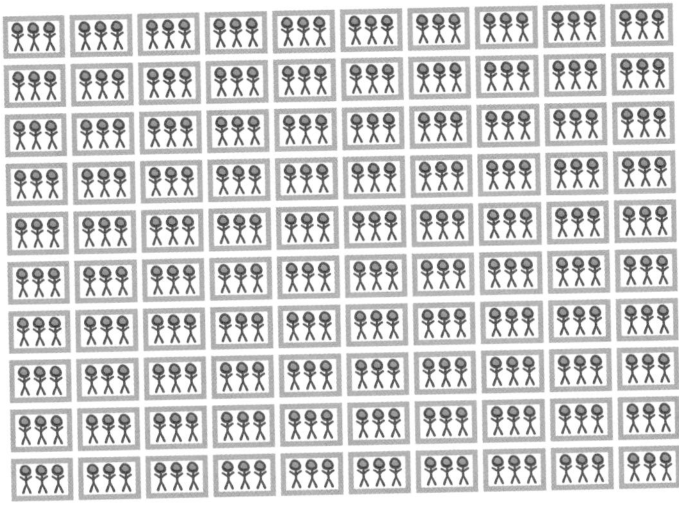

1. Color one group blue.

   What percent of the students is this?

   What number of students is this?

2. Color four groups red.

   What percent of the students is this?

   What number of students is this?

3. Color 17 groups green.

   What percent of the students is this?

   What number of students is this?

4. Color 9% of the students yellow.

   What number of students is this?

5. Color 24% of students orange.

   What number of students is this?

6. Color 35% of the students purple.

   What number of students is this?

▶ Find a Percent of a Number

Three students had different ideas about how to solve the following problem.

Show your work on your paper or in your journal.

Of the 300 students at a school, 35% say they are going on a field trip. How many students are going on the field trip?

Use each idea to solve the problem.

7. **Anna's idea:** I will divide 300 by 100 to find 1% of 300. Then, I will multiply that answer by 35 to find 35% of 300.

8. **Rantavious's idea:** I will use the fact that 35% of 300 means $\frac{35}{100}$ times 300.

9. **Jon's idea:** If f is the number of students going on the trip, then the fraction of students going is $\frac{f}{300}$, and it is also $\frac{35}{100}$. I can write and solve a proportion.

10. What is 80% of 300 students? Solve in two ways.

11. What is 26% of 1,200 students? Solve in two ways.

7–9
Class Activity

Use Activity Workbook page 161.

▶ Percent as a Ratio

Now the students at the school are in 3 groups of 100.

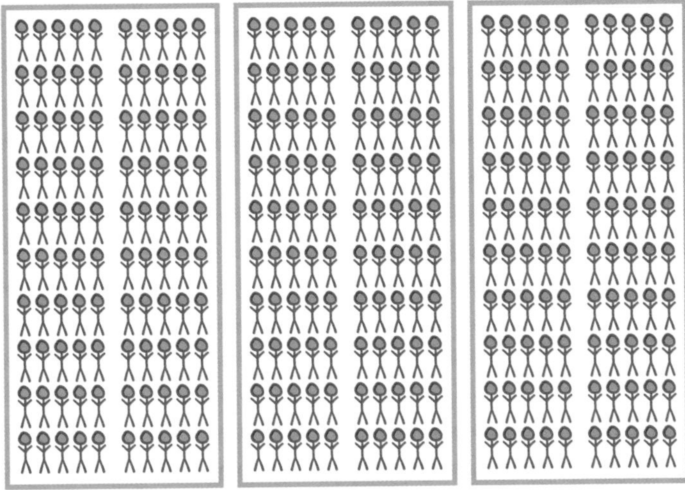

12. Circle one student from each group in blue.

    What percent of the students is this?

    What number of students is this?

13. Circle four students from each group in red.

    What percent of the students is this?

    What number of students is this?

14. Circle 45% of the students in green.

    How many students is this? Why?

15. Circle 82% of the students in yellow.

    How many students is that? Why?

▶ Methods for Finding a Percent of a Number

Five students had different ideas about how to solve the problem below.

Of the 300 students at a school, 99% say they are going to the school party. How many students is this?

Use each idea to solve the problem.

16. **Hilda's idea:** 99% means 99 for each 100. So, I will use a 99% ratio table.

99% ratio table

portion	99		
whole	100	200	300

17. **Anna's idea:** I will divide 300 by 100 to find 1% of 300. Then, I will multiply that answer by 99 to find 99% of 300.

18. **Rantavious's idea:** I will use the fact that 99% of 300 means $\frac{99}{100}$ times 300.

19. **Jon's idea:** If p is the number of students going to the party, then the fraction of students going is $\frac{p}{300}$, and it is also $\frac{99}{100}$. I can write and solve a proportion.

20. **Gregory's idea:** 99% is 100% minus 1%, so I will take 1% of the 300 students away from 100% of 300.

Solve.

21. What is 51% of 600 students?

22. What is 49% of 500 students?

▶ Percents of Numbers

The adult dose of a medicine is 8 milliliters. The child dose is 75% of the adult dose. How many milliliters is the child dose?

1. Complete the double number line to help you solve this problem.

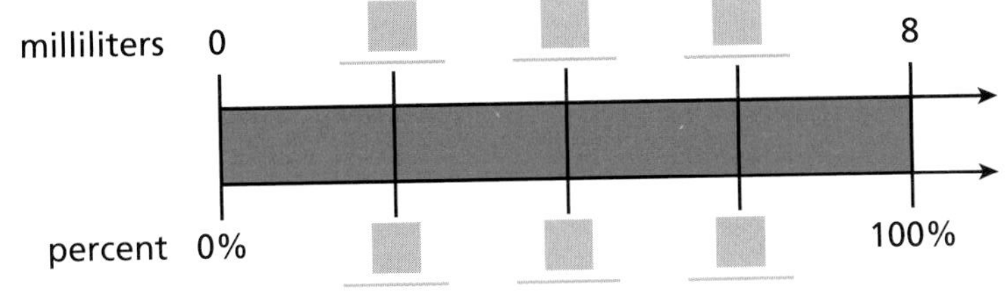

2. Discuss and complete these solutions.

Trey's Reasoning About Parts

100% is 4 parts, which is 8 mL.

25% is 1 part, which is 8 mL ÷ 4 = 2 mL.

75% is 3 parts and is ______.

Quowanna's Factor Puzzle

	percent	milliliters
	25	
portion	75	
whole	100	8

Tomaslav's Equation

m is 75% of 8.

$m = \frac{75}{100} \bullet 8 =$ ______

Jessica's Proportion

	percent		milliliters
portion / whole	$\frac{75}{100}$	=	$\frac{m}{8}$
	$\frac{3}{4}$	=	$\frac{m}{8}$
	m	=	______

Solve in two ways.

3. The adult dose of a medicine is 6 milliliters. The child dose is 75% of the adult dose. How many milliliters is the child dose?

4. A chemist needs 20% of the 120 milliliters of solution in a beaker. How many milliliters of solution does the chemist need?

▶ Find the Whole from the Percent and the Part

If 12 milligrams is 60% of the recommended daily allowance for niacin, then what is the recommended daily allowance for niacin?

5. Complete the double number line to help you solve this problem.

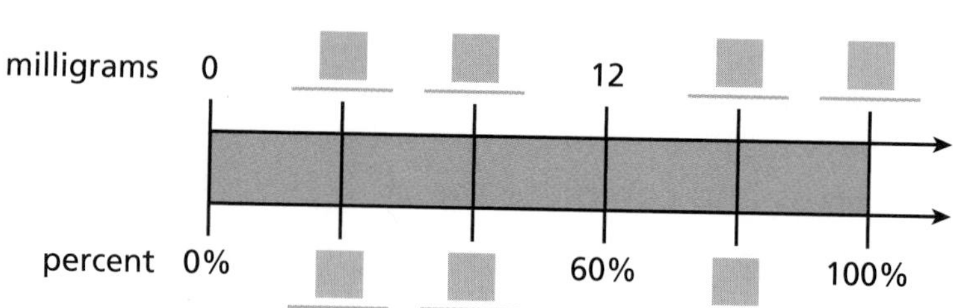

6. Discuss and complete these solutions.

Trey's Reasoning about Parts

60% is 3 parts and is 12 mg.

20% is 1 part, which is 12 mg ÷ 3 = 4 mg.

100% is 5 parts, which is ______.

Quowanna's Factor Puzzle

	percent	milliliters
portion	60	12
whole	100	

Tomaslav's Equation

60% of g is 12.

$\frac{60}{100} \bullet g = 12$

Jessica's Proportion

	percent		milliliters
portion / whole	$\frac{60}{100}$	=	$\frac{12}{g}$

Solve.

7. A chemist poured 12 mL of chemicals into water to make a solution. The chemicals make up 80% of the solution. How many milliliters is the full solution?

8. What is 40% of 70?

9. 40% of what number is 70?

10. 30% of what number is 120?

11. What is 30% of 120?

12. If 75% of the recommended daily allowance of vitamin C is 45 mg, what is the recommended daily allowance of vitamin C?

▶ Use Percents to Compare

Using percents can help you compare two groups when the sizes of the groups are different.

Appling School has 300 students and 45 students have the flu. Baldwin School has 500 students and 55 students have the flu.

1. Discuss and complete these methods for calculating the percent of students at Appling School who have the flu.

Alex's Equation

$f\%$ is $\frac{45}{300}$.

$\frac{f}{100} = \frac{45}{300}$

Jordan's Equation

$f\%$ of 300 is 45.

$\frac{f}{100} \bullet 300 = 45$

Aliya's Factor Puzzle

	percent	students
portion	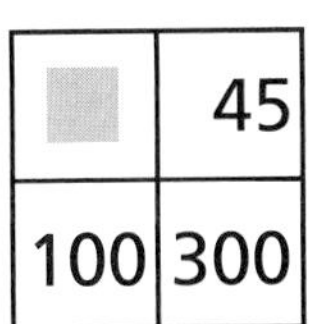	45
whole	100	300

Rachel's Idea of Going through 1%

300 students is 100%.

$300 \div 100 = 3$; 3 students is 1%.

$45 \div 3 = 15$; 45 students is 15 groups of 3 students,

which is ______%.

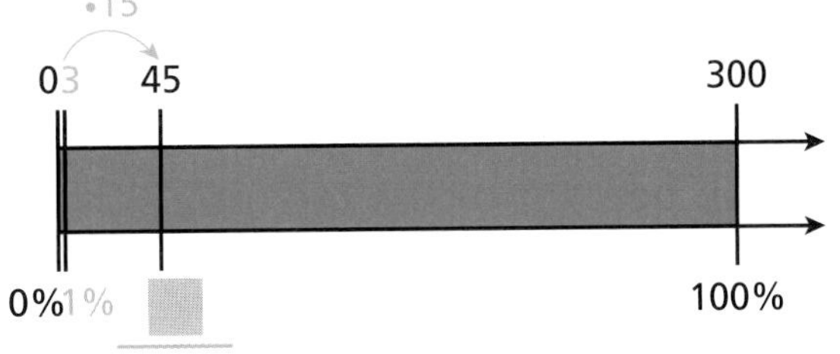

2. Use two methods to calculate the percent of students at Baldwin School who have the flu.

▶ Mixed Percent Problems

3. 26 is what percent of 130?

4. 25% of what number is 225?

5. What is 75% of 280?

6. 70% of what number is 595?

Solve.

Show your work on your paper or in your journal.

7. A company spent $4,500 of its $18,000 advertising budget on Internet ads. What percent of its advertising budget did the company spend on Internet ads?

8. If 30% of a company's advertising budget is $7,200, then what is the full advertising budget?

9. Another company's advertising budget is $7,200. The company spent 30% of their budget on newspaper ads. How much did the company spend on newspaper ads?

10. If a gasoline-ethanol mixture made with 24 liters of ethanol is 15% ethanol, then how many liters is the whole mixture?

11. If 3 gallons of antifreeze is mixed with 2 gallons of water, what percent of the mixture is antifreeze?

    What percent of the mixture is water?

12. If a pharmacist needs to mix 800 mL of antibiotic with water so that the mixture is 40% antibiotic, then how much water does the pharmacist need to add?

▶ Convert Between Centimeters and Millimeters

1. Label the double number line to show how centimeters (cm) and millimeters (mm) are related.

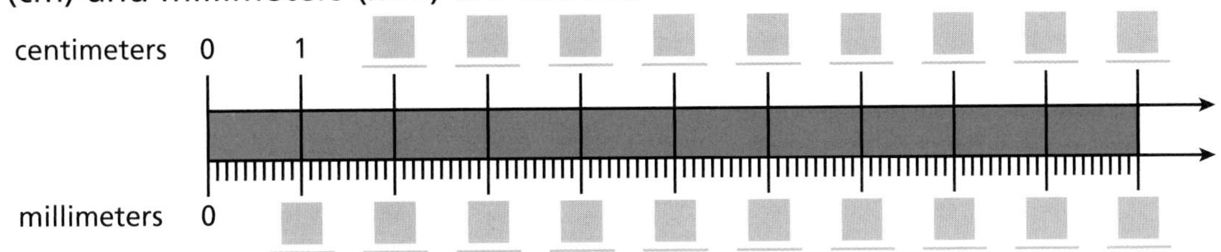

We can write two unit rates comparing centimeters to millimeters.

There are 10 millimeters per centimeter.

We can write this unit rate as $10 \frac{mm}{cm}$.

There is $\frac{1}{10}$ centimeter per millimeter.

We can write this unit rate as $\frac{1}{10} \frac{cm}{mm}$.

Unit rates are helpful for converting measurements from one unit to another.

2. Compare these methods of converting 52 centimeters to millimeters.

Write and Solve a Proportion

$$\frac{1 \text{ cm}}{10 \text{ mm}} = \frac{52 \text{ cm}}{x \text{ mm}}$$

$$52 \bullet 10 = 1 \bullet x$$

$$520 = x$$

So, 52 cm = 520 mm.

Use a Unit Rate

$$52 \cancel{\text{cm}} \bullet 10 \frac{\text{mm}}{\cancel{\text{cm}}} = 520 \text{ mm}$$

There are 52 cm, and there are 10 mm in each cm.

The unit cm cancels, leaving the unit mm.

3. Complete these methods for converting 85 millimeters to centimeters.

Write and Solve a Proportion

$$\frac{1 \text{ cm}}{10 \text{ mm}} = \frac{x \text{ cm}}{85 \text{ mm}}$$

So, 85 mm = ______ cm.

Use a Unit Rate

$$85 \cancel{\text{mm}} \bullet \frac{1}{10} \frac{\text{cm}}{\cancel{\text{mm}}} = \_\_\_\_\_\_ \text{ cm}$$

There are 85 mm, and there is $\frac{1}{10}$ cm in each mm.

▶ Convert Between Feet and Inches

4. Label the double number line to show how feet and inches are related.

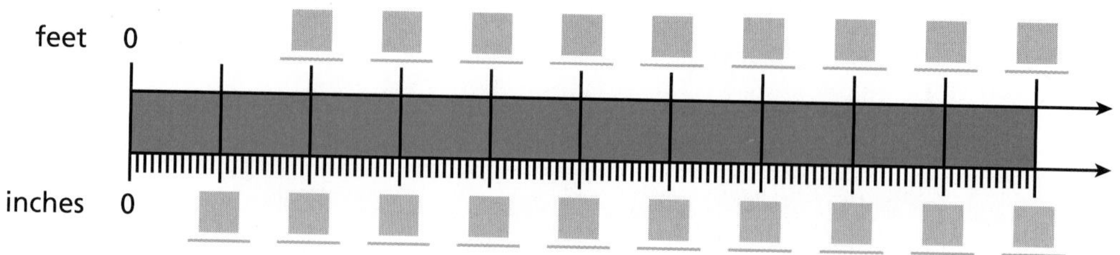

5. What are the two unit rates in this situation?

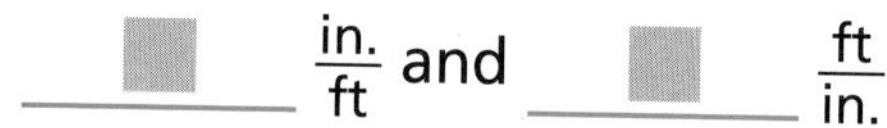

6. Convert 132 inches to feet by multiplying by a unit rate. Show your work.

132 in. = ______ ft

7. Convert $6\frac{1}{2}$ feet to inches by multiplying by a unit rate. Show your work.

$6\frac{1}{2}$ ft = ______ in.

▶ Practice Converting Units of Length

8. What two unit rates relate centimeters (cm) and meters (m)?

9. Convert 7.9 meters to centimeters using any method.

7.9 m = ______ cm

10. Convert 42 centimeters to meters using any method.

42 cm = ______ m

11. What two unit rates relate feet (ft) and yards (yd)?

12. Convert 16 feet to yards using any method.

16 ft = ______ yd

13. Convert 24 yards to feet using any method.

24 yd = ______ ft

▶ Find Area When Units Are Different

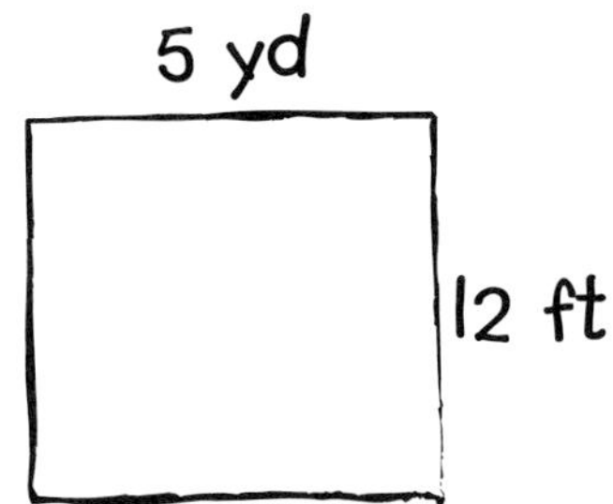

Riley and Kelsey wanted to find the area of their rectangular bedroom. Riley measured the length and Kelsey measured the width. They made the sketch at the right to show their measurements.

Below are the girls' area calculations.

Riley's Calculation

I want to find the area in square yards, so I have to change 12 feet to yards.

$12 \text{ ft} \bullet \frac{1}{3} \frac{\text{yd}}{\text{ft}} = 4 \text{ yd}$

Now, I can use the area formula.

$A = lw = 4 \text{ yd} \bullet 5 \text{ yd} = 20 \text{ yd}^2$

Kelsey's Calculation

I want to find the area in square feet, so I have to change 5 yards to feet.

$5 \text{ yd} \bullet 3 \frac{\text{ft}}{\text{yd}} = 15 \text{ ft}$

Now, I can use the area formula.

$A = lw = 15 \text{ ft} \bullet 12 \text{ ft} = 180 \text{ ft}^2$

14. Discuss Riley and Kelsey's calculations.

15. Explain how the diagram at the right shows that $1 \text{ yd}^2 = 9 \text{ ft}^2$.

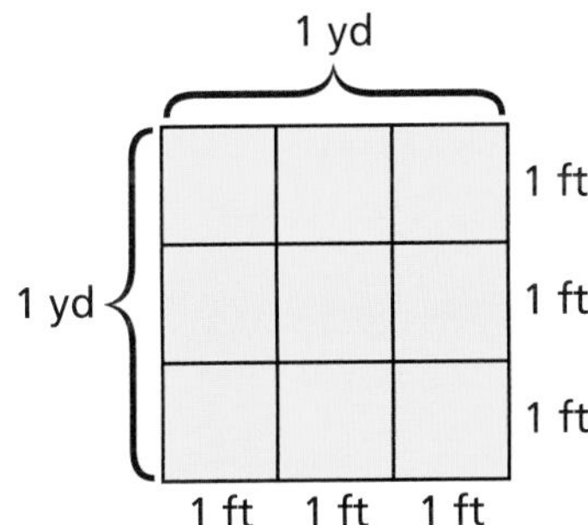

16. Write two unit rates relating square yards and square feet.

_____ $\frac{\text{ft}^2}{\text{yd}^2}$ and _____ $\frac{\text{yd}^2}{\text{ft}^2}$

17. Use one of the unit rates from Exercise 16 to convert Riley's area of 20 yd^2 to square feet. Does the answer agree with the area Kelsey got?

$20 \text{ yd}^2 =$ _____

▶ Practice Solving Area Problems

Solve.

18. A rectangle has a base length of 3 meters and a height of 15 decimeters. Find the area of the rectangle. Be sure to specify the unit in your answer.

19. Find the surface area of the rectangular prism at the right. Be sure to specify the unit in your answer.

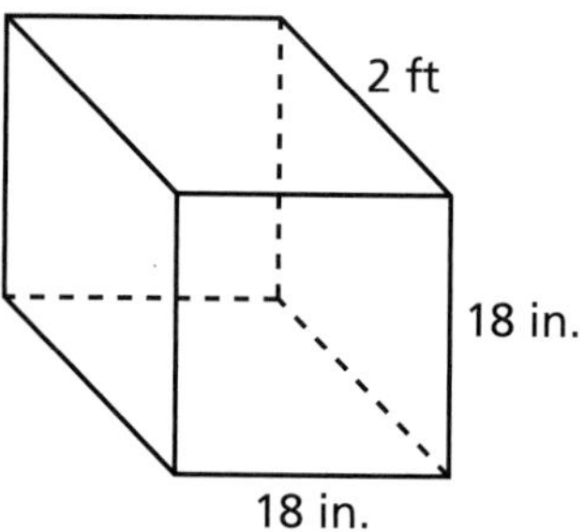

▶ What's the Error?

Dear Math Students,

The school nurse said that I am 42 inches tall. I wanted to figure out how many feet this is. Here's what I did:

$42 \text{ in.} \cdot 12 \frac{\text{in.}}{\text{ft}} = 504 \text{ ft}$

I know I am not 504 feet tall! Please help me figure out what I did wrong and help me find my real height in feet.

Thank you.

Puzzled Penguin

20. Write a response to Puzzled Penguin.

Vocabulary
liquid volume

▶ Converting Metric Units of Liquid Volume

The most common metric units of **liquid volume**, or capacity, are milliliters and liters.

1. Label the double number line to show how liters (L) and milliliters (mL) are related.

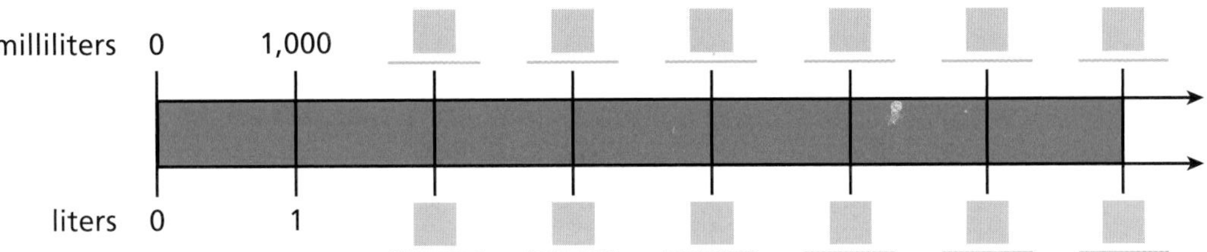

2. What two unit rates relate liters and milliliters?

3. A can holds 344 mL of seltzer. How many liters is this? Find your answer in two ways: by writing and solving a proportion and by using a unit rate.

Write and Solve a Proportion	Use a Unit Rate

344 mL = ______ L

Solve using any method.

4. A bottle contains 1.89 liters of water. How many milliliters is this?

5. A soap dispenser holds 220 mL of soap. A refill bottle of soap contains 1.76 L. How many times can the dispenser be refilled from the bottle?

▶ Converting Customary Units of Liquid Volume

Units of liquid volume, or capacity, in the customary system include cups, pints, quarts, and gallons.

Customary Units of Liquid Volume
2 cups = 1 pint
2 pints = 1 quart
4 quarts = 1 gallon

6. Write two unit rates relating quarts (qt) and gallons (gal).

7. How many quarts would it take to fill a $2\frac{3}{4}$-gallon punch bowl?

8. One of the cows on Tessa's farm produces an average of 22 quarts of milk each day. How many gallons is this?

9. How many pints are in 1 gallon?

10. Use your answer to Question 9 to help you write two unit rates relating pints (pt) and gallons (gal).

11. The school cafeteria sells 300 half-pint cartons of milk every day. How many gallons of milk is this?

12. Which is more, 72 cups or 20 quarts? Explain how you found your answer.

▶ Converting Units of Mass

The most common units of mass are grams (g) and kilograms (kg).

13. Complete.

    1 kg = ________ g   1 g = ________ kg

14. Write two unit rates relating grams and kilograms.

15. Convert 3,575 grams to kg.

    3,575 g = ________ kg

16. Convert 3,575 kg to grams.

    3,575 kg = ________ g

17. A nickel has a mass of 5 g. A bag contains 2 kg of nickels. How many nickels are in the bag? Explain.

▶ Converting Units of Weight

The most common units of weight are ounces (oz) and pounds (lb).

18. There are 16 ounces in 1 pound. Write two unit rates relating ounces and pounds.

19. Convert 420 pounds to ounces.

    420 lb = ________ oz

20. Convert 420 ounces to pounds.

    420 oz = ________ lb

21. Donelle adopted two puppies. Daisy weighs $7\frac{1}{2}$ pounds. Bandit weighs 108 ounces. Which puppy weighs more? Explain.

▶ Conversion Word Problems

Solve.

Show your work on your paper or in your journal.

22. A box of FruitBlaster cereal contains 450 g of cereal.

    a. How many kilograms of cereal will the company need to fill 15,000 boxes?

    b. How many boxes of FruitBlaster cereal can the company fill with 15,000 kg of cereal?

23. A perfume bottle holds 5 mL. The perfume company wants to fill 25,000 bottles. How many liters of perfume will the company need?

24. Zeke's little sister is trying to fill her wading pool using a 1-cup container that she fills at the bathroom sink. If the pool holds 70 gallons, how many times will she have to fill her container to completely fill the pool?

25. There are 75 sixth grade students at Wilson Middle School. Each student has a science book that is 5 cm thick. If all the sixth graders stacked their science books on top of each other, would the stack be as tall as the 4-meter-tall school building? Explain.

Vocabulary

bar graph
circle graph

▶ Math and Collections

The **bar graph** and the **circle graph** show data about Sahil's postcard collection.

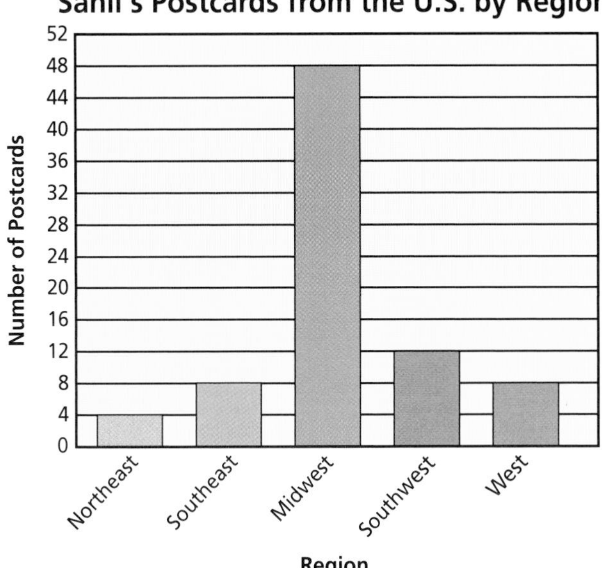

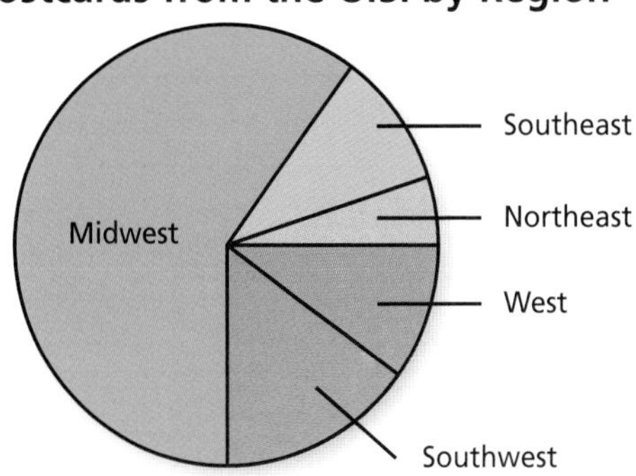

Solve. Use the bar graph.

1. What is the ratio of cards from the Northeast to cards from the West?

2. What is the ratio of cards from the West to cards from the Northeast?

Solve. Use the circle graph.

3. Are more or fewer than 50% of Sahil's cards from the Midwest?

4. Are more or fewer than 25% of Sahil's cards from the Southwest?

5. How could you check your answers to Problems 3 and 4 by using the bar graph?

▶ Choose Graphs to Solve

Isabel has a collection of souvenirs from U.S. presidential elections. The graphs below show the kinds of souvenirs she has collected and the dates of the presidential elections for her souvenirs.

Isabel's Presidential Election Souvenirs

Number of Souvenirs: 0, 2, 4, 6, 8, 10, 12, 14, 16, 18, 20, 22

Buttons, Bumper stickers, Pens, Posters, Other

Kind of Souvenir

Presidential Elections of Isabel's Souvenirs

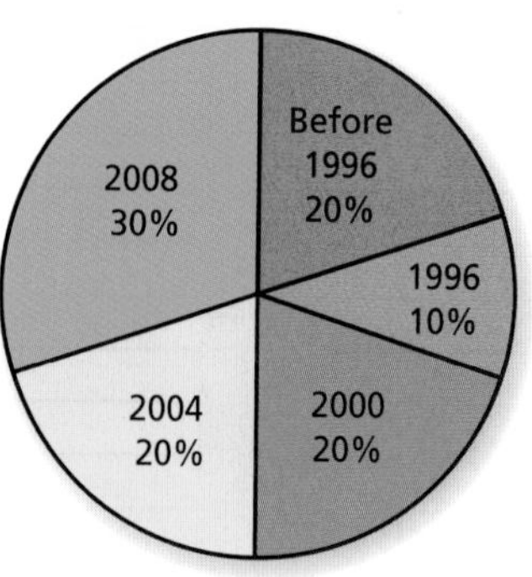

Solve. For Problems 6–8, write whether you used the bar graph, the circle graph, or both.

6. What percent of Isabel's souvenirs are buttons?

7. What percent of Isabel's souvenirs are from elections in 2000 or later?

8. How many of her souvenirs are from the 2008 election?

9. Hector says that the graphs make it clear that 6 of the buttons must be from the 2008 election. Do you agree? Explain.

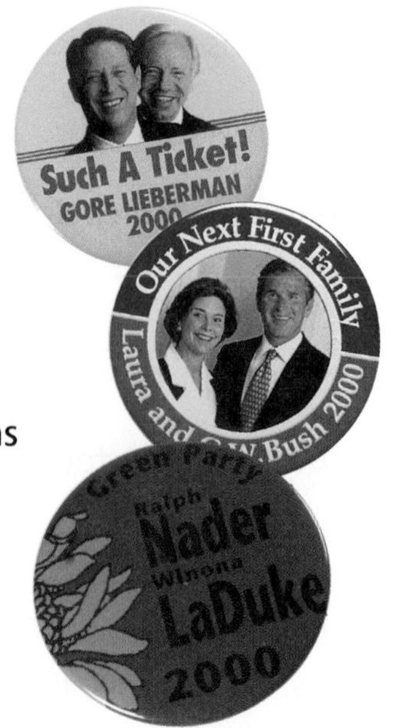

Use the Activity Workbook Unit Test on pages 169–172.

▶ Vocabulary

Choose the best term from the box.

Vocabulary
unit rates
equivalent ratios
percent
line

1. Twenty ___?___ means *twenty out of 100.* (Lesson 7-8)
2. When ratios equivalent to 2:3 are graphed as points in the coordinate plane, the points lie along a ___?___. (Lesson 7-1)
3. *Three-fourths cup of flour per cup of water* and *100 cm per meter* are examples of ___?___. (Lessons 7-2, 7-12)

▶ Concepts and Skills

4. How are comparing two fractions and comparing two ratios alike? How are they different? (Lesson 7-1)

5. Complete the double number line and explain your method. Then explain how you can use the double number line to find 75% of 24 grams. (Lesson 7-10)

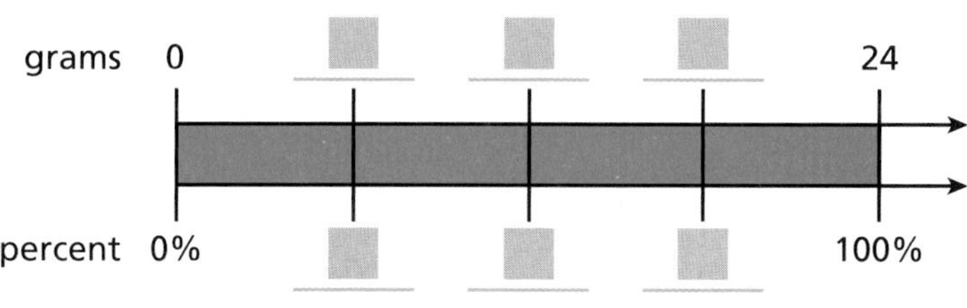

Write the unit rate. (Lessons 7-2, 7-6, 7-13)

6. Dotti's potato salad uses 5 large potatoes and 2 eggs.

   Her salad uses ______ potatoes for each egg.

7. Carly buys 4 pounds of strawberries for $9.00. The

   strawberries cost ______ per pound.

8. There are 4 quarts in 1 gallon. There is ______ gallon per quart.

9. A paint mixture is 4 parts red and 5 parts white. For

   every 1 gallon of paint, ______ gallon is red

   and ______ gallon is white.

Solve each proportion. (Lessons 7-2, 7-3, 7-4)

10. $4{:}x = 3{:}5$

    $x =$

11. $\frac{1}{7} = \frac{b}{18}$

    $b =$

12. $\frac{3}{2} = \frac{5}{c}$

    $c =$

Solve. (Lessons 7-8, 7-9, 7-10, 7-11)

13. 14 is what percent of 56?

14. 25% of what number is 35?

15. What is 15% of 40?

16. Convert 8 meters to centimeters. (Lesson 7-12)

17. Convert 8,900 mL to L. (Lesson 7-13)

▶ Problem Solving

Solve.

18. In a lab, Chemical A and Chemical B are mixed in a ratio of 3 to 5. How much of Chemical B is needed to mix with 18 liters of Chemical A? (Lessons 7-5, 7-7)

19. Orange and pineapple juice are mixed in a ratio of 4 to 5. How much of each juice is needed to make 36 gallons of orange-pineapple juice? (Lessons 7-5, 7-7)

    Orange juice: ▢

    Pineapple juice: ▢

20. Savitri buys 3 pounds of sliced turkey for $12. At that rate, how much sliced turkey can she buy for $25? (Lessons 7-2, 7-7)

21. Of the 120 pizzas sold at Pizza Place on Saturday, 30% were plain pizzas. How many plain pizzas were sold? (Lessons 7-10, 7-11, 7-14)

22. If 35% of a company's advertising budget is $7,000, what is the full advertising budget for the company? (Lessons 7-10, 7-11)

23. A rectangle has a base length of 4 feet and a height of 18 inches. Find the area of the rectangle in square feet. (Lesson 7-12)

24. A bottle of olive oil holds 750 mL. How many bottles could be filled with 4.5 L of olive oil? (Lesson 7-13)

25. Extended Response Arun's Honey-Mustard Sauce has 3 cups honey and 4 cups mustard. Ben's Honey-Mustard Sauce has 5 cups honey and 8 cups mustard.

a. Graph and label a line to represent each ratio.

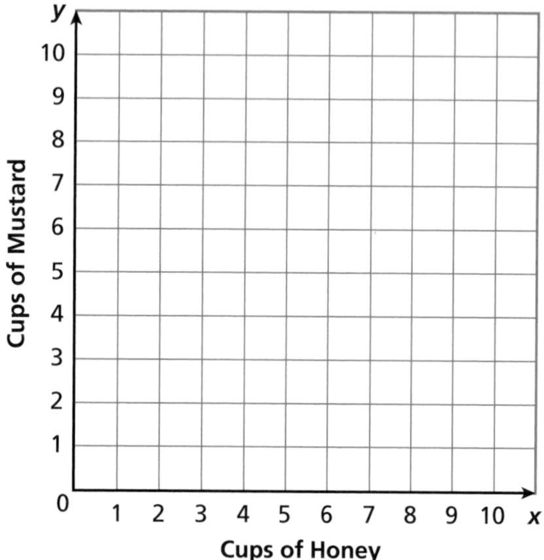

b. Explain how to use the two lines and a straightedge to determine whose Honey-Mustard sauce is more honey-tasting. **(Lesson 7-1)**

Share with your family the Family Letter on Activity Workbook page 173.

Dear Family,

Your child will be learning about numbers throughout the school year. The math unit your child is beginning to study now involves numerical data in the form of statistics.

Important Words

mean or average

median

range

interval

quartiles

clusters

peaks

gaps

Some of the important words we will be working with in this unit are shown at the left. Some of the data displays we will be working with are shown below.

Histogram

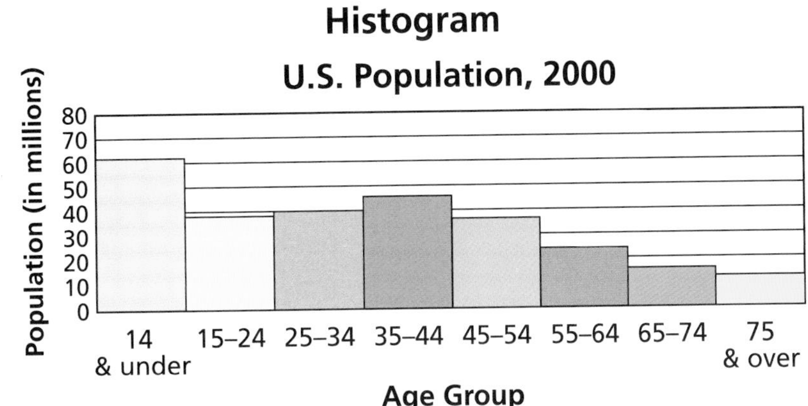

Dot Plot

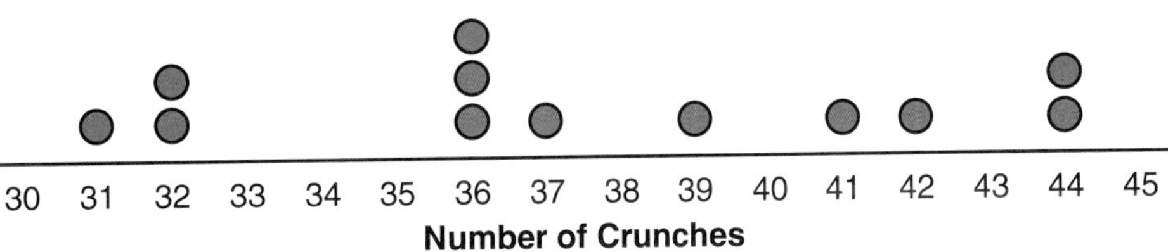

Box Plot

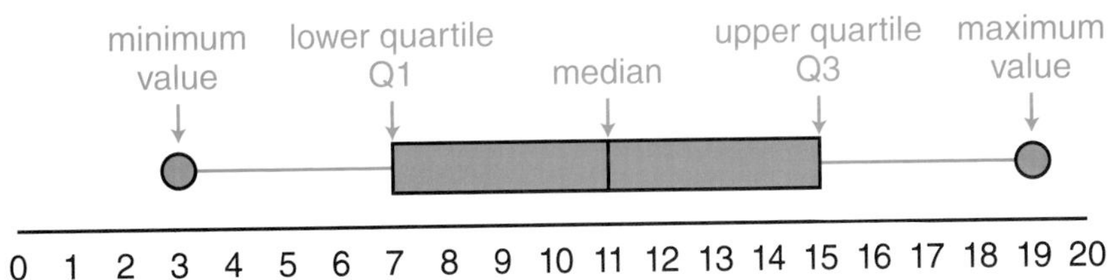

In addition to learning about ways to display data, your child will be learning about ways to analyze and summarize it. In other words, we will be exploring ways to make sense of data and statistics.

If you have any questions or comments, please call or write to me.

Sincerely,
Your child's teacher

This unit includes the Common Core Standards for Mathematical Content for Statistics and Probability 6.SP.1, 6.SP.2, 6.SP.3, 6.SP.4, 6.SP.5, 6.SP.5a, 6.SP.5b, 6.SP.5c, 6.SP.5d and all Mathematical Practices.

Muestra a tu familia la Carta a la familia de la página 174 del Cuaderno de actividades y trabajo.

Estimada familia,

Su hijo aprenderá diferentes conceptos relacionados con los números durante el año escolar. La unidad de matemáticas que estamos comenzando a estudiar trata de datos numéricos en forma de estadísticas.

Algunas de las palabras importantes que usaremos en esta unidad se muestran a la izquierda. Algunas de las representaciones de datos que estaremos usando se muestran debajo.

Palabras importantes

media o promedio

mediana

rango

intervalo

cuartiles

agrupamientos

valores pico

brechas

Histograma

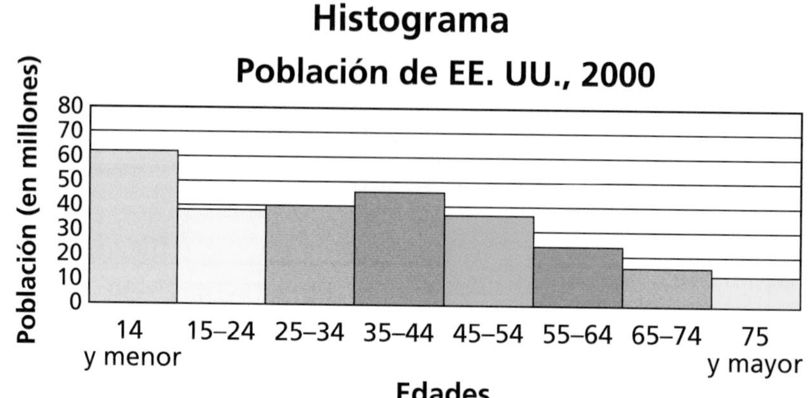

Diagrama de puntos

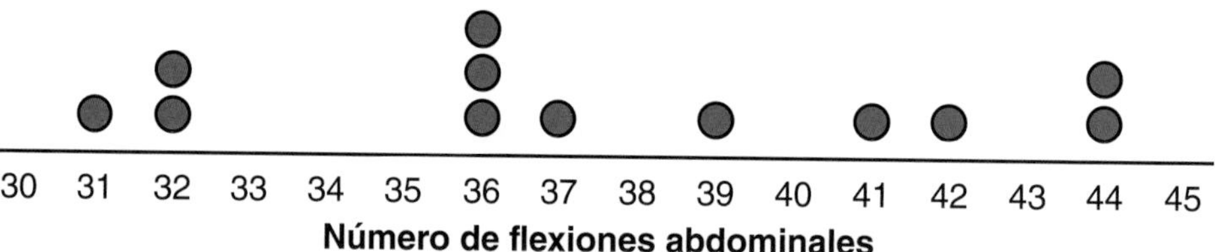

Diagrama de caja y brazos

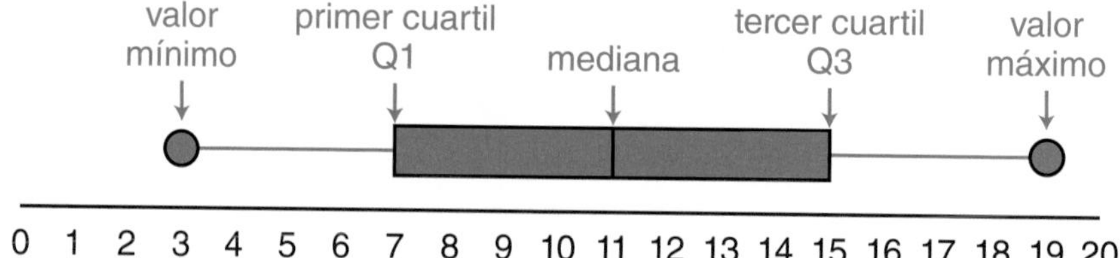

Además de aprender acerca de diferentes maneras de representar datos, su hijo aprenderá cómo analizarlos y resumirlos. En otras palabras, explorará maneras de interpretar mejor los datos y las estadísticas.

Si tiene preguntas o comentarios, por favor comuníquese conmigo.

Atentamente,
El maestro de su hijo

Esta unidad incluye los Common Core Standards for Mathematical Content for Statistics and Probability 6.SP.1, 6.SP.2, 6.SP.3, 6.SP.4, 6.SP.5, 6.SP.5a, 6.SP.5b, 6.SP.5c, 6.SP.5d and all Mathematical Practices.

Vocabulary

numerical data

▶ Numerical Data Can Vary

Numerical data involve numbers and quantities. One example of numerical data is the number of students in your class. The answers to these questions involve numerical data: How many students are in your class? How does the number of students in your class compare to the number of students in other classes in your school, or in your city or state?

For each group of people named below, describe a kind of numerical data that could be collected. Then decide if you would expect all of the data to be the same or if you would expect it to vary. Explain why. Exercise 1 shows you an example.

1. For each student in your school:

   The length of time it takes each student to travel to school in the morning. These times will vary because students live different distances from school.

2. For each student in your class:

3. For each sixth grade student in your state:

4. For each teacher in your school:

5. Write your own example.

▶ Compare Numerical Data

Fitness testing sometimes involves the number of crunches that can be completed in a given length of time. (Crunches are sometimes called sit-ups.) The data below show how many crunches a group of sixth grade students from two classes were able to complete in 1 minute.

Ms. Jackson's Class	
Student	**Number of Crunches**
Lucas	36
Ava	32
Tyler	44
Alexis	36
Jada	37
Chase	41
Sabrina	39

Mr. Ryan's Class	
Student	**Number of Crunches**
Reyna	32
Julien	42
Lia	36
Omar	44
Jorge	31

Use the data from the tables.

6. Consider the question "Which class did better in crunches?" Why is the question difficult to answer?

7. What are different ways you could display the two sets of data so the sets would be easier to compare?

8. Choose one of the ways you named in Exercise 7. Why would that way make the data easier to compare?

Vocabulary

dot plot

▶ Numerical Data and Dot Plots

Look again at the crunch data. The data are numerical.

Ms. Jackson's Class	
Student	**Number of Crunches**
Lucas	36
Ava	32
Tyler	44
Alexis	36
Jada	37
Chase	41
Sabrina	39

Mr. Ryan's Class	
Student	**Number of Crunches**
Reyna	32
Julien	42
Lia	36
Omar	44
Jorge	31

A **dot plot** displays the frequency of numerical data. It uses dots to show how often numbers occur.

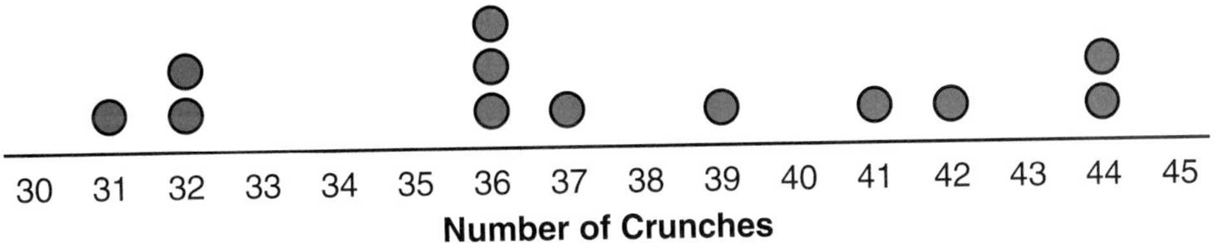

9. The data tables show how many crunches various students completed. Is the number of students shown in the tables the same as the number of dots in the plot?

10. How does the dot plot represent the data in the tables?

11. In the dot plot, there are three dots above 36. Which three students do the dots represent? Explain how you know.

▶ Analyze a Dot Plot

Use the dot plot below for Exercises 12–15. The dot plot shows how many letters are in the last names of a group of students.

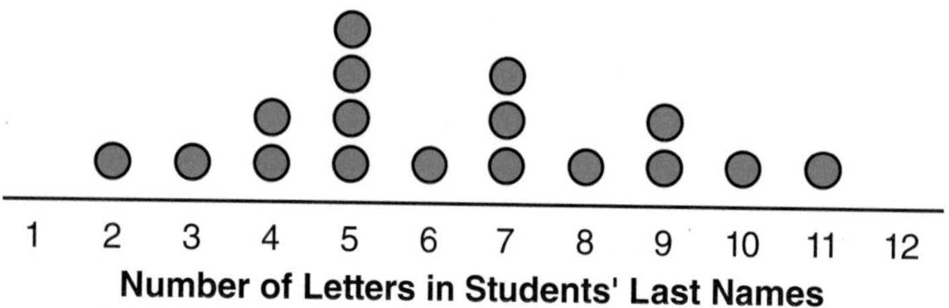

12. How many students does the dot plot represent? Explain how you know.

13. How many letters do most students have in their last name? Explain your answer.

14. Do more students have short last names or long last names? Explain your reasoning.

15. Write your own question about the dot plot. Exchange papers with a classmate and answer each other's questions.

8–2
Class Activity

Use Activity
Workbook page 175.

▶ Make a Dot Plot

The data below show the number of hours a group of students spent doing homework last week.

5, 4, 1, 6, 0, 5, 3, 3, 5, 6, 1, 3, 8, 5, 4

1. Draw a dot plot to represent the data. Title your display.

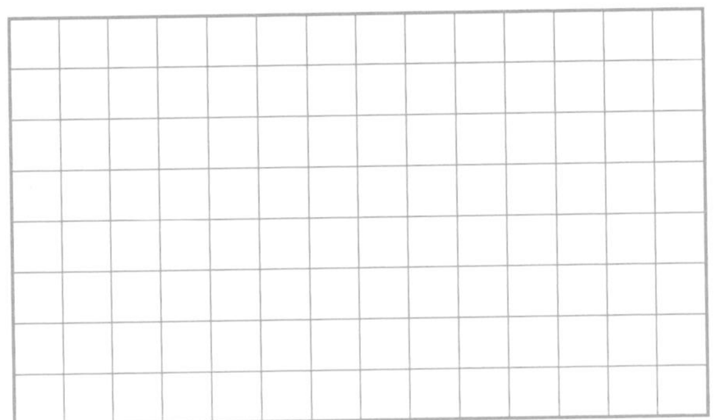

2. How many students does your dot plot represent? Explain how you know that number of students is correct.

3. **Analyze** Why are no dots shown at 2 and at 7?

4. **Analyze** Why do you think 5 hours is the most frequent number of hours? Explain.

5. **Predict** The data represent 15 students. Would the scale of the plot change if it included more students? Explain.

6. **Predict** Suppose the data represent sixth grade students. Would the data change if it represented high school students? Explain.

▶ What's the Error?

Dear Math Students,

The dot plot at the right displays data about kites that were seen at the beach.

I interpreted the dot plot to show that 2 kites had tails with five bows on each tail, and 4 kites had tails with one bow on each tail.

Did I interpret the dot plot correctly? Explain.

Your friend,

Puzzled Penguin

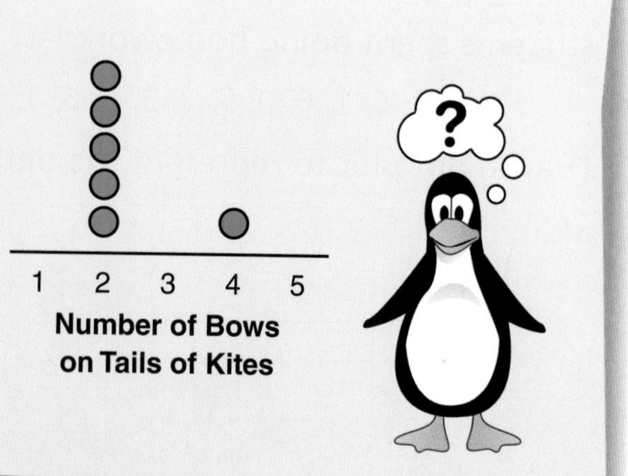

7. Write a response to Puzzled Penguin.

Dear Math Students,

Five of my friends made a dot plot to show the number of times they ate hot lunch at school last month.

My three friends represented by the dots on the left side of the plot said that altogether they ate hot lunch more times than my two friends represented by the dots on the right side of the plot.

Can you help me decide if they are correct?

Your friend,

Puzzled Penguin

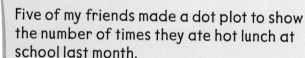

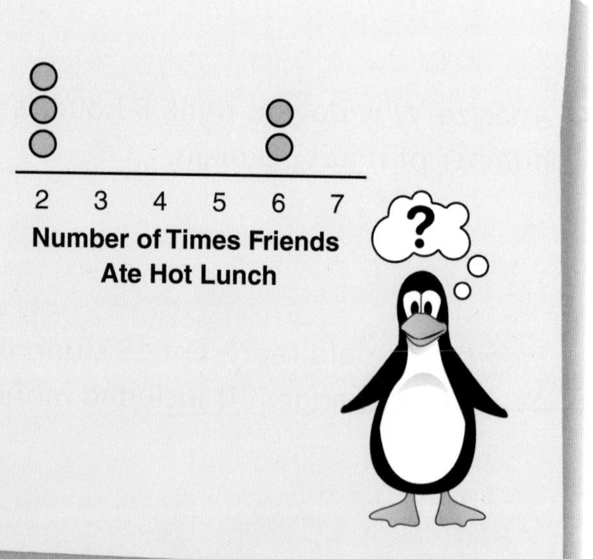

8. Write a response to Puzzled Penguin.

Vocabulary

histogram
interval

▶ Read a Histogram

A **histogram** is a frequency display that uses bars to show the distribution of data in a set. The data are presented in intervals. An **interval** is a range of numbers.

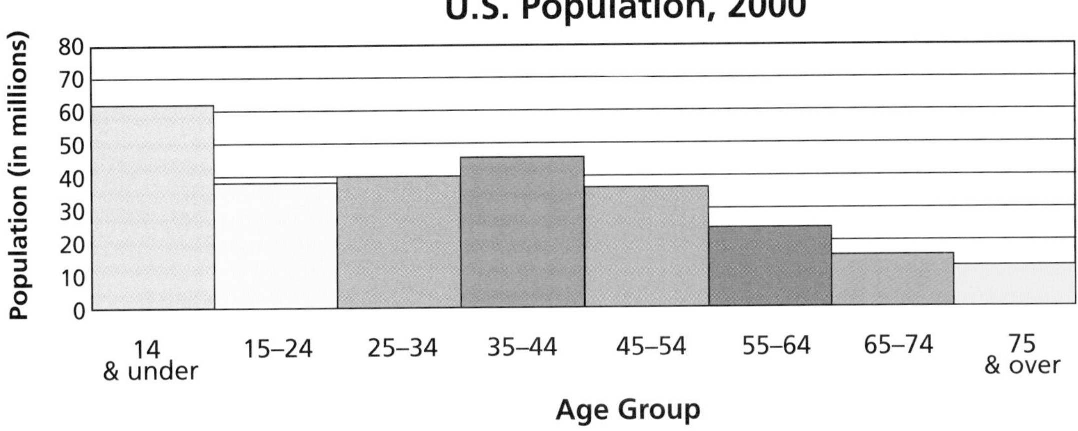

A histogram is used when we want to graphically display a large set of data. The intervals are usually the same size. The bars touch so all the data in the set are included.

Height and width are two important characteristics of the bars. The vertical height (*y*-axis) of a bar shows the frequency, or number of times a data value occurs. The horizontal width (*x*-axis) shows the intervals into which the data are grouped.

Use the histogram above for Exercises 9–13.

9. Which age group has the least number of people?

10. Which age groups have nearly the same numbers of people?

11. What age group has about 15 million people?

12. About how many people are 14 & under or 75 & older?

13. **Discuss** Where do you think a person that is $34\frac{1}{2}$ is included in the graph?

8–2
Class Activity

Use Activity Workbook page 176.

▶ Make a Histogram

The table below shows the lengths of various U.S. rivers.

Selected Rivers of the United States				
River	**Length (miles)**		**River**	**Length (miles)**
Connecticut	407		Savannah	314
Hudson	306		Illinois	273
Mobile	45		Roanoke	410
Potomac	287		Yazoo	169
Apalachicola	90		Saint Johns	285
Monongahela	129		Kanawha	97
Sacramento	374		Delaware	367

14. On the grid below, draw and label a histogram of the data.

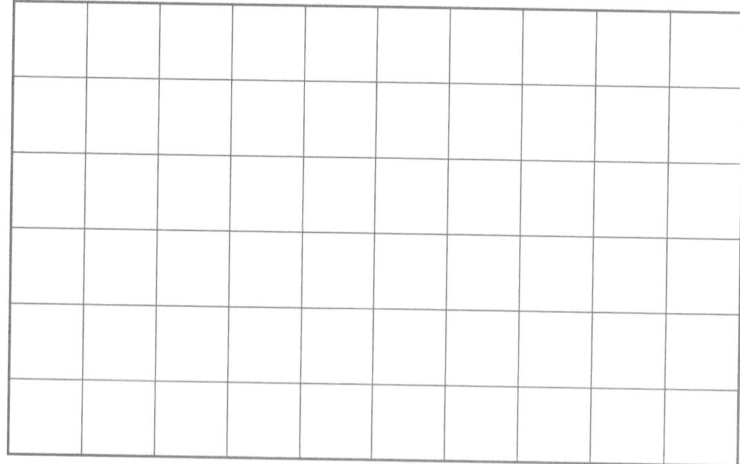

8–3
Class Activity

Use Activity
Workbook page 177.

Vocabulary

mean

▶ Leveling Out and Fair Shares

The **mean** is a measure of the center for a set of numerical data. It summarizes all of its values with a single number. Use the three groups of cubes shown below for Exercises 1 and 2.

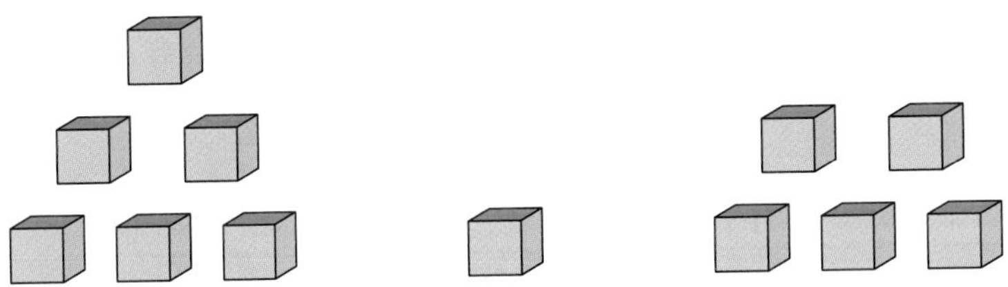

1. Suppose two cubes are moved from the left group to the center group, and two cubes are moved from the right group to the center group. Will the groups be leveled out and represent fair shares? Explain.

2. Explain how to level out the three groups so that each group represents a fair share. Use the words *add* and *subtract* in your answer. Then sketch the fair shares in the space at the right.

▶ Calculate the Mean

Eight students took a 10-question quiz. The number of correct answers each student scored is shown in the table at the right. Use the table for Exercises 3 and 4.

3. What is the quotient when the sum of the scores is divided by the number of scores?

4. What is the mean of the data? Explain.

Quiz Scores

Student	Score (Number Correct)
Blaise	6
Dani	7
Olivia	8
Jamaal	9
William	5
Shanika	8
Cora	6
Enrico	7

▶ What's the Error?

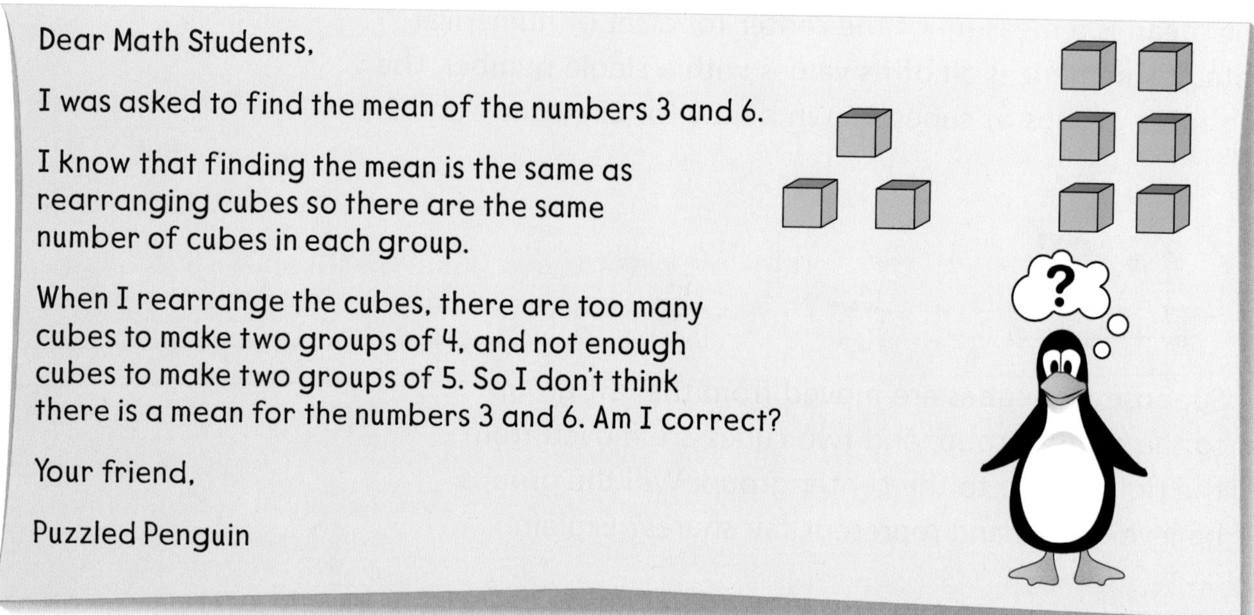

Dear Math Students,

I was asked to find the mean of the numbers 3 and 6.

I know that finding the mean is the same as rearranging cubes so there are the same number of cubes in each group.

When I rearrange the cubes, there are too many cubes to make two groups of 4, and not enough cubes to make two groups of 5. So I don't think there is a mean for the numbers 3 and 6. Am I correct?

Your friend,

Puzzled Penguin

5. Write a response to Puzzled Penguin.

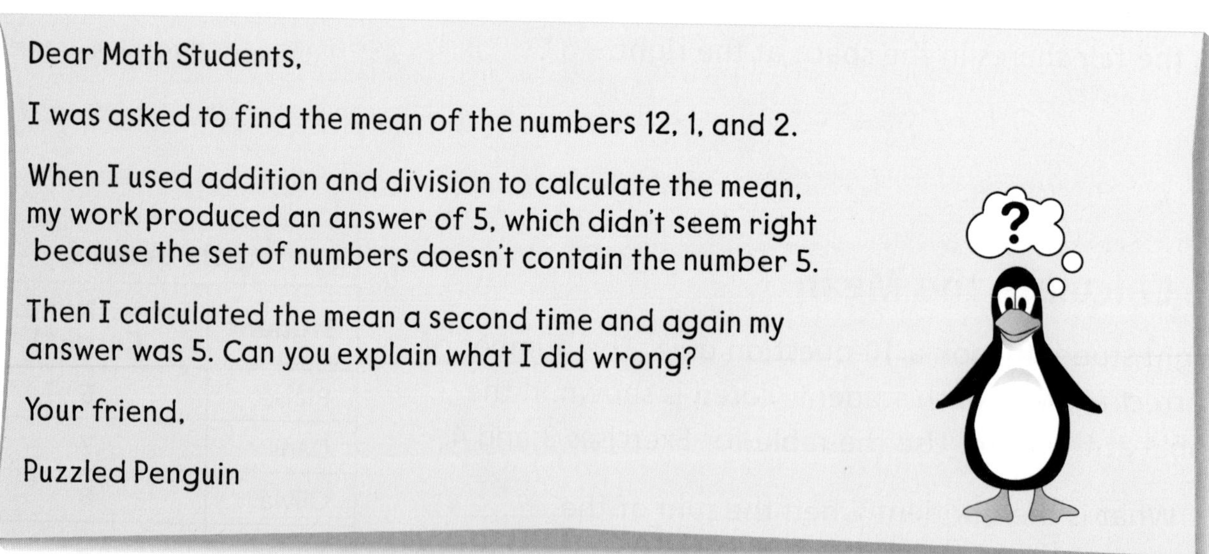

Dear Math Students,

I was asked to find the mean of the numbers 12, 1, and 2.

When I used addition and division to calculate the mean, my work produced an answer of 5, which didn't seem right because the set of numbers doesn't contain the number 5.

Then I calculated the mean a second time and again my answer was 5. Can you explain what I did wrong?

Your friend,

Puzzled Penguin

6. Write a response to Puzzled Penguin.

▶ Summarize Data

One way to summarize a set of data is to use the mean. If all the data values were the same, the common value would be the mean.

Homework Scores	
Day	**Score**
Monday	90
Tuesday	84
Wednesday	93
Thursday	97
Friday	91

1. Hannah wants to tell her family about her homework scores, shown in the table at the right. Hannah believes it would be easier for her family to make sense of the mean score than it would be to make sense of the individual scores.

   Using words, explain how to find the mean score.

2. Calculate the mean score.

3. Write a sentence to explain what your answer to Exercise 2 represents. Include your answer to Exercise 2 in your sentence.

▶ Compare Sets of Data

One way to compare two sets of data is to compare the mean of one set to the mean of the other set.

Points Scored		
Game	**Player A**	**Player B**
1	5	
2	8	
3	1	11
4	12	7
5	9	6
6	4	6
7	10	8
8	7	10

4. The number of points two basketball players scored is shown in the table at the right. One player missed the first two games of the season.

   Which player made a greater contribution of points to the team on a game-by-game basis? Give a reason to support your answer.

▶ Solve Real World Problems

Solve.

5. In Ms. Dixon's science class, the mean of four quiz scores and a final test score determine the quarterly grade. During the first quarter, Yunhee's four quiz scores were 95, 99, 86, and 94.

   a. What is the sum of Yunhee's four quiz scores?

   b. What must the sum of Yunhee's *five* scores be for her to average 90 or more on all four quizzes and the test? Explain your answer.

   c. What is the minimum score Yunhee must earn on the final test to have an average score of at least 90 for the quarter? Explain your answer.

6. The average age in years of the four people in Jorge's family is 25. Jorge is 12 years old, his mom is 38 years old, and his dad is 41 years old. How old is Jorge's sister?

7. The fuel economy of Jo's car is 32 miles per gallon on the highway and 26 miles per gallon in the city. For the two trips shown in the chart at the right combined, did Jo drive more often on the highway, or more often in the city? Give a reason to support your answer.

Jo's Trips

Miles Driven	Fuel Used (in gallons)
420	14
190	6

▶ Draw Models to Unlevel Data

In this lesson, the mean is shown as a balance point.

Draw a dot plot to show the new arrangement of dots.

1. Move one dot to the left and move one dot to the right so the balance point remains the same.

2. Move all of the dots so the balance point remains the same.

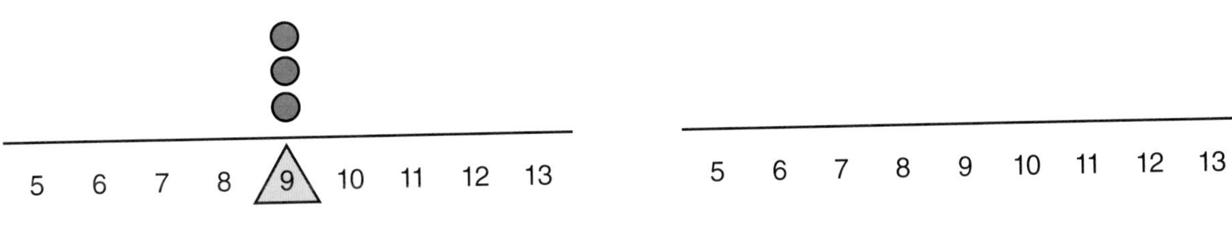

3. Move all of the dots so that the balance point changes to a different whole number. Draw the new balance point.

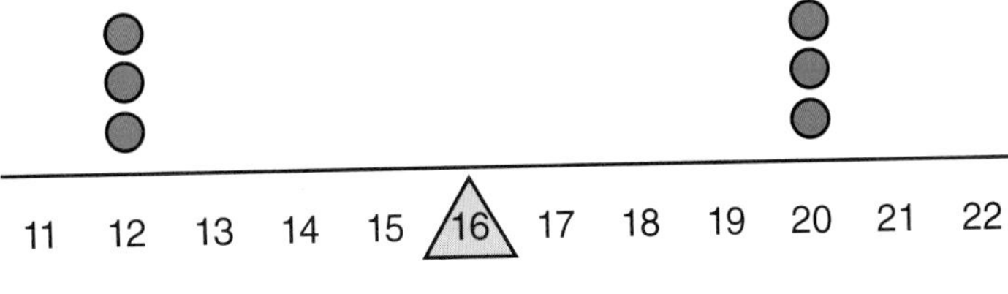

11 12 13 14 15 16 17 18 19 20 21 22

4. Move all of the dots so that the balance point is 6.

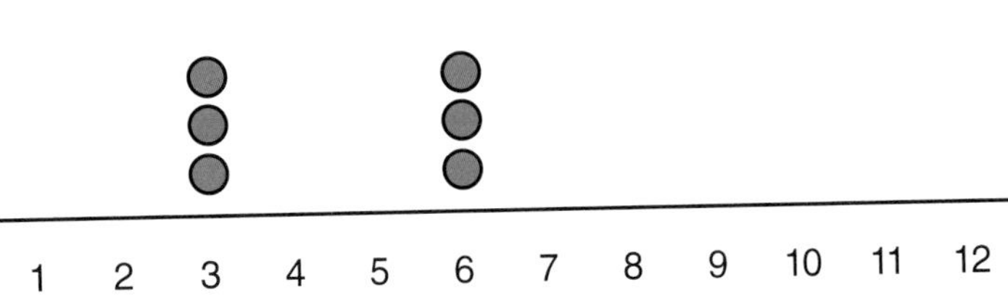

1 2 3 4 5 6 7 8 9 10 11 12

▶ Predict the Mean

Plot the given data. Draw a balance point to predict where you think the mean will be located. Then calculate the mean to check your prediction.

5. 10, 17, 9, 18, 11

8 9 10 11 12 13 14 15 16 17 18

mean: ▢

6. 8, 10, 7, 5, 10, 2

1 2 3 4 5 6 7 8 9 10

mean: ▢

▶ What's the Error?

Dear Math Students:

I was asked to decide if the balance point of the dot plot at the right was correct.

The numbers to the left of the balance point are 4, 4, and 5, which add to 13. The numbers to the right of the balance point are 8 and 9, which add to 17.

I decided the balance point is not correct because the total on one side of the balance point is not the same as the total on the other side.

Can you help correct my thinking?

Your friend,

Puzzled Penguin

7. Write a response to Puzzled Penguin.

Vocabulary

median

▶ Find the Median

The **median** is a single number that summarizes the center of a set of numerical data. The median is the middle number, or the mean of the two middle numbers, when the data are arranged from least to greatest or greatest to least.

10 21 22 37 46

1. The numbers at the right are ordered from least to greatest. Find the median.

2. The dot plot at the right displays 10 data values. Find the median of the data.

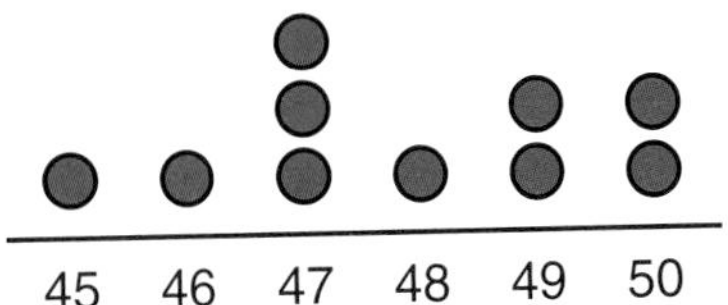

3. Some animals can move very fast for short distances. The table at the right shows the top speeds at which some animals can move. Find the median speed.

Animal	Speed (mph)
Giraffe	32
Rabbit	35
Squirrel	12
Wildebeest	50
Elephant	25
Gray Fox	42
Zebra	40
Wart Hog	30

A set of data may have an odd number of values or an even number of values.

4. Using words, describe the median of a numerical set of data when there are an odd number of values in the set.

5. Using words, describe the median of a numerical set of data when there are an even number of values in the set.

▶ What's the Error?

Dear Math Students,

I was asked to find the median of the set of numbers at the right.

7 4 5 1 6 8 9

By counting, I discovered that there are three numbers to the left of 1 and three numbers to the right of 1. So I decided that 1 is the median because it is the middle number.

Can you tell me what I did wrong?

Your friend,

Puzzled Penguin

6. Write a response to Puzzled Penguin.

Dear Math Students,

I wrote the two sets of numbers shown at the right to help a friend understand how to find the median of a set of numbers.

205 142 110

56 40

I explained that the median of the top set of numbers was 142 because 142 was the number in the middle.

Then I explained that the bottom set of numbers had no median because there was no number in the middle.

Did I provide my friend with correct advice?

Your friend,

Puzzled Penguin

7. Write a response to Puzzled Penguin.

Vocabulary

symmetric

▶ Same Mean and Median

Compare the dot plots below. Plot A has a line of symmetry. The data in Plot A are **symmetric** because the shape of the data on one side of the line of symmetry is the same as the shape of the data on the other side of the line. Plot B has the same number of data values as Plot A, but when compared to Plot A, some values in Plot B have been shifted to the left.

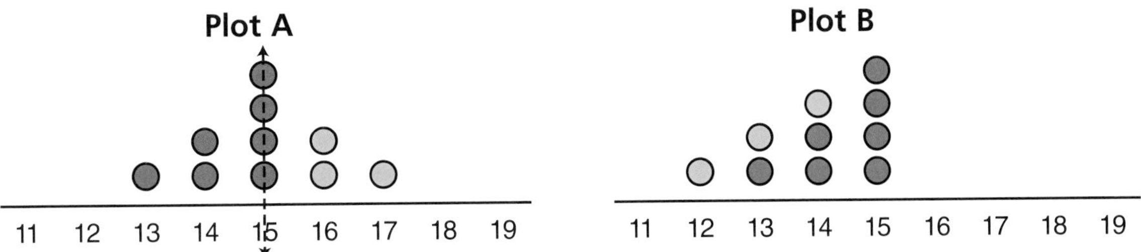

8. Calculate the mean and the median of Plot A.

   Plot A mean: ☐ Plot A median: ☐

9. Plot A is a symmetric dot plot. How is the line of symmetry related to the mean and the median of the data?

10. Using words, predict how the mean and the median of Plot B may be different than the mean and the median of Plot A.

11. Calculate the mean and the median of Plot B. Was the prediction you made in Exercise 10 correct?

12. Why do you think the shift of dots to the left as is shown in Plot B decreased the mean and median of Plot A?

▶ Same Median, Different Mean

Compare these two dot plots. Two data values in symmetric Plot A have been shifted to the right.

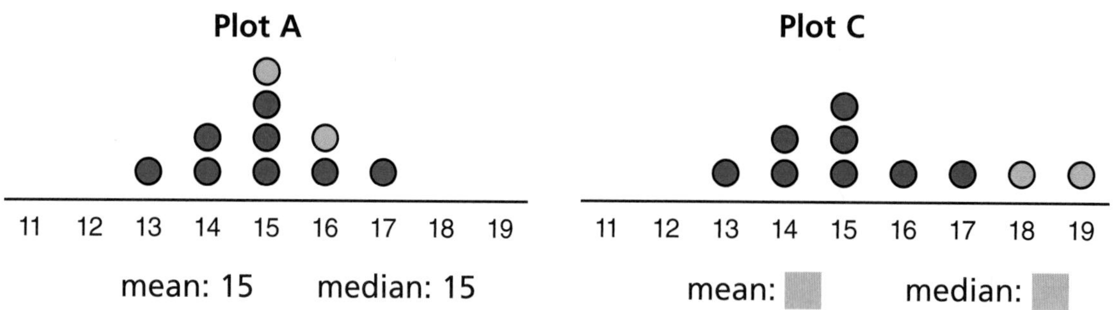

13. Calculate the mean and median of Plot C.

14. How did the shift of dots to the right as is shown in Plot C affect the mean and median of Plot A?

15. Why does a shift to the right increase the mean?

Compare these two dot plots. Two data values in symmetric Plot A have been shifted to the left.

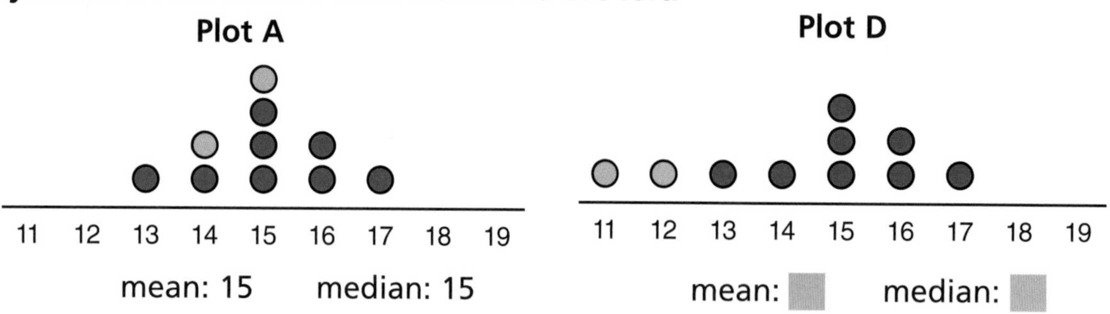

16. Calculate the mean and median of Plot D.

17. How did the shift of the dots to the left as is shown in Plot D affect the mean and median of Plot A?

18. Why does a shift to the left decrease the mean?

▶ Different Mean and Median

Compare these two dot plots. Three data values in symmetric Plot A have been shifted to the right.

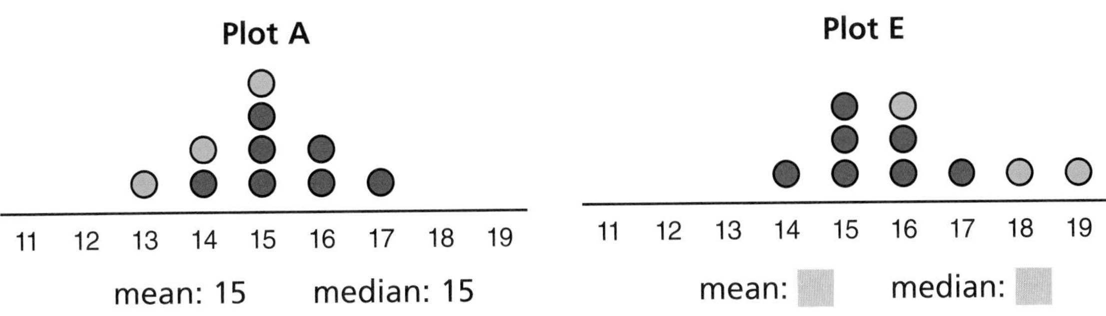

19. Calculate the mean and median of Plot E.

20. How did the shift of the dots to the right as is shown in Plot E affect the mean and median of Plot A?

21. Why did the shift increase the mean and the median?

Compare these two dot plots. Three data values in symmetric Plot A have been shifted to the left.

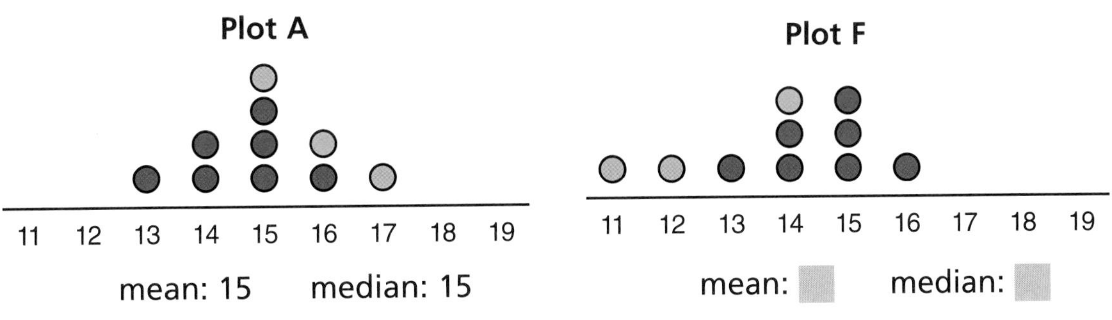

22. Calculate the mean and median of Plot F.

23. How did the shift of the dots to the left as is shown in Plot F affect the mean and median of Plot A?

24. Why did the shift decrease the mean and the median?

▶ Choose the Best Measure

Solve.

Estimates of the populations of seven cities in Colorado are shown in the table at the right. The populations have been rounded to the nearest thousand.

City	Population
Durango	17,000
Montrose	18,000
Windsor	17,000
Loveland	66,000
Erie	17,000
Canon City	16,000
Golden	17,000

25. Calculate the mean of the data.

26. Find the median of the data.

27. How could you summarize the populations of all seven cities using only one number? Would you choose the mean, or the median, to summarize the populations? Give a reason to support your answer.

Rachel has a new part-time summer job. She works 3 days per week. Her earnings for the first two weeks are shown in the table at the right.

Earnings	
Week 1	**Week 2**
$20	$40
$40	$10
$30	$40

28. Calculate the mean earnings per day for each week.

Week 1:  Week 2:

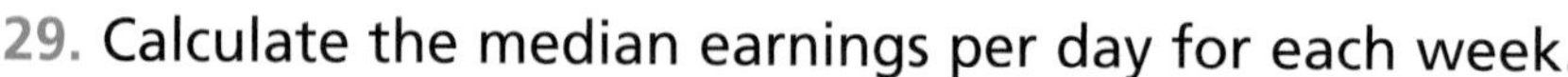

29. Calculate the median earnings per day for each week.

Week 1:  Week 2:

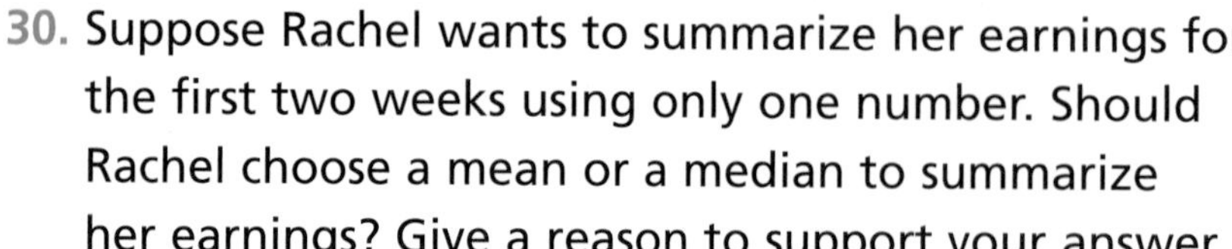

30. Suppose Rachel wants to summarize her earnings for the first two weeks using only one number. Should Rachel choose a mean or a median to summarize her earnings? Give a reason to support your answer.

Vocabulary

range

▶ Calculate Range

Jayla and Sophie are members of a sixth grade basketball team. The dot plots below show the number of points scored by each player during the first 10 games of the season.

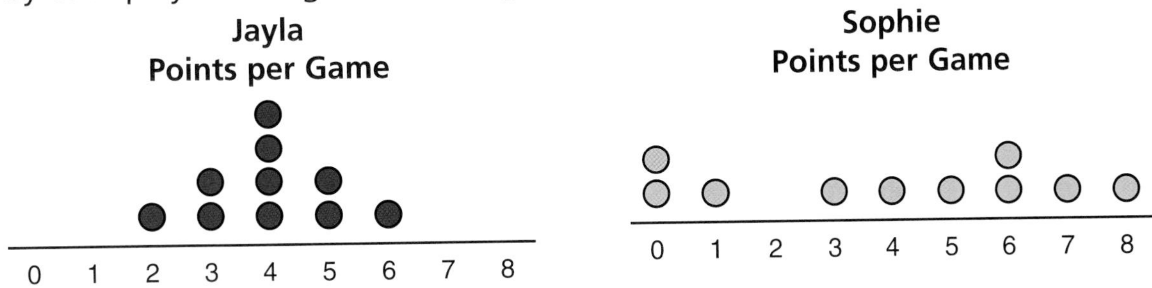

The range is a single number that summarizes the variability of a set of data. You can calculate the **range** of a set of numbers by subtracting the least number from the greatest number in the set.

1. Calculate the range of each dot plot.

   Jayla: range ______ Sophie: range ______

2. Calculate the mean and the median number of points per game for Jayla and for Sophie.

   Jayla: mean ______ median ______

   Sophie: mean ______ median ______

3. Suppose you calculated the mean and the median for each of the other players on the team. Would your answers be the same as the mean and median for Jayla and Sophie, or would your answers be different? Explain.

4. All three measures—mean, median, and range—describe the data in some way. What does the range tell you about the data?

Vocabulary

quartiles
first quartile
third quartile

▶ What are Quartiles?

A set of numerical data is shown below. The median is the mean or average of the two middle numbers.

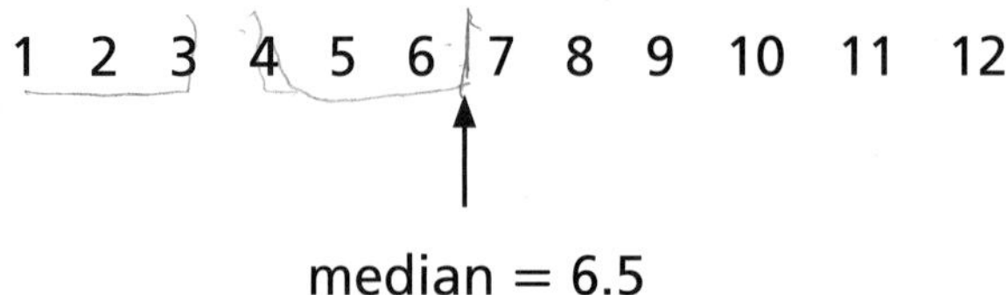

5. Into how many equal parts does the median divide the data?

Quartiles are the values of the points that separate a set of data into four equal parts. The **first quartile** separates the lower half of the data into two equal parts. The **third quartile** separates the upper half of the data into two equal parts.

Look below at the numbers to the *left* of the median. The first quartile is the mean or average of the two middle numbers.

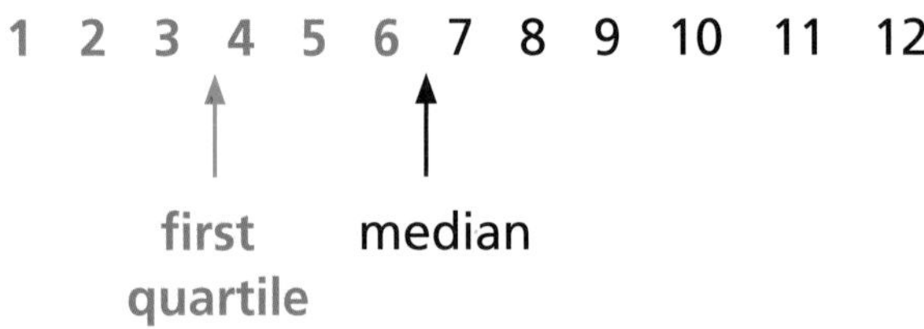

6. Into how many equal parts does the first quartile divide the data to the left of the median?

7. What number represents the first quartile?

Look below at the numbers to the *right* of the median. The third quartile is the mean or average of the two middle numbers.

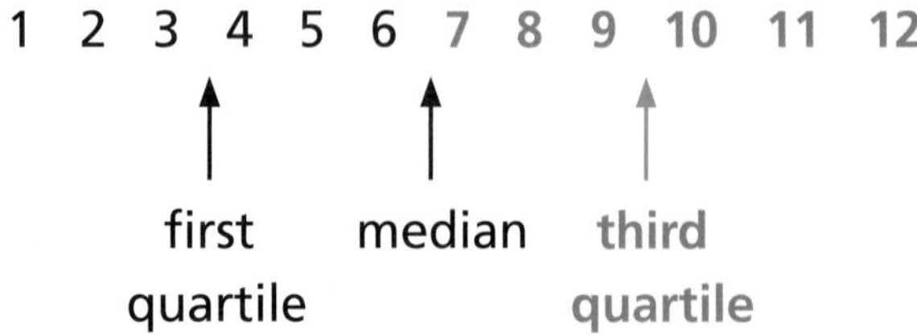

8. Into how many equal parts does the third quartile divide the data to the right of the median?

9. What number represents the third quartile?

▶ Find Quartiles

Look at Set A. When a set of data has an odd number of values, the median is a value in the set.

Set A

	101
first quartile →	133
	137
median →	210
	212
third quartile →	275
	284

10. What number is the median, or middle number, of the set?

11. Explain why 133 is the first quartile of the set and 275 is the third quartile.

Look at Set B. When a set of data has an even number of values, the median is not a value in the set.

Set B

	26
first quartile →	28
	51
median →	
	55
third quartile →	64
	87

12. Explain how to calculate the median, or middle number, of the set. Then calculate the median.

13. Explain why 28 is the first quartile of the set and 64 is the third quartile.

Find the median, first quartile, and third quartile of the data on each dot plot.

Plot A

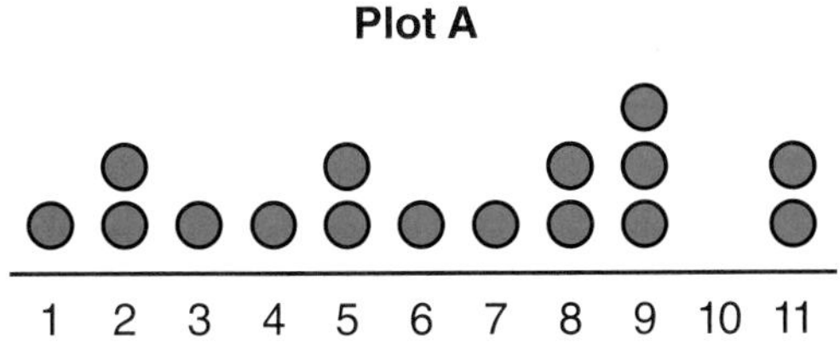

Plot B

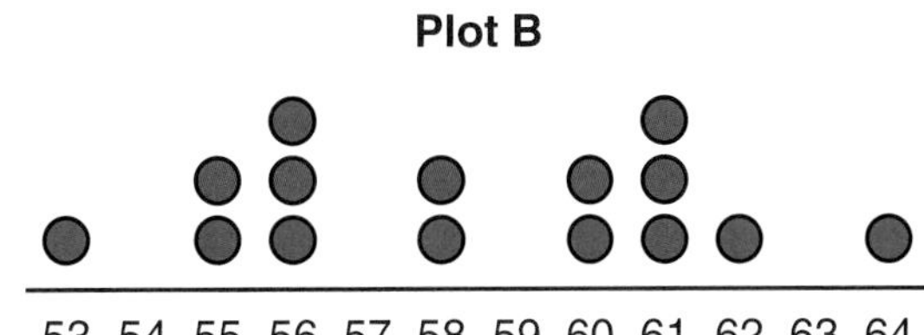

14. Plot A: median:

first quartile:

third quartile:

15. Plot B: median:

first quartile:

third quartile:

▶ What's the Error?

Dear Math Students,

I can use mental math to calculate the range and the median of the numbers at the right.

The range is 60 because $70 - 10 = 60$. And the median is 30 because $60 \div 2 = 30$. Is this correct?

Your friend,

Puzzled Penguin

16. Write a response to Puzzled Penguin.

Dear Math Students,

I was asked to calculate the first quartile of the set of data that is shown at the right.

2, 2, 3, 4, 4, 6, 8, 8, 8, 10

To calculate the first quartile, I divided the range by 4, like this:

First Quartile = Range ÷ 4
First Quartile = $(10 - 2) \div 4$
First Quartile = $8 \div 4$
First Quartile = 2

So I decided that the first quartile is 2. Can you explain what I did wrong, and explain how I can correctly calculate the first quartile?

Your friend,

Puzzled Penguin

17. Write a response to Puzzled Penguin.

Vocabulary

box plot

▶ Compare a Dot Plot and a Box Plot

The dot plot and box plot below represent the same set of data. A **box plot** is a graphic summary that shows the median, quartiles, and minimum and maximum values of a set of data.

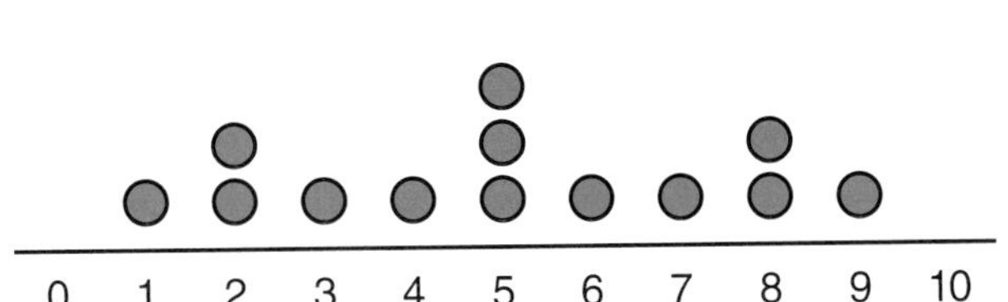

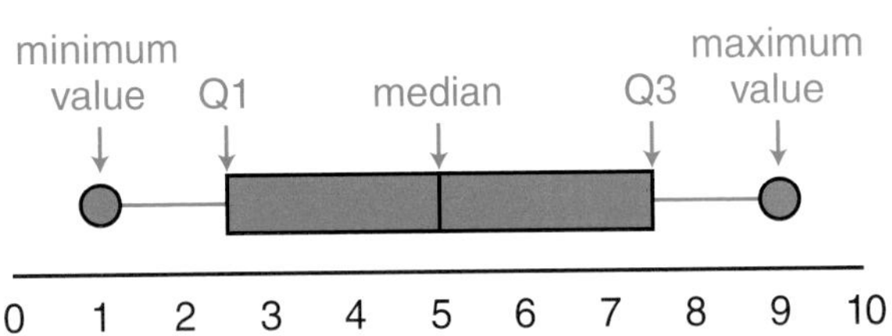

1. In which display, the dot plot or the box plot, is it easier to identify the median and quartiles of the data? Give a reason to support your answer.

2. Use the box plot to name the median, the quartiles, and the minimum and maximum values of the data. Explain how you know.

3. In which display, the dot plot or the box plot, is it easier to identify the range into which one half the data can be found? Explain your answer.

▶ Make a Box Plot

4. Make a box plot to represent the dot plot data.

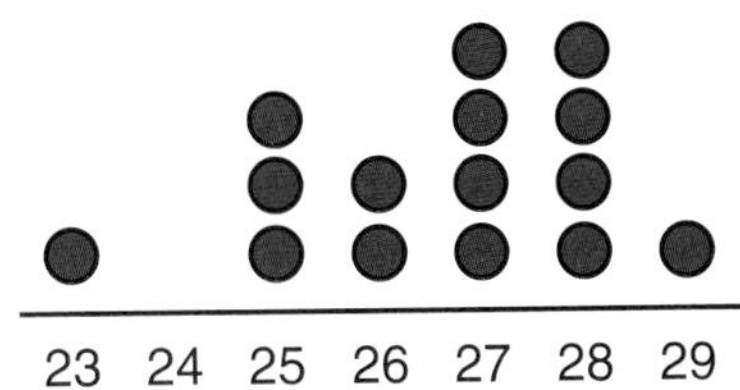

23 24 25 26 27 28 29

▶ Interpret a Box Plot

Compare the box plots shown below. The box plot at the left shows the number of times the students in Mr. Rayburn's class wore shorts during September. The box plot at the right shows the number of times the students wore shorts during October.

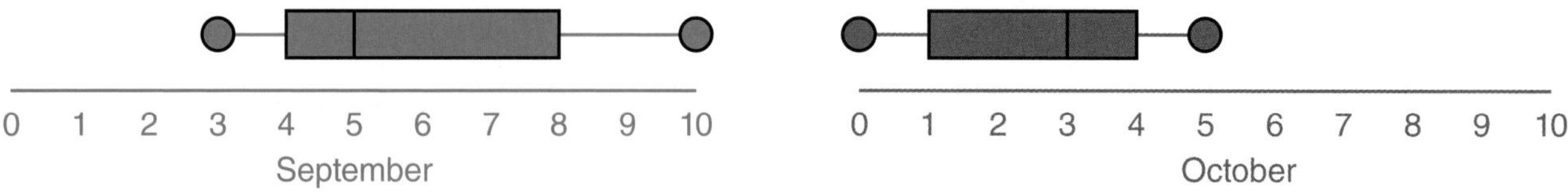

Use the box plots for Exercises 5 and 6.

5. How do the median and quartiles for September compare to the median and quartiles for October?

6. What does your answer for Exercise 5 suggest about the September and October temperatures? Explain your answer.

Three summaries of data displayed by a box plot are shown at the right. Use the summaries for Exercises 7 and 8.

Q1 = 13.5
median = 16.02
Q3 = 44

7. Suppose 37.79 is a value in the set of data. Where in the set is 37.79? Explain your answer.

8. How does the range from the median to Q1 compare to the range from the median to Q3, and what does this suggest about the spread of the data?

8–8
Class Activity

Vocabulary

interquartile range

▶ Introduce Interquartile Range

In a box plot, Q1 is often called the lower quartile and Q3 is often called the upper quartile. The **interquartile range** (or IQR) is the difference between the upper and lower quartiles, and it is a way to describe the spread of data in a set.

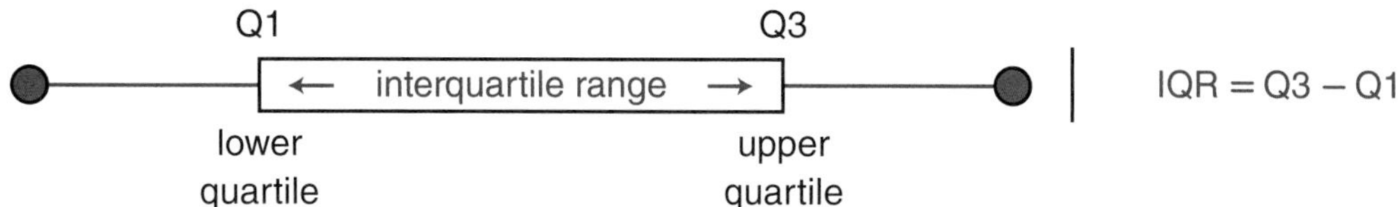

IQR = Q3 − Q1

Use the box plots below for Exercises 9–11.

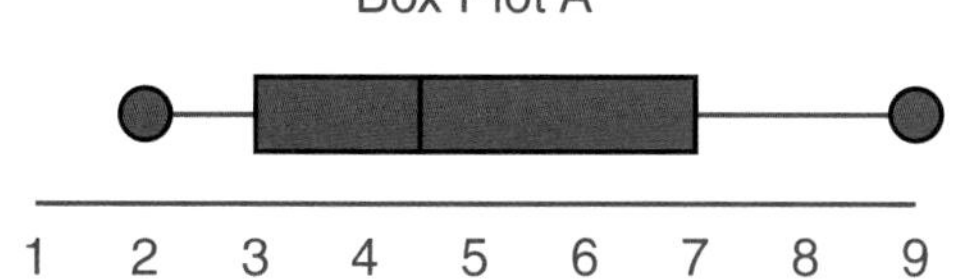

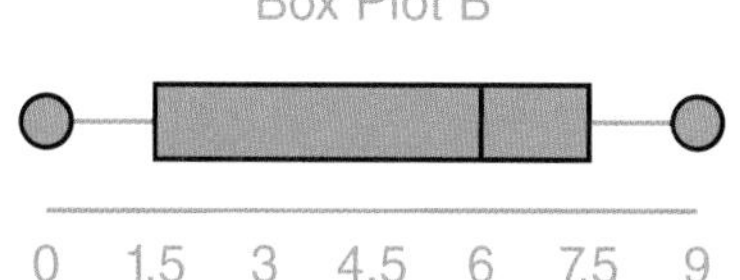

9. Calculate the IQR of Box Plot A.

10. Calculate the IQR of Box Plot B.

11. Compare the IQR of Box Plot A to the IQR of Box Plot B. What does the comparison suggest about the spread of data in Plot A when compared to the spread of data in Plot B?

The data at the right summarize the quiz scores for two math classes. The quiz was the same for each class, and each class has the same number of students.

Morning Class	Afternoon Class
Q1 = 74 median = 87 Q3 = 89	Q1 = 81 median = 87 Q3 = 95

12. Suppose a score of 90 or more earns a grade of A. Which class earned more A's? Give a reason to support your answer.

▶ What's the Error?

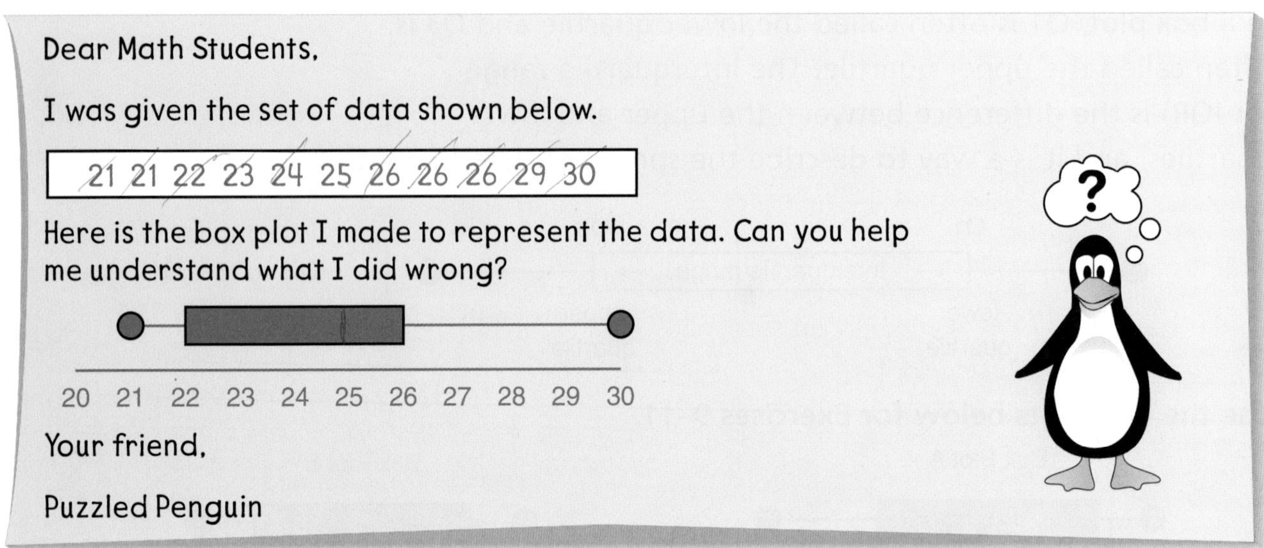

Dear Math Students,
I was given the set of data shown below.
21 21 22 23 24 25 26 26 26 29 30
Here is the box plot I made to represent the data. Can you help me understand what I did wrong?
20 21 22 23 24 25 26 27 28 29 30
Your friend,
Puzzled Penguin
?

13. Write a response to Puzzled Penguin.

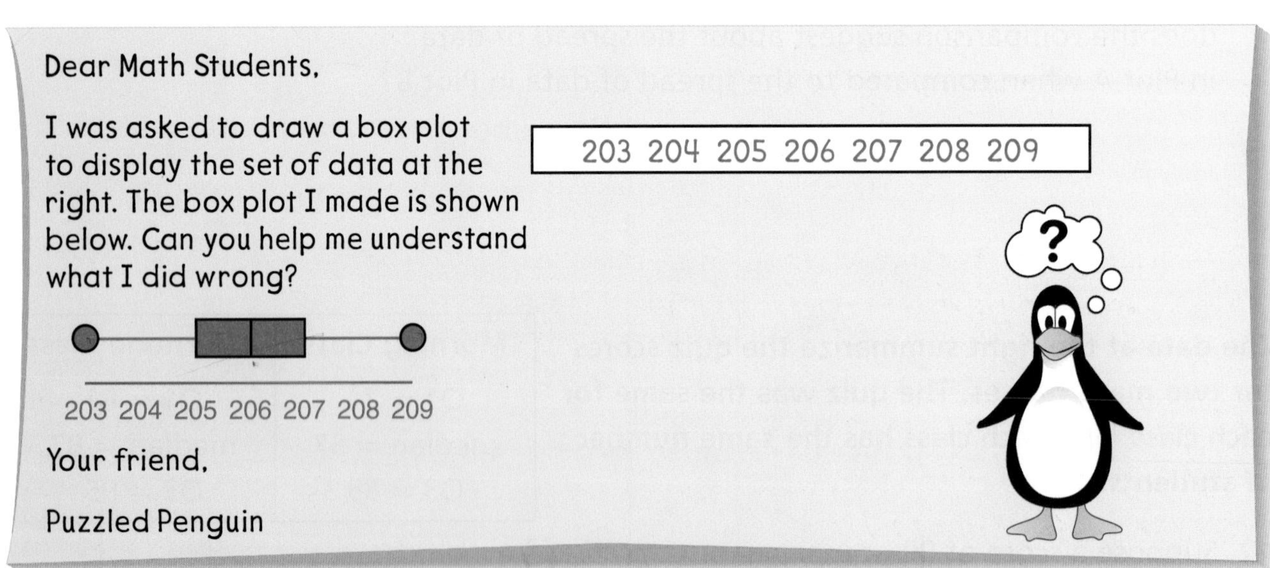

Dear Math Students,
I was asked to draw a box plot to display the set of data at the right. The box plot I made is shown below. Can you help me understand what I did wrong?
203 204 205 206 207 208 209
203 204 205 206 207 208 209
Your friend,
Puzzled Penguin
?

14. Write a response to Puzzled Penguin.

▶ Determine Distance from the Mean

This dot plot shows six values. The mean of the values is 5.

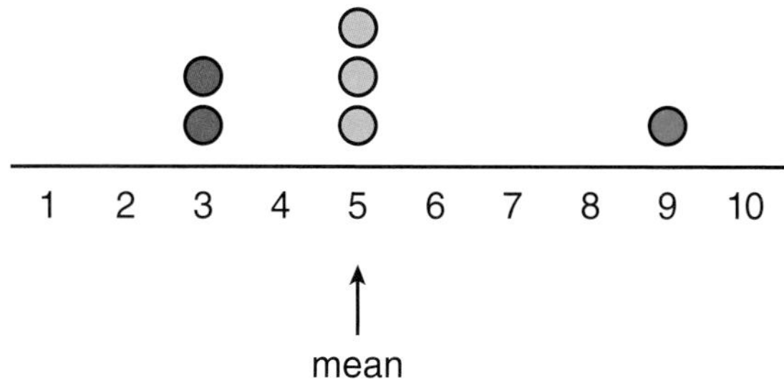

The numbers below represent each dot's distance from the mean.

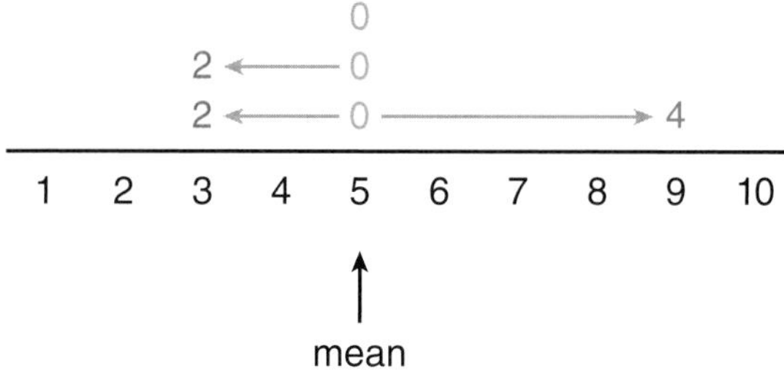

1. Why is 5 the mean?

2. What subtraction is used to calculate distance from the mean to each blue dot?

3. What subtraction is used to calculate distance from the mean to the green dot?

4. Calculate the mean of the dot plot below and label it. Then in the space at the right, write a number for each dot that represents the dot's distance from the mean.

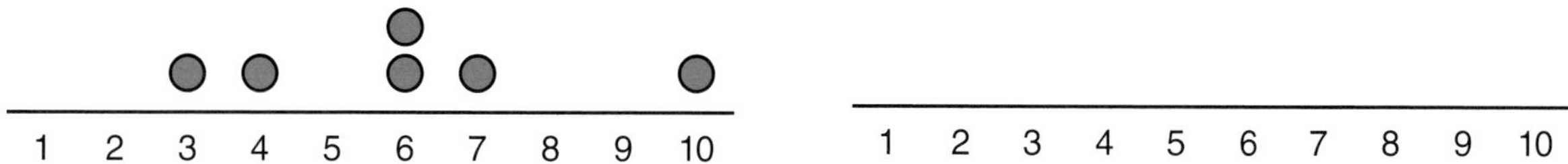

Vocabulary

mean absolute deviation

▶ Find the Mean Absolute Deviation

Each display below represents the same set of data. The display at the right shows a number in green to indicate each dot's distance from the mean. Use the displays for Exercises 5–7.

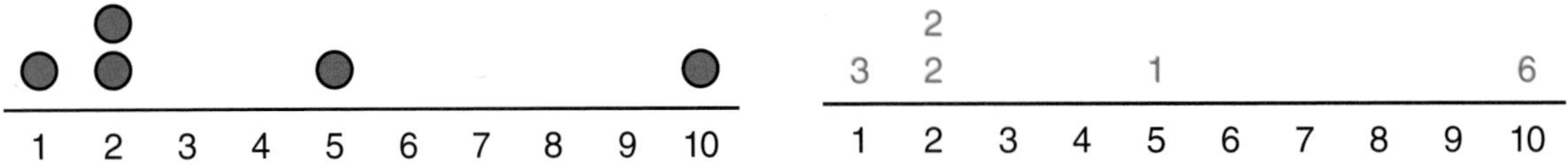

5. Find the sum of the distances from the mean.

6. Divide the sum of the distances from the mean by the number of values.

7. What does the answer to Exercise 6 represent?

In a set of data, the **mean absolute deviation** is the mean or average distance each data value is from the mean. The mean absolute deviation is a measure of the variability or spread of data in a set.

Follow the steps below to calculate the mean absolute deviation of the set of data shown at the right.

1	1	3	5	9	9	10	10

8. Find the mean of the data.

9. Find the distance each value is from the mean.

10. Write the sum of the distances.

11. Calculate the mean absolute deviation by dividing the sum of the distances by the number of values.

12. Which set has data that is more spread out from the mean?

Write your answers on Activity Workbook page 182.

▶ Compare Mean Absolute Deviations

A basketball team consists of two groups of players with five players in each group. The tables at the right show the number of points the players have scored so far this season.

Group A	Points Scored
Nick	10
Kurtis	31
Raul	68
Cory	26
Hector	45

Group B	Points Scored
Casey	29
Pedro	43
Zack	32
Andre	45
Tommy	31

13. Calculate the mean number of points scored by the players in each group.

    Group A mean: ▢

    Group B mean: ▢

14. Calculate each player's distance from the mean number of points scored and write the distances in the table at the right.

Group A	Distance from Mean
Nick	
Kurtis	
Raul	
Cory	
Hector	

Group B	Distance from Mean
Casey	
Pedro	
Zack	
Andre	
Tommy	

15. Calculate the mean absolute deviation of each group. What does your calculation suggest?

    Group A mean absolute deviation: ▢ Group B mean absolute deviation: ▢

16. Which player in each group has the greatest deviation from the mean?

    Group A player: ▢ Group B player: ▢

17. What does the greatest deviation from the mean suggest about the two players you named in Exercise 16?

8–9
Class Activity

Use Activity Workbook page 183.

▶ What's the Error?

Dear Math Students,

On the last day of school, the students in a sixth grade class were asked how many days they were absent that year.

The table shows the data that were collected.

I calculated the mean absolute deviation for each set of data.

I concluded that the data for the girls showed more variability than the data for the boys.

I was told my conclusion was wrong. Can you tell me why?

Your friend,

Puzzled Penguin

Number of Days Absent	
Boys	**Girls**
2	0
0	3.5
8	1
5	3
0	4
3	0
0	4.5
9	3
0	5
1	2

?

18. Write a response to Puzzled Penguin.

Number of Days Absent	
Distance from the mean	Distance from the mean
Boys	Girls

Vocabulary

cluster
peak
gap
outlier

▶ Analyze the Shape of Data

A set of data can be described by its shape. A **cluster** is a group of data values. A **peak** is the value that appears most often. A **gap** is an interval with no data. An **outlier** is an extreme or distant value.

Use the dot plot below for Exercises 1–4.

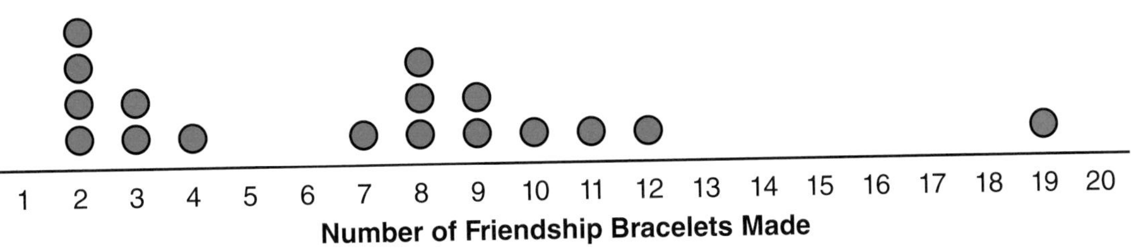

1. Describe the shape of the data. Use the words *clusters, peaks, gaps,* and *outliers* in your answer.

2. The median of the data is 8. Would the median change if it was calculated a second time without including the value at 19? Explain why or why not.

3. The mean of the data is 7. Would the mean change if it was calculated a second time without including the value at 19? Explain why or why not.

4. Which measure, mean or median, best describes the set of data? Give a reason to support your answer.

8–10
Class Activity

Use Activity
Workbook page 184.

▶ Display and Summarize Data

Twenty-five sixth graders were surveyed and asked "In the morning, how long does it take you to get ready for school?" Their answers are shown in the table at the right.

Number of Minutes
30
60
45
60
25
90
55
60
50
60
30
60
10
45
25
45
30
60
50
60
45
90
60
30
50

Use the table for Exercises 5–7.

5. In the space below make a display of the data that enables you to see its overall shape.

6. Describe the shape of the data. Use the words *clusters*, *peaks*, *gaps*, and *outliers* in your answer.

7. Which measure—mean, median, range, interquartile range, or mean absolute deviation—best describes the data? Include a reason to support your answer.

▶ Collect and Record Data

1. **Investigate** Write the question you are investigating.

2. **Predict** How far do you think a paper airplane can fly? Record your prediction.

3. Perform the steps shown at the right.

4. **Compare** Look at the prediction you made in Exercise 2 and compare it to the data that were collected during the investigation. Was your prediction reasonable? Explain your answer.

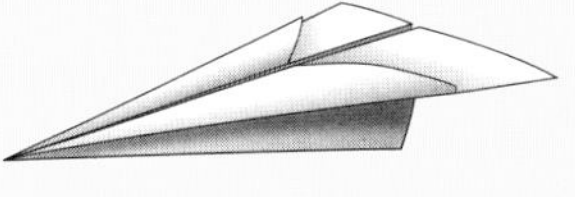

Investigation Steps

- Review the question to be answered.
- Use the steps on Student Book page 354 or use your own design to make a paper airplane.
- Measure the distance the paper airplane flies.
- Record the data you collect.
- With your classmates, make a graphic display of the data.
- Analyze the data.
- Form a conclusion.

5. **Summary** Look at the data that were collected during the investigation. Write a summary of the data. Include the distance a paper airplane can fly in your summary.

6. **Choose a Measure** Which statistical measure of the data would you use to best describe the distance a paper airplane can fly? Explain your reasoning.

▶ Make a Paper Airplane

You are going to make a paper airplane to answer the question "How far will a paper airplane fly?"

If you know how to make a paper airplane, make one of your own design. Or, make the paper airplane shown below.

Step 1 Fold a sheet of paper in half.

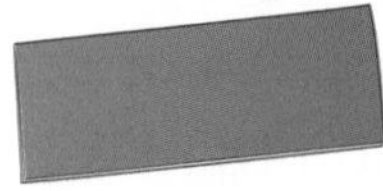

Step 2 Open it. Fold in two corners.

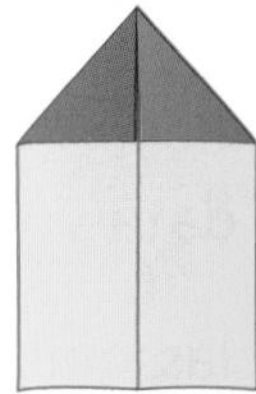

Step 3 Fold in two sides.

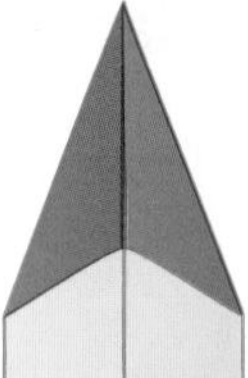

Step 4 Fold in half.

Step 5 Fold both sides in half.

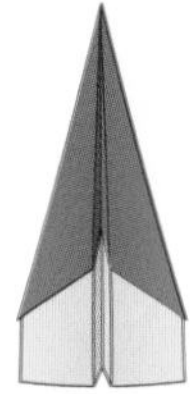

Step 6 Write your name on the airplane.

▶ Math and Handprints

If you've ever traced an outline of your hand, you may have traced it with your fingers spread apart.

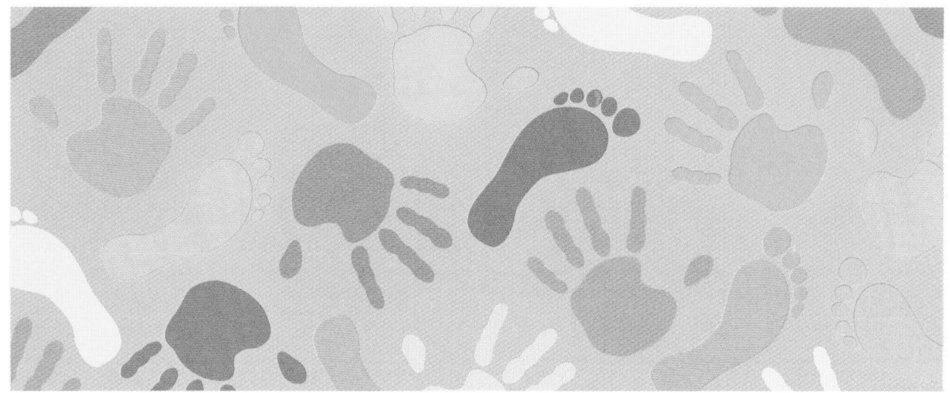

In today's activity, you will estimate the area of your hand with your fingers together.

1. **Predict** What do you think the area of your hand might be? Record your prediction in square centimeters.

2. **Predict** Do you think the data collected by your class will vary? Give a reason to support your answer.

3. Perform the steps shown at the right.

4. **Compare** Look at the data collected by your class. Was your prediction in Exercise 1 reasonable? Explain.

5. **Choose a Measure** Which statistical measure of the data best describes the area of a typical sixth grader's hand? Explain your reasoning.

Investigation Steps

- Review the goal of the activity.
- Trace your hand.
- Estimate by counting.
- Record the data you collect.
- With your classmates, make a graphic display of the data.
- Analyze the data.
- Form a conclusion.

▶ Informal Measurement Tools and Units

Before the invention of formal measuring tools and standard units of measure, ancient civilizations used informal tools and units, such as spans.

Span

An example of a *span* is the distance across your hand, from the tip of the thumb to the tip of the little finger, with your fingers spread apart as far as possible.

Solve.

6. **Estimate** What is a reasonable estimate in inches of one span of your hand?

7. **Compare** Measure your hand span in inches. Was the estimate you made in Exercise 6 reasonable? Explain.

8. **Predict** What is a reasonable estimate in hand spans of the length and the width of your classroom?

9. **Measure** Using hand spans, measure and record the length and width of your classroom. Were the predictions you made in Exercise 8 reasonable? Explain.

10. **Decide** Do you think using a hand span is a precise way to measure? Explain why or why not.

Use the Activity Workbook Unit Test on pages 185–188.

▶ Vocabulary

Vocabulary

mean
quartile
range
median

Choose the best term from the box.

1. The ___?___ is the middle number, or the average of the two middle numbers, in a set of numerical data. (Lesson 8-6)

2. The ___?___ of a set of data is calculated by subtracting the least value from the greatest. (Lesson 8-7)

3. The ___?___ is a single number that summarizes all the values in a set of numerical data. (Lesson 8-3)

▶ Concepts and Skills

Complete.

4. Write a statistical question that is likely to show variability in its answer. (Lesson 8-1)

5. Suppose the data in one dot plot are symmetric and the data in a related dot plot are not symmetric. How would the dot plots look different? (Lesson 8-6)

6. Why do the quartiles of a set of data divide the data into four equal parts? (Lesson 8-7)

7. Explain why you can think of finding a mean as unleveling and leveling data. (Lessons 8-3, 8-4, 8-5)

The dot plot below shows the number of correct answers a group of students scored on a quiz. Use the dot plot for Exercises 8–14.

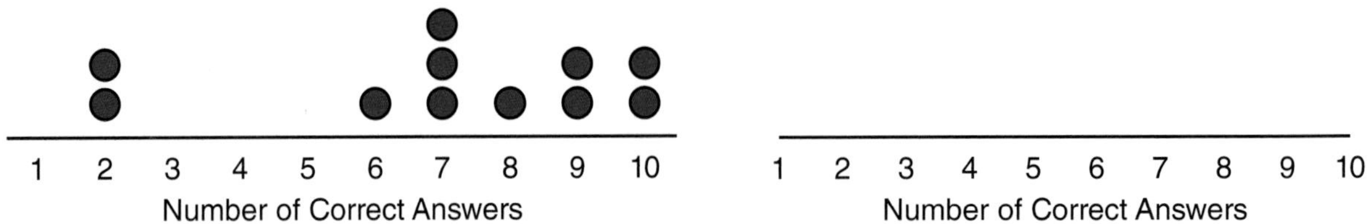

8. Calculate the mean absolute deviation of the data. **(Lesson 8-9)**

9. Consider the shape of the dot plot data. Does the dot plot display a *cluster* or *clusters* of data? Explain. **(Lesson 8-10)**

10. Write a sentence that describes the *peak* or *peaks* of the data. **(Lesson 8-10)**

11. Write a sentence that describes the *gap* or *gaps* in the display. **(Lesson 8-10)**

12. Are any of the data values outliers? Explain why or why not. **(Lesson 8-10)**

13. To the right of the dot plot, make a box plot for the data. **(Lesson 8-8)**

14. Calculate the interquartile range of the data. **(Lesson 8-8)**

▶ Problem Solving

15. The table below shows the length of the shorelines of various states. On the grid, draw a histogram of the data. (Lesson 8-2)

Shorelines of Selected States

State	Length (miles)
Texas	3,359
Rhode Island	384
Georgia	2,344
California	3,427
Hawaii	1,052
Alabama	607
New Jersey	1,792
Maine	3,478
Oregon	1,410
South Carolina	2,876
Connecticut	618
Massachusetts	1,519
Washington	3,026
New York	1,850

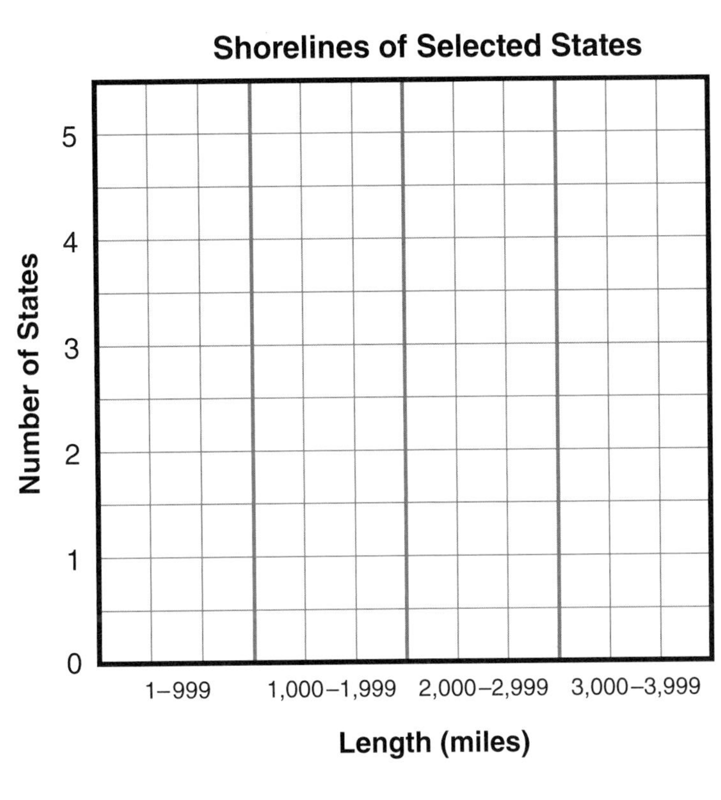

16. Write a conclusion about the data displayed by the histogram. (Lesson 8-2)

17. Suppose you wanted to investigate the size of a typical sixth grader's foot. (Lessons 8-11, 8-12)

a. What unit of measure would you use?

b. How would you do the measuring?

18. Calculate the quartiles (Q1 and Q3) of the data. (Lesson 8-7)

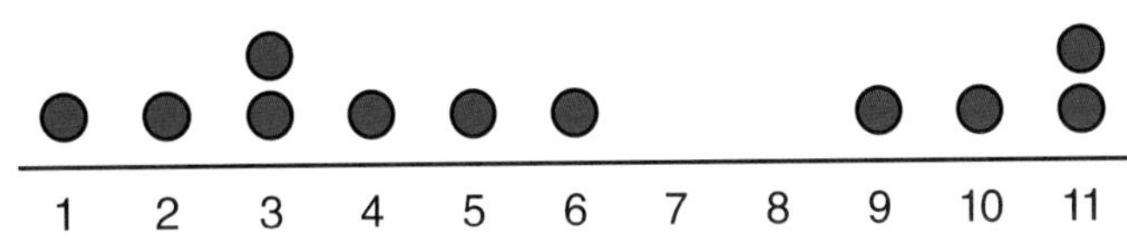

The set of data below shows the number of brothers and sisters each student in a sixth grade class has. Use the data for Exercises 19–25.

2	0	3	1	5	2	0	4	0	3	2	3	2	1	2

0 1 2 3 4 5
Number of Brothers and Sisters

19. In the space at the right, make a dot plot to to display the data. (Lesson 8-2)

20. How many students does the dot plot represent? Explain how you can check your answer. (Lessons 8-1, 8-2)

21. Calculate the mean of the data. (Lessons 8-3, 8-4, 8-5, 8-7)

22. Calculate the median of the data. (Lesson 8-6)

23. Calculate the range of the data. (Lesson 8-7)

24. Suppose fifteen students in a different sixth grade class are asked "How many brothers and sisters do you have?" Will a dot plot showing their answers be the same as the dot plot at the top of this page? Or is it likely to be different? Explain. (Lessons 8-1, 8-7)

25. **Extended Response** Which measure—mean, median, or range—is an appropriate measure for summarizing the data? Explain your answer. (Lessons 8-6, 8-7)

Share with your family the Family Letter on Activity Workbook page 189.

Dear Family,

Your child will be learning about numbers throughout the school year. The math unit your child is beginning to study now introduces rational numbers. A rational number can be positive, negative, or zero. Examples of rational numbers include integers, fractions, and decimals.

Some of the lessons and activities in the unit will involve number lines. An example of a number line is shown below.

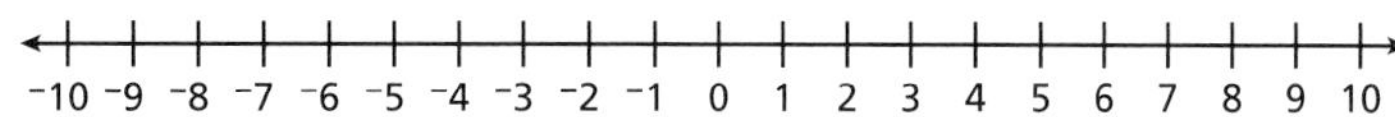

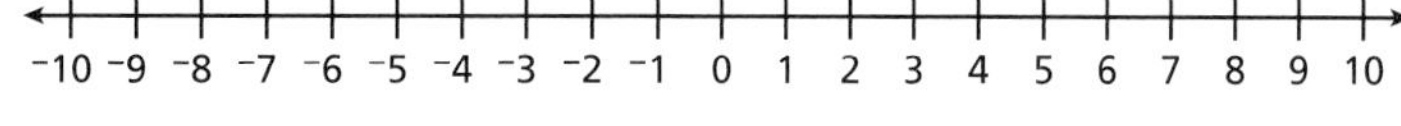

Your child will learn to plot and locate points on a number line, and use a number line to compare and order numbers.

This unit will also introduce your child to a four-quadrant coordinate plane, shown below. The plane is formed by the intersection of two number lines.

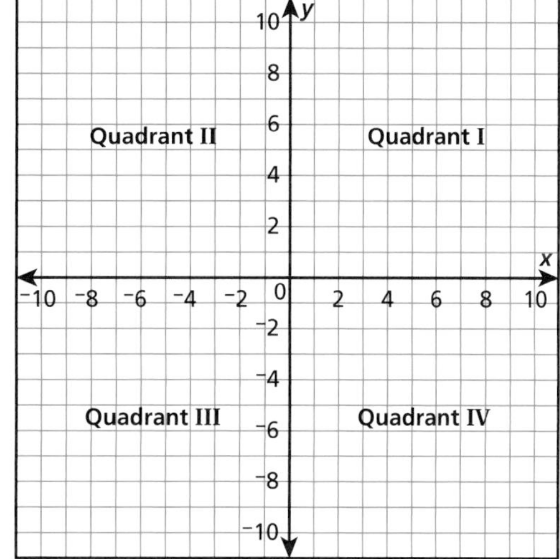

In previous units, your child has plotted and located points for ordered pairs in Quadrant I of the coordinate plane. In this unit, your child will be working in all four quadrants of the plane.

If you have any questions or comments, please call or write to me.

Sincerely,
Your child's teacher

Examples of Rational Numbers

Integers

$^{-}8$ 0 $^{+}3$

Fractions

$-\frac{1}{2}$ $\frac{3}{4}$

Decimals

$^{-}0.5$ 6.29

Examples of Ordered Pairs in the Coordinate Plane

(2, 1) (x, y) $(^{-}7, ^{-}4)$

This unit includes the Common Core Standards for Mathematical Content for The Number System, 6.NS.5, 6.NS.6, 6.NS.6a, 6.NS.6b, 6.NS.6c, 6.NS.7, 6.NS.7a, 6.NS.7b, 6.NS.7c, 6.NS.7d, 6.NS.8; Geometry, 6.G.3 and all Mathematical Practices.

Muestra a tu familia la Carta a la familia de la página 190 del Cuaderno de actividades y trabajo.

Estimada familia,

Su hijo aprenderá diferentes conceptos relacionados con los números durante el año escolar. La unidad de matemáticas que estamos comenzando a estudiar presenta los números racionales. Un número racional puede ser positivo, negativo o puede ser cero. Ejemplos de números racionales incluyen enteros, fracciones, y decimales.

Algunas de las lecciones y actividades tendrán rectas numéricas. Abajo se muestra un ejemplo de una recta numérica.

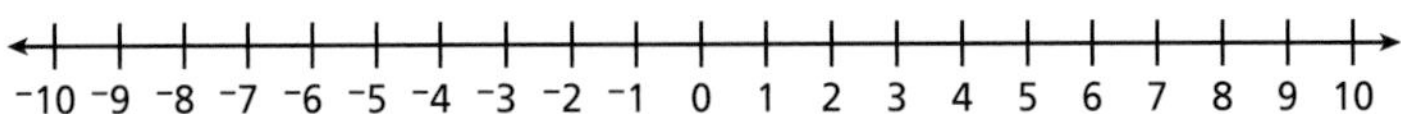

Su hijo aprenderá a localizar y marcar puntos en rectas numéricas. También aprenderá a usarlas para comparar y ordenar números.

En esta unidad también se introduce un plano de coordenadas dividido en cuatro cuadrantes, como el que se muestra abajo. El plano se forma por la intersección de dos rectas numéricas.

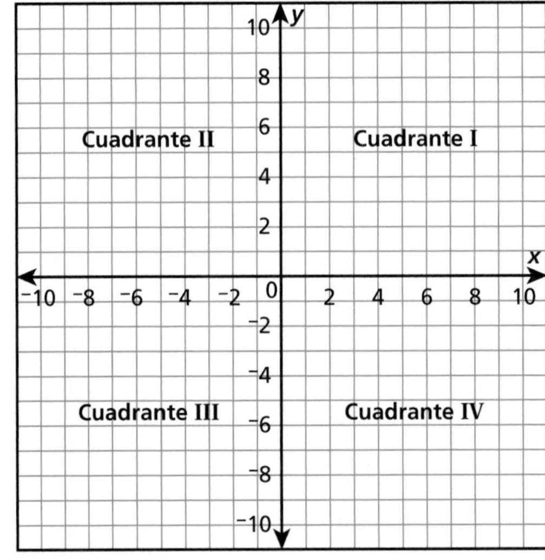

En unidades anteriores, su hijo ha localizado y marcado puntos para pares ordenados en el Cuadrante I del plano de coordenadas. En esta unidad trabajará en los cuatro cuadrantes del plano de coordenadas.

Si tiene preguntas o comentarios, por favor comuníquese conmigo.

Atentamente,
El maestro de su hijo

Ejemplos de números racionales

Números enteros

$^{-}8$ 0 $^{+}3$

Fracciones

$^{-}\frac{1}{2}$ $\frac{3}{4}$

Decimales

$^{-}0.5$ 6.29

Ejemplos de pares ordenados en el plano de coordenadas

(2, 1) (x, y) ($^{-}7$, $^{-}4$)

Esta unidad incluye los Common Core Standards for Mathematical Content for The Number System, 6.NS.5, 6.NS.6, 6.NS.6a, 6.NS.6b, 6.NS.6c, 6.NS.7, 6.NS.7a, 6.NS.7b, 6.NS.7c, 6.NS.7d, 6.NS.8; Geometry, 6.G.3 and all Mathematical Practices.

▶ Discuss Real World Situations

Discuss each situation and diagram.

1. The cliff diver below is poised to dive from the top of a cliff that is 60 feet above sea level.

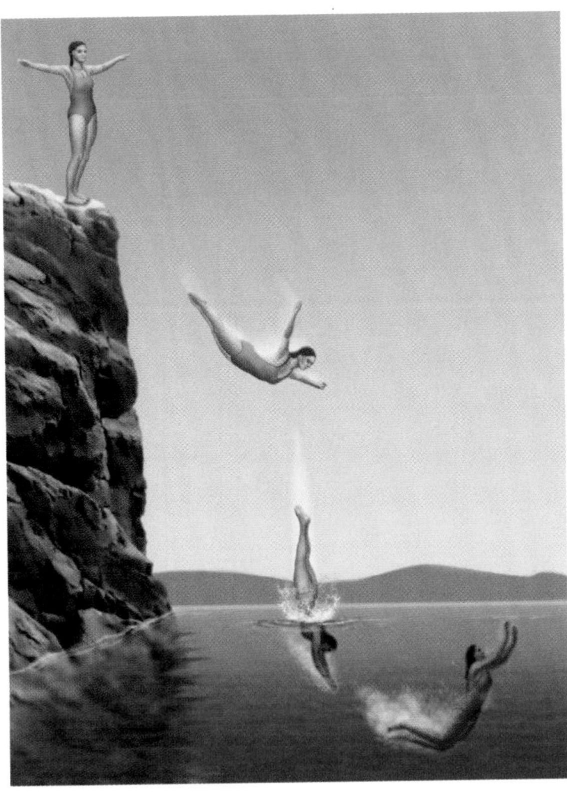

If the distance she travels underwater is about $\frac{1}{4}$ of the distance she travels above water, how would you describe her location at the deepest part of the dive?

2. Protons and electrons are parts of an atom. A proton has a positive (+) electrical charge, and an electron has a negative (–) electrical charge.

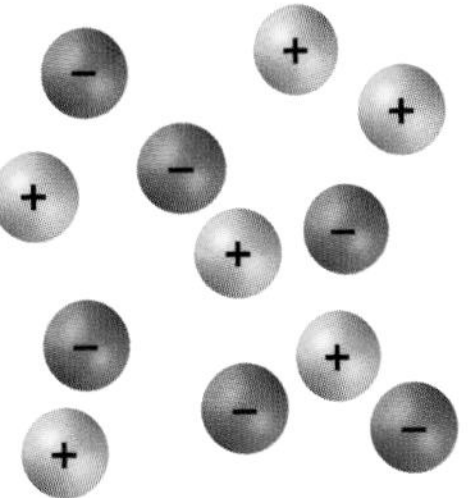

In this illustration, is there a positive electrical charge for every negative electrical charge? Explain.

3. A checking account has a balance of $80.

Check Number	Amount	Balance
		$80.00

Suppose a check is written for $100.

Check Number	Amount	Balance
		$80.00
409	$100.00	–$100.00

Using words, describe the new balance.

Vocabulary

opposites

▶ Identify and Write Opposite Temperatures

Two numbers are **opposites** if they are the same distance from zero on a number line, but in opposite directions. If two temperatures are opposites, they are the same distance from zero on a thermometer. If one temperature is above zero, the other will be below zero. The opposite of zero is zero.

Each arrow on the Fahrenheit thermometer points to a temperature. Write the temperature.

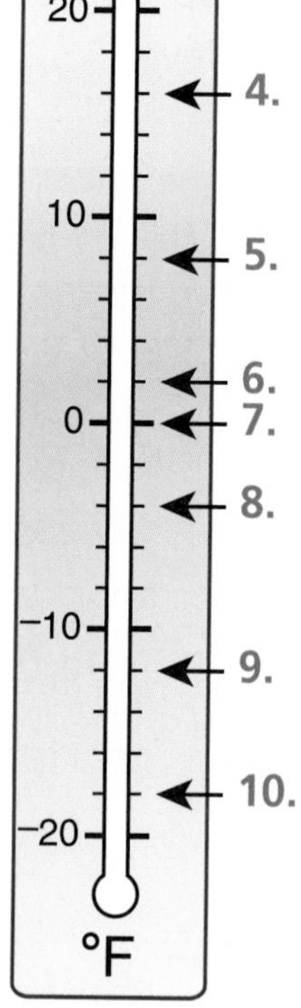

4.

5.

6.

7.

8.

9.

10.

Each arrow on the Celsius thermometer points to a temperature. Write the *opposite* temperature.

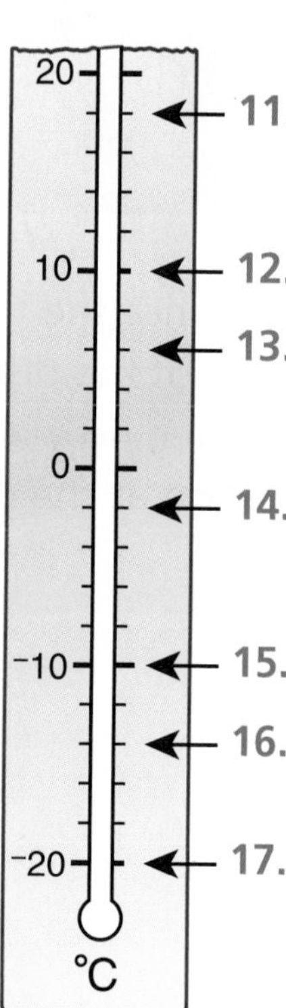

11.

12.

13.

14.

15.

16.

17.

▶ Understand Number Lines

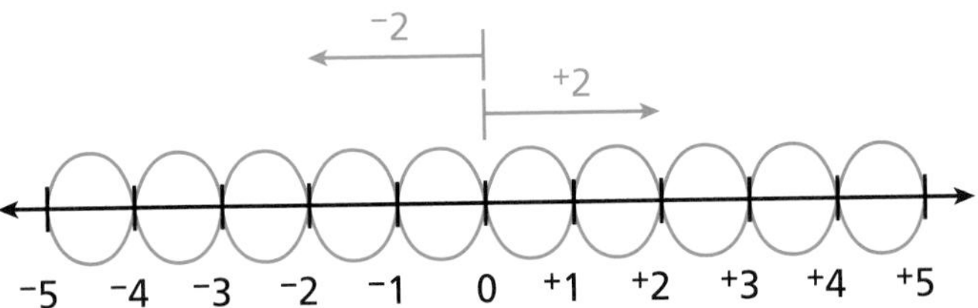

Vocabulary

origin
positive numbers
negative numbers
integers

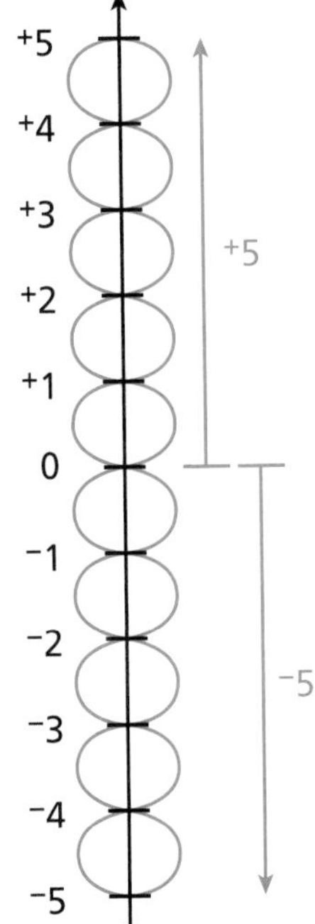

The **origin** of a number line is the point at 0. **Positive numbers** are to the right of, or above, the origin. **Negative numbers** are to the left of, or below, the origin.

The set of **integers** includes whole numbers, their opposites, and zero. Integers represent both *distance* measured in unit lengths (shown by the numeral), and *direction* (shown by + or –).

1. What do the loops on each number line show?

2. On the horizontal number line, how do the arrows for $^{+}2$ and $^{-}2$ show both *direction* and *distance*?

3. On the vertical number line, how do the arrows for $^{+}5$ and $^{-}5$ show both *direction* and *distance*?

4. Are $^{+}2$ and $^{-}2$, and $^{+}5$ and $^{-}5$ opposite integers? Explain.

5. What do the arrows at the end of each number line mean?

6. Write a 3-digit number and its opposite.

9–2
Class Activity

Use Activity Workbook page 191.

▶ Distance and Points on a Number Line

One way to represent distance on a number line is to circle unit lengths. Another way is to mark points. The number lines on this page use tick marks and points to show the origin and unit lengths.

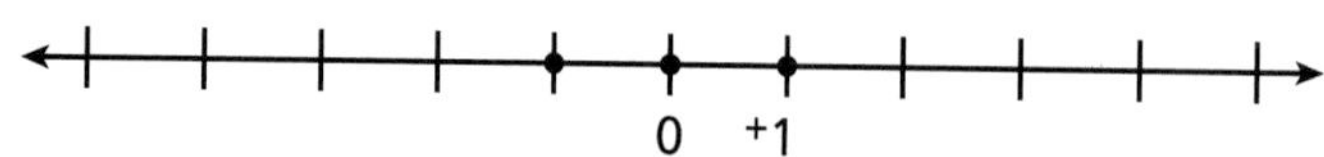
0
+1

+1
0

7. One point on each number line is not labeled. Label each point with an integer, and explain why you chose that integer.

8. On each number line, draw a point at each tick mark. Label each point.

▶ What's the Error?

Dear Math Students,

Today I drew two number lines to show the integers from $^{+}2$ to $^{-}2$.

Number Line *A*

+2 +1 0 −1 −2

Number Line *B*

+2
+1
0
−1
−2

My friends say that I did not draw either number line correctly.

Can you tell me what I did wrong?

Your friend,

Puzzled Penguin

9. For each number line, write a response to Puzzled Penguin.

Number Line *A*:

Number Line *B*:

▶ Compare and Order Integers

Use the number line below for Exercises 1–22.

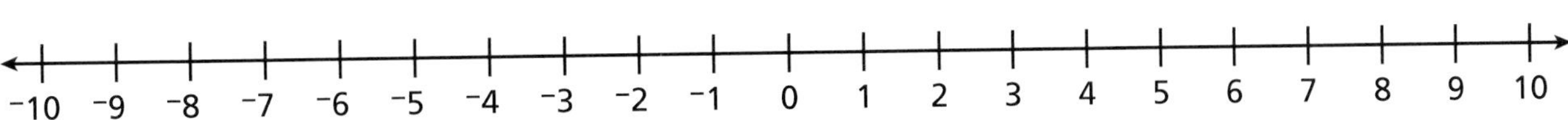

This number line has two directions—left and right.

1. As you move to the right on the number line, do the numbers increase or decrease?

2. As you move to the left on the number line, do the numbers increase or decrease?

3. If two numbers are placed on a number line, is the number farther to the right the *greater* number, or the *lesser* number?

4. If two numbers are placed on a number line, is the number farther to the left the *greater* number, or the *lesser* number?

Compare. Write <, >, or =.

5. $^{-}1$ ◯ $^{-}4$
6. 2 ◯ $^{-}2$
7. 4 ◯ 5
8. $^{-}5$ ◯ 5
9. 0 ◯ $^{-}7$
10. $^{-}3$ ◯ $^{-}2$
11. $^{-}2$ ◯ $^{-}6$
12. $^{-}4$ ◯ 0
13. $^{-}3$ ◯ 1
14. $^{-}8$ ◯ $^{-}8$
15. 9 ◯ 7
16. $^{-}1$ ◯ $^{-}7$

Write the numbers in order from *least* to *greatest*.

17. $^{-}2$, 0, $^{-}1$
18. 6, $^{-}3$, 7
19. $^{-}9$, $^{-}1$, $^{-}6$

Write the numbers in order from *greatest* to *least*.

20. $^{-}3$, 0, 5, $^{-}1$
21. $^{-}10$, $^{-}7$, $^{-}5$, 6
22. $^{-}1$, $^{-}9$, 0, $^{-}2$

Vocabulary
absolute value

▶ Absolute Value

The symbol | | is used to indicate absolute value. **Absolute value** is a measure of the distance a number is from zero on a number line.

This number line shows that 4 is a distance of 4 unit lengths from zero.

Because 4 is 4 unit lengths from zero, the absolute value of 4 is 4, and we record that fact by writing $|4| = 4$.

Since absolute value is a measure of distance, and the distance between two points can never be a negative number, absolute value is never a negative number.

This number line shows that $^-3$ is 3 unit lengths from zero.

Because $^-3$ is 3 unit lengths from zero, the absolute value of $^-3$ is 3, and we record that fact by writing $|^-3| = 3$.

Absolute value is a measure of the distance a number is from zero on a number line. So, the absolute value of zero is zero.

Write the absolute value of each number.

23. $|5| =$ ▒
24. $|^-1| =$ ▒
25. $|2| =$ ▒
26. $|^-4| =$ ▒
27. $|^-2| =$ ▒
28. $|3| =$ ▒
29. $|0| =$ ▒
30. $|^-5| =$ ▒

Rewrite each sentence using only integers and symbols.

31. The absolute value of positive ten equals ten.

32. The absolute value of negative eighteen equals eighteen.

33. The absolute value of twenty-five equals twenty-five.

34. The absolute value of negative thirty is thirty.

▶ Absolute Value and Opposites

Use the number line below for Exercises 35–37.

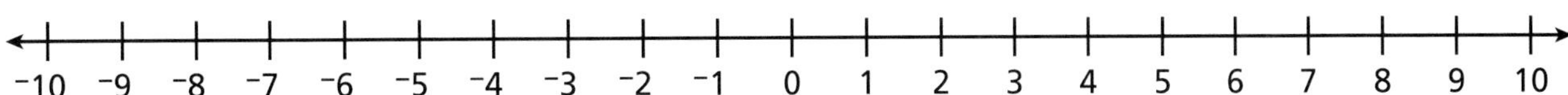

35. Plot a point at 8 and plot a point at $^{-}8$.
    What is the absolute value of each number? $|8| = \square$ $|^{-}8| = \square$

36. Are 8 and $^{-}8$ opposite integers? Explain why or why not.

37. Write a generalization about the absolute values of opposite integers.

▶ Use Absolute Value to Compare

Use absolute value to compare the numbers. Then write $<$, $>$, or $=$.

38. $^{-}5 \bigcirc {}^{-}4$
39. $^{-}1 \bigcirc {}^{-}3$
40. $^{-}2 \bigcirc {}^{-}5$
41. $^{-}6 \bigcirc {}^{-}6$

▶ What's the Error?

Dear Math Students,

I was asked to use absolute value to compare two positive integers and two negative integers. The positive integers were 10 and 5, and the negative integers were $^{-}10$ and $^{-}5$.

I know that 10 is the absolute value of both 10 and $^{-}10$, and I know that 5 is the absolute value of both 5 and $^{-}5$.

I decided that the greater absolute value is the greater number. So I wrote $10 > 5$ and $^{-}10 > {}^{-}5$.

Can you explain to me what I did wrong?

Your friend,

Puzzled Penguin

42. Write a response to Puzzled Penguin.

▶ Compare and Order Integers in Real World Situations

Solve. Use the situation below for Exercises 43 and 44.

A thermometer shows a temperature of $^{-}10$°F. A nearby thermometer shows a temperature of $^{-}12$°F.

43. Explain how a number line can be used to find the *warmer* temperature. Then name the warmer temperature.

44. Explain how absolute value can be used to find the *cooler* temperature. Then name the cooler temperature.

Solve. Use the situation below and the table for Exercises 45–47.

In a game played by five friends, points can be added to a score, or points can be taken away. The table shows the points earned by each player halfway through the game. The game ends when a player earns 50 points.

Player	Score
A	$^{-}15$
B	30
C	0
D	15
E	$^{-}35$

45. The scores of which two players are opposite integers?

46. Which player needs to earn the least number of points to win the game? Explain how a number line can be used to find the answer.

47. Write the scores in order from least to greatest.

Vocabulary

coordinate plane

▶ Graph in the Coordinate Plane

A **coordinate plane** is formed by two perpendicular number lines that intersect at the origin, 0.

Use the coordinate plane at the right for Exercises 1–8.

Write the location of each point.

1. Point *A*
2. Point *B*
3. Point *C*
4. Point *D*

Plot and label each point.

5. Point *E* at (0, 4)
6. Point *F* at ($^-$9, $^-$2)
7. Point *G* at (7, 9)
8. Point *H* at (9, $^-$6)

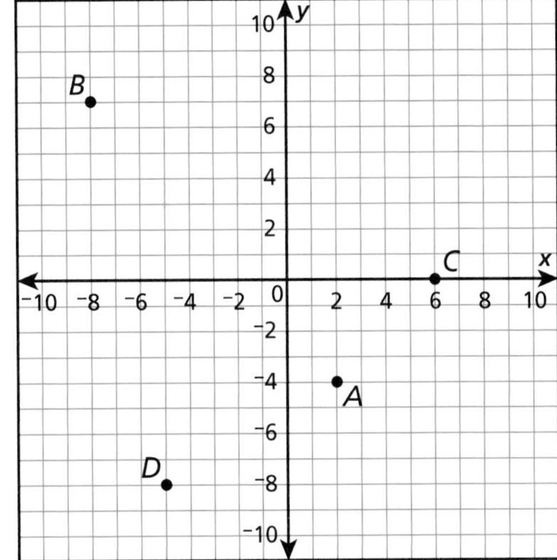

▶ What's the Error?

Dear Math Students,

I was asked to graph a point at ($^-$3, $^-$6) in the coordinate plane. My work is shown at the right.

I was told that I did not plot the point in the correct location. Can you explain to me what I did wrong, and explain how to plot the point correctly?

Your friend,

Puzzled Penguin

9. Write a response to Puzzled Penguin.

Use Activity Workbook page 197.

Vocabulary

quadrant

▶ Quadrants of the Coordinate Plane

The two perpendicular number lines (the *x*- and *y*-axes) divide the coordinate plane into four regions called **quadrants**. Beginning in the upper right quadrant and moving in a counterclockwise direction, the quadrants are numbered using the Roman numerals I, II, III, and IV.

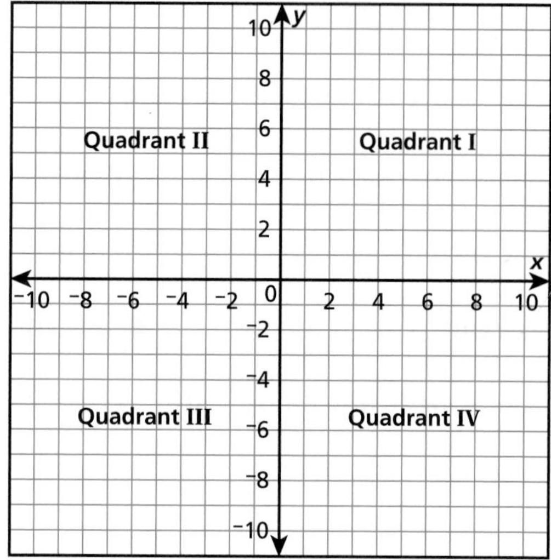

In which quadrant is each point located?

10. (5, 4)

11. $(^-5, ^-4)$

12. $(5, ^-4)$

13. $(^-5, 4)$

A coordinate is a number that determines the horizontal or vertical position of a point in the coordinate plane. An ordered pair consists of two coordinates.

14. The signs of the coordinates of an ordered pair are (–, +). In which quadrant is the point located? Explain your answer.

15. The signs of the coordinates of an ordered pair are (+, –). In which quadrant is the point located?

16. The signs of the coordinates of an ordered pair are (–, –). In which quadrant is the point located?

17. The signs of the coordinates of an ordered pair are (+, +). In which quadrant is the point located?

18. On the coordinate plane above, plot Point *T* at (0, 0).

▶ The Coordinate Plane and a Cross-Section

A research team is studying cave crickets. A drawing of a cross-section of one passage of the cave is shown on the coordinate plane at the right. Points *A*, *B*, *C*, *D*, and *E* represent locations in the passage where research is being performed.

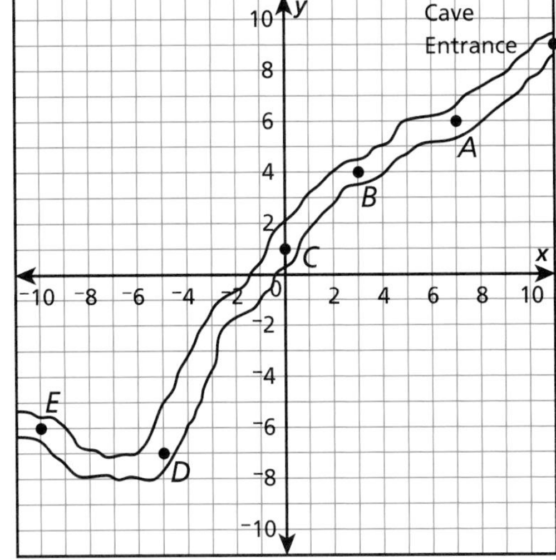

19. Write an ordered pair to represent each research location, and the location of the cave entrance.

20. The researchers are thinking about performing research in a new location. Does a location that has no sign for its *x*-coordinate and a negative *y*-coordinate represent a possible research location? Why or why not?

A typical cave cricket has up to a 2-inch-long body and 4-inch-long hind legs.

Suppose the side of each unit square in the coordinate plane represents 10 feet. The elevation of the cave entrance is 640 feet above sea level. The five research locations in the cave each represent an elevation that is less than 640 feet above sea level.

21. What is the location of Point *A*, and how far below the cave entrance is its elevation?

22. Which research location has an elevation of 560 feet above sea level? What ordered pair describes its location?

23. Which research location shown is at the lowest elevation? What ordered pair describes its location, and what is its elevation?

▶ The Coordinate Plane and a Map

The coordinate plane below represents a map. Use the map to solve these problems.

24. A family's home is located at (4, $^-5$). Draw a point at that location, and write "Home" next to the point.

25. The family begins their vacation by leaving home and driving to a restaurant at ($^-7$, $^-5$). Draw a point at that location, and write "Restaurant" next to the point. In what direction did the family drive?

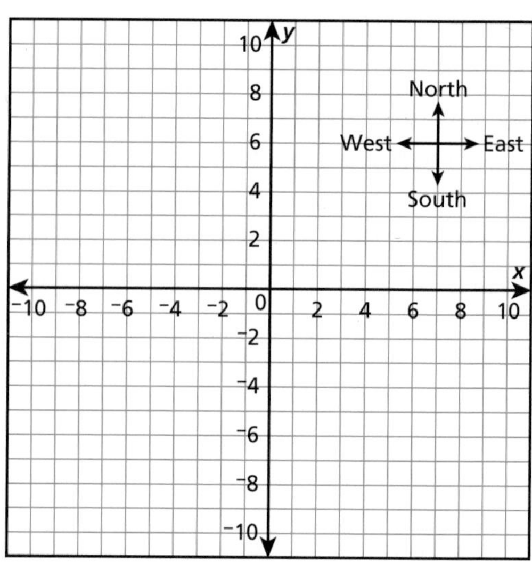

26. From the restaurant, the family drove to a campground at ($^-7$, 1). Draw a point at that location, and write "Campground" next to the point. In what direction did the family drive?

27. From the campground, the family drove to a rest area at ($^-3$, 1). Draw a point at that location, and write "Rest Area" next to the point. In what direction did the family drive?

28. From the rest area, the family drove to ($^-3$, 9), to (2, 9), and then to their destination at (2, 10). Plot points at each location, and write "Destination" next to the point at (2, 10). During this portion of the trip, in which directions did the family *not* drive?

29. Starting from home, draw line segments to show the path the family traveled. Suppose that each side of every unit square represents 25 miles. What is a reasonable estimate of the number of miles the family traveled from home to their destination?

Use Activity Workbook page 199.

Vocabulary

rational number

▶ Fractions on a Number Line

Use the number line below for Exercises 1–8.

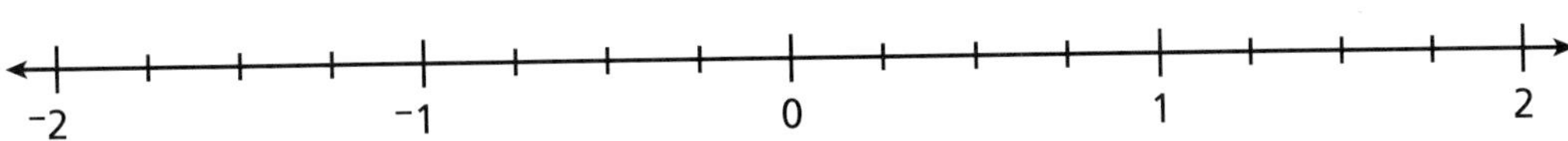

1. How many equal lengths are between 0 and 1?
2. What fractional unit does the number line show?
3. Label each tick mark of the number line with a fraction or mixed number in simplest form.
4. Draw a point at $^{-}\frac{1}{4}$. Label it *A*.
5. Draw a point at $\frac{3}{4}$. Label it *B*.
6. Draw a point at $^{-}1\frac{1}{2}$. Label it *C*.
7. Draw a point at $\frac{6}{4}$. Label it *D*.

A **rational number** is any number that can be expressed as a fraction $\frac{a}{b}$, where a and b are integers and $b \neq 0$.

8. Do Points *C* and *D* represent *opposite* rational numbers? Explain. Draw arrows above the number line to justify your answer.

Write the opposite rational number.

9. $^{-}\frac{2}{3}$
10. $\frac{7}{10}$
11. $^{-}\frac{11}{12}$
12. $\frac{1}{6}$

Simplify.

13. $^{-}(^{-}\frac{3}{5})$
14. $^{-}(1\frac{3}{4})$
15. $^{-}(^{-}1\frac{2}{5})$
16. $^{-}(\frac{4}{7})$

Draw and label a number line from $^{-}2$ to 2 by thirds. Then use it to plot and label each point.

17. Point *E* at $^{-}1\frac{2}{3}$
18. Point *F* at $1\frac{1}{3}$
19. Point *G* at $\frac{2}{3}$
20. Point *H* at $^{-}\frac{1}{3}$

▶ Decimals on a Number Line

Use the number line below for Exercises 21–26.

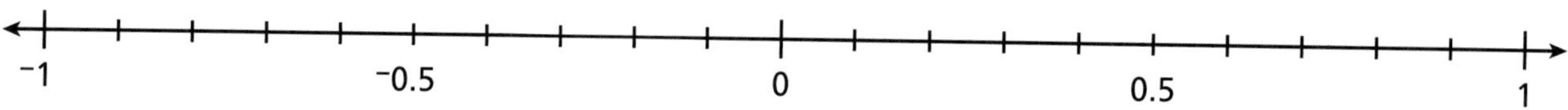

21. How many equal lengths are between 0 and 1?

22. What decimal place does the number line show?

23. Label each tick mark on the number line with a decimal.

24. Draw a point at ⁻0.3. Label it *B*.

25. Draw a point at 0.7. Label it *C*.

26. Draw a point at 0.2 and label it *M*. Draw a point at its opposite and label it *N*. Draw arrows above the number line to show that the numbers are opposites.

▶ What's the Error?

Dear Students:

I was asked to write a sentence about opposite numbers. Here's what I wrote:

A number and its opposite are the same number.

I wrote the sentence because I know that the opposite of zero is zero. Since the opposite of zero is zero, I thought it made sense for me to say that a number and its opposite are the same number. Can you help correct my thinking?

Your friend,

Puzzled Penguin

27. Write a response to Puzzled Penguin.

▶ Compare and Order Rational Numbers

A horizontal number line has two directions—left and right. A vertical number line has two directions—above and below.

1. Suppose two rational numbers are plotted on a *horizontal* number line. Is the number farther to the left the greater number, or the lesser number?

2. Suppose two rational numbers are plotted on a *vertical* number line. Is the number that is above the other number the greater number, or the lesser number?

Use the number line below for Exercises 3–20.

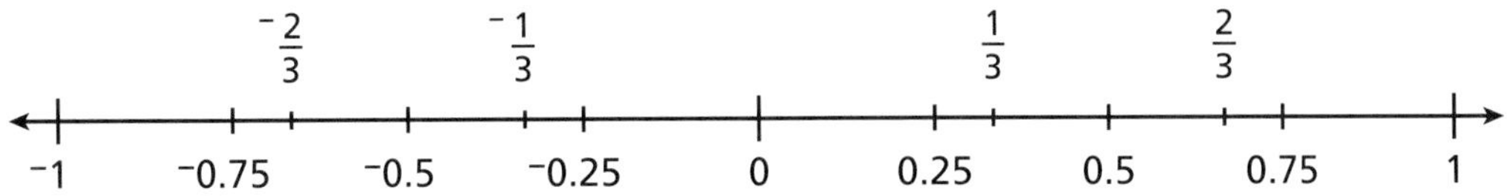

Compare. Write <, >, or =.

3. $^-0.5$ ◯ $^-1$
4. $\frac{2}{3}$ ◯ 0.75
5. 0 ◯ $\frac{-1}{3}$
6. $^-0.5$ ◯ $^-0.25$
7. $\frac{1}{3}$ ◯ $\frac{-1}{3}$
8. $|^-0.5|$ ◯ $|^-0.75|$
9. $^-1$ ◯ 1
10. $|\frac{-2}{3}|$ ◯ $|^-0.5|$
11. $\frac{-1}{3}$ ◯ $^-(^-0.5)$
12. $\frac{2}{3}$ ◯ $^-|\frac{-2}{3}|$
13. $\frac{1}{3}$ ◯ $^-(^-0.75)$
14. $\frac{1}{4}$ ◯ $^-(^-0.25)$

Write the numbers in order from *greatest* to *least*.

15. $^-0.25$, $^-1$, $^-0.75$
16. $\frac{1}{3}$, $\frac{-2}{3}$, $\frac{-1}{3}$
17. 0, $\frac{2}{3}$, $^-0.5$

Write the numbers in order from *least* to *greatest*.

18. $\frac{1}{3}$, 0, $^-0.5$, $\frac{-1}{3}$
19. $\frac{-2}{3}$, 0, $^-1$, $^-0.5$
20. $^-0.75$, $\frac{2}{3}$, 0.5, $^-0.25$

▶ Compare and Order Rational Numbers in the Real World

Solve. Use the situation below for Exercises 21–23.

At the beginning of a science experiment, the temperature of a liquid was $^-19.4$°F. Five minutes later, the temperature was $^-8.7$°F.

21. Suppose you plot $^-19.4$ on a horizontal number line. Explain how knowing the location of $^-8.7$ can help you decide if the temperature increased or decreased.

22. Explain how a number line can be used to find the cooler temperature. Then name the cooler temperature.

23. Explain how absolute value can be used to find the *warmer* temperature. Then name the warmer temperature.

Solve. Use the situation below and the table for Exercise 24.

Five classmates are playing a game that involves rational numbers.

Whenever possible, the scores are recorded in terminating decimals. If the decimals are repeating, the scores are recorded in fractions.

The table at the right shows the points earned by each player halfway through the game.

Player	Score
A	0.5
B	$^-\frac{1}{3}$
C	1.25
D	$^-\frac{5}{6}$
E	$^-0.6$

24. Write the scores in order from greatest to least.

Vocabulary

reflected point

▶ Distance in the Coordinate Plane

On the coordinate grid, an airport is located at Point *A*. Points *B* and *C* are airplanes. Use the grid for Exercises 1–4.

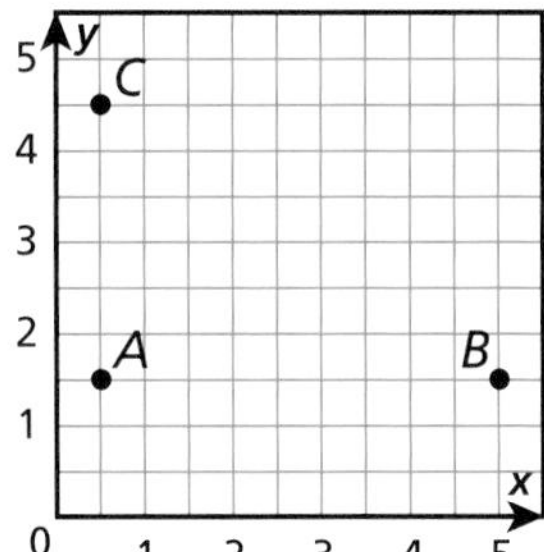

1. Write the location of each point.

   Point *A* Point *B* Point *C*

2. Explain how subtraction can be used to find the number of unit lengths the plane at Point *B* is from the airport. Then write the distance.

3. Explain how subtraction can be used to find the number of unit lengths the plane at Point *C* is from the airport. Then write the distance.

4. Plane *B* is 225 miles east of the airport. How many miles north of the airport is plane *C*?

▶ Reflections in the Coordinate Plane

A given point and its **reflected point** are mirror images across the *x*-axis, the *y*-axis, or both axes of the coordinate plane.

5. Suppose a point at $(^-1\frac{3}{4}, ^-2\frac{1}{4})$ is reflected across the *x*-axis. Explain how to find the location of the reflected point, and then write its location.

6. Suppose a point at $(1\frac{1}{2}, ^-1\frac{1}{4})$ is reflected across the *y*-axis. Explain how to find the location of the reflected point, and then write its location.

▶ Graph Real World Situations

Victor's checking account has a balance of $10 and is assessed a $2 service charge at the end of each month.

7. Suppose Victor never uses the account. Complete the table below to show the balance in the account each month for 6 months. Then use the data to plot points on the coordinate plane to show the decreasing balance over time.

Month	Balance (in dollars)
0	10
1	8
2	6
3	
4	
5	
6	

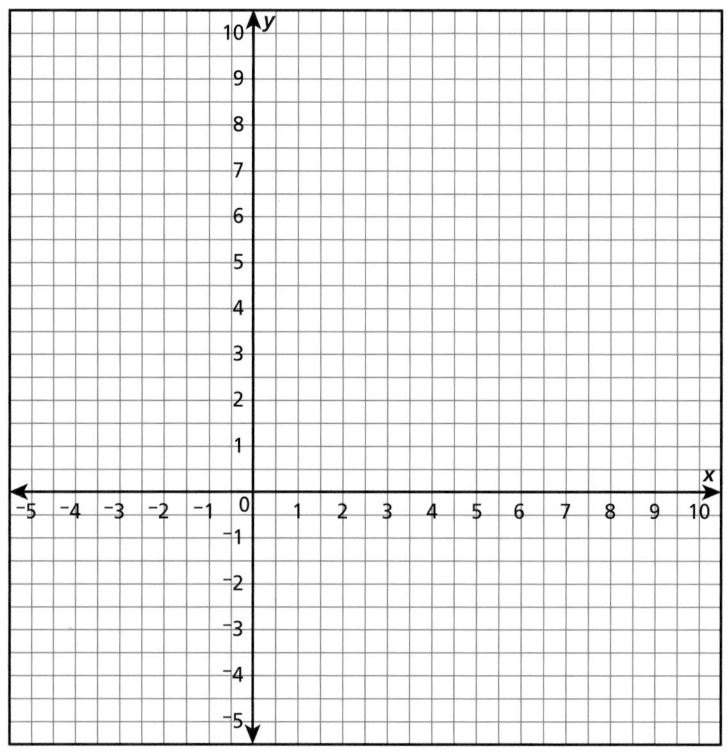

8. Add points to the graph showing what Victor's balance would be each month if the service charge was $2.50, instead of $2.00.

9. How do the graphs for the $2.00 service charge and the $2.50 service charge compare?

▶ Math and Global Positioning

On Earth, latitude is measured north and south of the Equator. Longitude is measured east and west of the Prime Meridian. Latitude and longitude is a coordinate system that enables every location on Earth to be identified by an ordered pair of numbers. A Global Positioning System (GPS) uses this coordinate system.

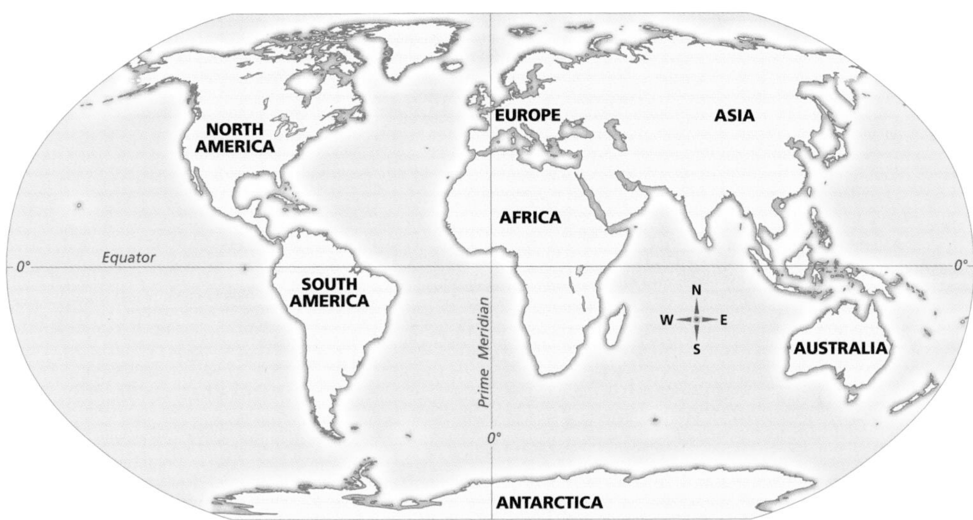

The first coordinate in an ordered pair is a measure of latitude. If a location is north of the Equator, the sign of the coordinate is +. If a location is south of the Equator, the sign of the coordinate is −.

The second coordinate in an ordered pair is a measure of longitude. If a location is east of the Prime Meridian, the sign of the coordinate is +. If a location is west of the Prime Meridian, the sign of the coordinate is −.

For example, the signs of the coordinates that identify the location of Chicago, Illinois, are (+, −). The first coordinate is + because Chicago is north of the Equator. The second coordinate is − because Chicago is west of the Prime Meridian.

Write the signs of the coordinates that identify the location of each country.

1. Canada
2. Australia
3. Argentina
4. India

▶ Locations and Ordered Pairs

In addition to a + or − sign, each coordinate of an ordered pair also identifies a number of degrees. The maximum number of degrees for the first coordinate, or measure of latitude, is 90°. The maximum number of degrees for the second coordinate, or measure of longitude, is 180°.

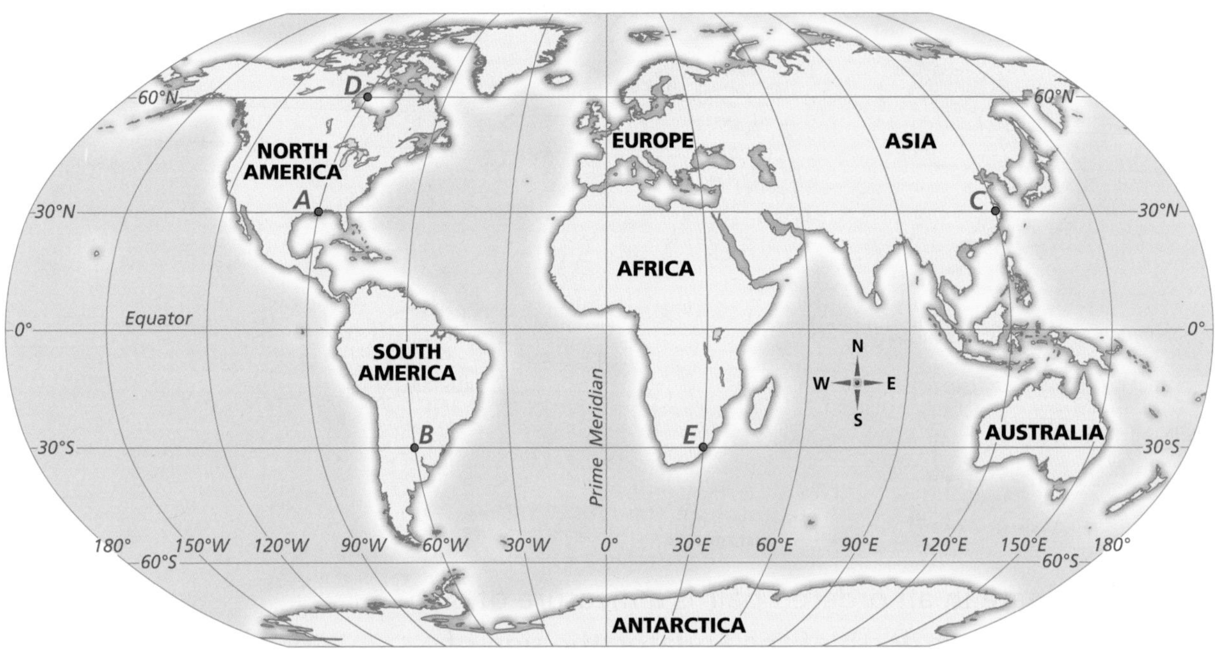

On the map above, the city of New Orleans, Louisiana is located near Point *A*. Since Point *A* is 30° north of the Equator, and 90° west of the Prime Meridian, the ordered pair ($^{+}30°$, $^{-}90°$) identifies the location of New Orleans.

Write an ordered pair to identify each location. Be sure to include a sign and a number of degrees for each coordinate you write.

5. The city of Goya, Argentina, located near Point *B*:
6. The city of Shanghai, China, located near Point *C*:
7. A ship in Hudson Bay, Ontario, located near Point *D*:
8. The city of Durban, South Africa, located near Point *E*:

Use the Activity Workbook Unit Test on pages 205–206.

▶ Vocabulary

Vocabulary

absolute value
integers
opposite
rational numbers

Choose the best term from the box.

1. Whole numbers, their opposites, and zero make up the set of ______?______. (Lesson 9-2)

2. The measure of the distance a number is from zero on a number line is called its ______?______. (Lesson 9-3)

3. Numbers that can be expressed as a fraction $\frac{a}{b}$ where a and b are integers and $b \neq 0$ are ______?______. (Lesson 9-5)

▶ Concepts and Skills

4. Simplify $^-(^-10)$. (Lesson 9-2)

5. Suppose two points in the coordinate plane have the same *x*-coordinate but different positive *y*-coordinates. Explain how subtraction can be used to find the distance between the points. (Lesson 9-7)

6. How will the *x*- and *y*-coordinates of a point in Quadrant I of the coordinate plane change if the point is reflected across the *x*-axis? (Lesson 9-7)

7. Write the value of Points *A*, *B*, and *C*. (Lesson 9-2)

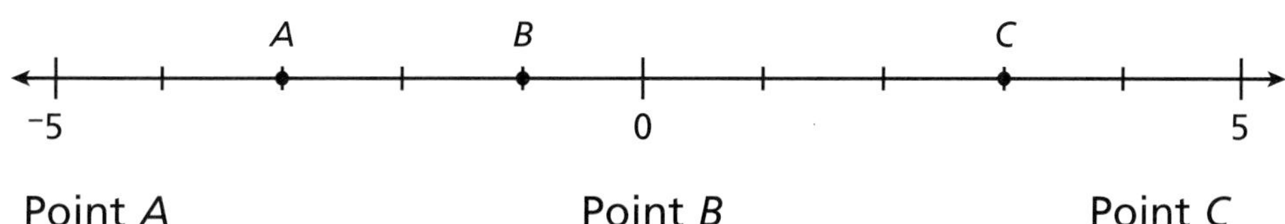

Point *A* Point *B* Point *C*

8. Label each tick mark of the number line with a decimal above and a fraction, in simplest form, below. (Lesson 9-5)

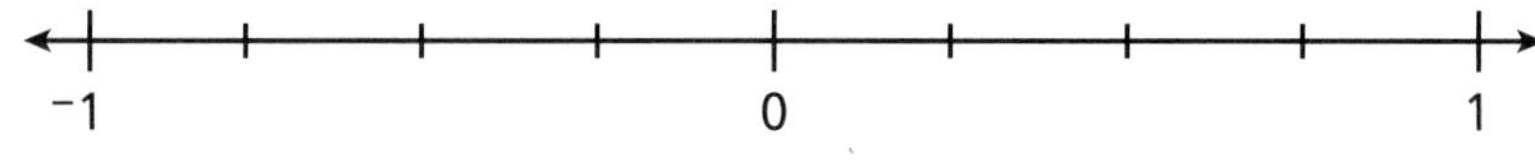

Compare. Write <, >, or =. (Lessons 9-3, 9-6)

9. $^-3.1$ ◯ $^-6.8$ 10. $|2|$ ◯ $|^-2|$ 11. $^-10$ ◯ $1\frac{1}{4}$ 12. $^-(^-5)$ ◯ $^-|5|$

Use the coordinate plane below for Exercises 13–18. (Lessons 9-4, 9-7)

Write the location of each point.

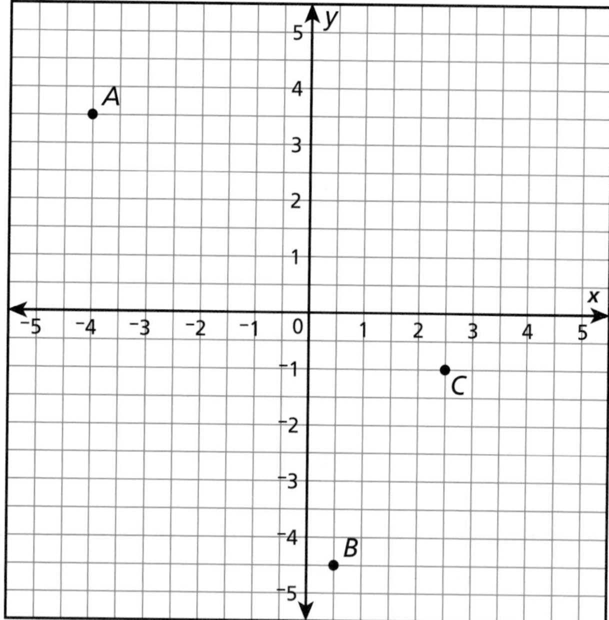

13. Point *A*

14. Point *B*

15. Point *C*

16. Reflect Point *A* across the *x*-axis. Label it Point *X*. Name its location.

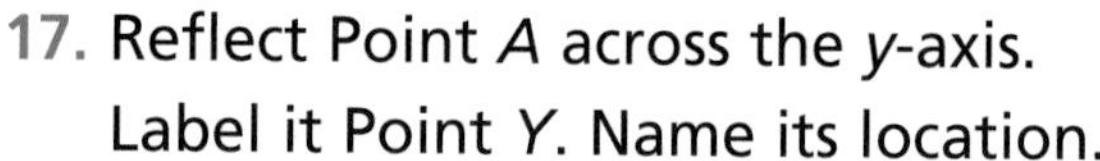

17. Reflect Point *A* across the *y*-axis. Label it Point *Y*. Name its location.

18. Use absolute value to find the distance from Point *A* to Point *X*.

▶ Problem Solving

19. A thermometer shows a temperature of $^-8.5$°F. A nearby thermometer shows a temperature of $^-7.5$°F. Explain how absolute value can be used to find the *warmer* temperature. (Lesson 9-6)

20. **Extended Response** Suppose that the ordered pairs (p, q) and (r, q) represent two points in the coordinate plane, and p, q, and r represent positive integers. If $p > r$ and $q = 2$, what expression represents the distance between the two points? Explain your answer. (Lesson 9-7)

Reference Tables

Table of Measures

Metric	Customary
Length/Area/Volume	
1 millimeter (mm) = 0.001 meter (m)	1 foot (ft) = 12 inches (in.)
1 centimeter (cm) = 0.01 meter	1 yard (yd) = 36 inches
1 decimeter (dm) = 0.1 meter	1 yard = 3 feet
1 dekameter (dkm) = 10 meters	1 mile (mi) = 5,280 feet
1 hectometer (hm) = 100 meters	1 mile = 1,760 yards
1 kilometer (km) = 1,000 meters	1 acre = 4,840 square yards
1 hectare (ha) = 1,000 square meters (m^2)	1 acre = 43,560 square feet
1 square centimeter = 1 cm^2 A metric unit for measuring area. It is the area of a square that is one centimeter on each side.	1 acre = $\frac{1}{640}$ square mile
1 cubic centimeter = 1 cm^3 A unit for measuring volume. It is the volume of a cube with each edge 1 centimeter long.	1 square inch = 1 in^2 A customary unit for measuring area. It is the area of a square that is one inch on each side.
	1 cubic inch = 1 in^3 A unit for measuring volume. It is the volume of a cube with each edge 1 inch long.
Capacity	
1 milliliter (mL) = 0.001 liter (L)	1 teaspoon (tsp) = $\frac{1}{6}$ fluid ounce (fl oz)
1 centiliter (cL) = 0.01 liter	1 tablespoon (tbsp) = $\frac{1}{2}$ fluid ounce
1 deciliter (dL) = 0.1 liter	1 cup (c) = 8 fluid ounces
1 dekaliter (dkL) = 10 liters	1 pint (pt) = 2 cups
1 hectoliter (hL) = 100 liters	1 quart (qt) = 2 pints
1 kiloliter (kL) = 1,000 liters	1 gallon (gal) = 4 quarts
Mass	**Weight**
1 milligram (mg) = 0.001 gram (g)	1 pound (lb) = 16 ounces
1 centigram (cg) = 0.01 gram	1 ton (T) = 2,000 pounds
1 decigram (dg) = 0.1 gram	
1 dekagram (dkg) = 10 grams	
1 hectogram (hg) = 100 grams	
1 kilogram (kg) = 1,000 grams	
1 metric ton = 1,000 kilograms	

Volume/Capacity/Mass for Water

1 cubic centimeter (cm^3) = 1 milliliter = 1 gram

1,000 cubic centimeters = 1 liter = 1 kilogram

Reference Tables (continued)

Table of Units of Time

Time	
1 minute (min) = 60 seconds (sec)	1 year = 365 days
1 hour (hr) = 60 minutes	1 leap year = 366 days
1 day = 24 hours	1 decade = 10 years
1 week (wk) = 7 days	1 century = 100 years
1 month, about 30 days	1 millennium - 1,000 years
1 year (yr) = 12 months (mo) or about 52 weeks	

Table of Formulas

Perimeter

Polygon	P = sum of the lengths of the sides
Rectangle	$P = 2(l + w)$ or $P = 2l + 2w$
Square	$P = 4s$

Area		Surface Area of a Polygon
Parallelogram	$A = bh$	(informal) SA = sum of the areas of the faces
Polygon	$A = \frac{1}{2}n \cdot s \cdot h$ or $A = \frac{n}{2} \cdot s \cdot h$	
Rectangle	$A = lw$ or $A = bh$	
Square	$A = s^2$	
Trapezoid	$A = \frac{1}{2}h\,(b_1 + b_2)$	
Triangle	$A = \frac{1}{2}bh$	

Volume of a Rectangular Prism

$V = lwh$ or $V = Bh$

(where B is the area of the base of the prism)

Distance Formula

$d = rt$

Properties of Operations

Associative Property of Addition

$(a + b) + c = a + (b + c)$ $(2 + 5) + 3 = 2 + (5 + 3)$

Commutative Property of Addition

$a + b = b + a$ $4 + 6 = 6 + 4$

Additive Identity Property of 0

$a + 0 = 0 + a = a$ $3 + 0 = 0 + 3 = 3$

Additive Inverse

For every a there exists ^{-}a so that $a + (^{-}a) = (^{-}a) + a = 0$.

For $a = 5$, $5 + (^{-}5) = (^{-}5) + 5 = 0$

Associative Property of Multiplication

$(a \cdot b) \cdot c = a \cdot (b \cdot c)$ $(3 \cdot 5) \cdot 7 = 3 \cdot (5 \cdot 7)$

Commutative Property of Multiplication

$a \cdot b = b \cdot a$ $6 \cdot 3 = 3 \cdot 6$

Multiplicative Identity Property of 1

$a \cdot 1 = 1 \cdot a = a$ $8 \cdot 1 = 1 \cdot 8 = 8$

Multiplicative Inverse

For every $a \neq 0$ there exists $\frac{1}{a}$ so that $a \cdot \frac{1}{a} = \frac{1}{a} \cdot a = 1$.

For $a = 5$, $5 \cdot \frac{1}{5} = \frac{1}{5} \cdot 5 = 1$.

Distributive Property of Multiplication over Addition

$a \cdot (b + c) = (a \cdot b) + (a \cdot c)$ $2 \cdot (4 + 3) = (2 \cdot 4) + (2 \cdot 3)$

Properties of Equality

Reflexive Property of Equality

$a = a$

Symmetric Property of Equality

If $a = b$, then $b = a$.

Transitive Property of Equality

If $a = b$ and $b = c$, then $a = c$.

Addition Property of Equality

If $a = b$, then $a + c = b + c$.

Subtraction Property of Equality

If $a = b$, then $a - c = b - c$.

Multiplication Property of Equality

If $a = b$, then $a \cdot c = b \cdot c$.

Division Property of Equality

If $a = b$ and $c \neq 0$, then $a \div c = b \div c$.

Problem Types

	Result Unknown	Change Unknown	Start Unknown
Add to	Six children were playing tag in the yard. Three more children came to play. How many children are playing in the yard now? *Situation and Solution Equation:* $6 + 3 = c$	Six children were playing tag in the yard. Some more children came to play. Now there are 9 children in the yard. How many children came to play? *Situation Equation:* $6 + c = 9$ *Solution Equation:* $6 + c = 9$ or $9 - 6 = c$	Some children were playing tag in the yard. Three more children came to play. Now there are 9 children in the yard. How many children were in the yard at first? *Situation Equation:* $c + 3 = 9$ *Solution Equation:* $3 + c = 9$ or $9 - 3 = c$
Take from	Jake has 10 trading cards. He gave 3 to his brother. How many trading cards does he have left? *Situation and Solution Equation:* $10 - 3 = t$	Jake has 10 trading cards. He gave some to his brother. Now Jake has 7 trading cards left. How many cards did he give to his brother? *Situation Equation:* $10 - t = 7$ *Solution Equation:* $10 - 7 = t$ or $7 + t = 10$	Jake has some trading cards. He gave 3 to his brother. Now Jake has 7 trading cards left. How many cards did he start with? *Situation Equation:* $t - 3 = 7$ *Solution Equation:* $7 + 3 = t$

	Total Unknown	Addend Unknown	Other Addend Unknown
Put Together/ Take Apart	Ana put 9 dimes and 4 nickels in her pocket. How many coins did she put in her pocket? *Situation and Solution Equation:* $9 + 4 = c$	Ana put 13 coins in her pocket. Nine coins are dimes and the rest are nickels. How many are nickels? *Situation Equation:* $13 = 9 + n$ *Solution Equation:* $13 - 9 = n$ or $9 + n = 13$	Ana put 13 coins in her pocket. Some coins are dimes and 4 coins are nickels. How many coins are dimes? *Situation Equation:* $13 = d + 4$ *Solution Equation:* $13 - 4 = d$ or $4 + d = 13$

	Difference Unknown	Bigger Unknown	Smaller Unknown
Compare[1]	Aki has 8 apples. Sofia has 14 apples. How many more apples does Sofia have than Aki? *Solution Equation:* $8 + a = 14$ or $14 - 8 = a$ Aki has 8 apples. Sofia has 14 apples. How many fewer apples does Aki have than Sofia? *Solution Equation:* $8 + a = 14$ or $14 - 8 = a$	**Leading Language** Aki has 8 apples. Sofia has 6 more apples than Aki. How many apples does Sofia have? *Solution Equation:* $8 + 6 = a$ **Misleading Language** Aki has 8 apples. Aki has 6 fewer apples than Sofia. How many apples does Sofia have? *Solution Equation:* $8 + 6 = a$	**Leading Language** Sofia has 14 apples. Aki has 6 fewer apples than Sofia. How many apples does Aki have? *Solution Equation*: $14 - 6 = a$ or $6 + a = 14$ **Misleading Language** Sofia has 14 apples. Sofia has 6 more apples than Aki. How many apples does Aki have? *Solution Equation:* $14 - 6 = a$ or $6 + a = 14$

[1]The comparing sentence can always be said in two ways: One uses more, and the other uses fewer. Misleading language suggests the wrong operation. For example, it says *Aki has 6 fewer apples than Sofia,* but you have to add 6 to Aki's 8 apples to get 14 apples.

	Unknown Product	Group Size Unknown	Number of Groups Unknown
Equal Groups	Seth has 5 bags with 2 apples in each bag. How many apples does Seth have in all? *Solution Equation:* $5 \cdot 2 = n$	Seth has 5 bags with the same number of apples in each bag. He has 10 apples in all. How many apples are in each bag? *Situation Equation:* $5 \cdot n = 10$ *Solution Equation:* $10 \div 5 = n$	Seth has some bags of apples. Each bag has 2 apples in it. He has 10 apples in all. How many bags of apples does Seth have? *Situation Equation:* $n \cdot 2 = 10$ *Solution Equation:* $10 \div 2 = n$

Problem Types (continued)

	Unknown Product	Unknown Factor	Unknown Factor
Arrays[2]	Jenna has 2 rows of stamps with 5 stamps in each row. How many stamps does Jenna have in all? *Solution Equation:* $2 \cdot 5 = s$	Jenna has 2 rows of stamps with the same number of stamps in each row. She has 10 stamps in all. How many stamps are in each row? *Situation Equation:* $2 \cdot s = 10$ *Solution Equation:* $10 \div 2 = s$	Jenna has a certain number of rows of stamps. There are 5 stamps in each row. She has 10 stamps in all. How many rows of stamps does Jenna have? *Situation Equation:* $r \cdot 5 = 10$ *Solution Equation:* $10 \div 5 = r$
Area	The floor of the kitchen is 2 meters by 5 meters. What is the area of the floor? *Solution Equation:* $2 \cdot 5 = a$	The floor of the kitchen is 2 meters long. The area of the floor is 10 square meters. How wide is the floor? *Situation Equation:* $2 \cdot s = 10$ *Solution Equation:* $10 \div 2 = s$	The width of the kitchen is 5 meters long. The area of the floor is 10 square meters. What is the length of the floor? *Situation Equation:* $r \cdot 5 = 10$ *Solution Equation:* $10 \div 5 = r$
Compare	Katie picked 5 times as many flowers as Benardo. Benardo picked 2 flowers. How many flowers did Katie pick? *Solution Equation:* $5 \cdot 2 = k$	Katie picked 5 times as many flowers as Benardo. Katie picked 10 flowers. How many flowers did Bernardo pick? *Situation Equation:* $5 \cdot b = 10$ *Solution Equation:* $10 \div 5 = b$	Katie picked 10 flowers. Bernardo picked 2 flowers. How many times as many flowers did Katie pick as Bernardo? *Situation Equation:* $m \cdot 2 = 10$ *Solution Equation:* $10 \div 2 = m$

[2]Array problems can also be stated using the number of rows and columns in the array: The apples in the grocery window are in 3 rows and 6 columns. How many apples are there?

Note: All of the division situations could also have the multiplication equation as the solution equation because you can solve division by finding the unknown factor.

Vocabulary Activities

MathWord Power

▶ Word Review PAIRS

Work with a partner. Choose a word from a current unit or a review word from a previous unit. Use the word to complete one of the activities listed on the right. Then ask your partner if they have any edits to your work or questions about what you described. Repeat, having your partner choose a word.

Activities

- Give the meaning in word or gestures.
- Use the word in the sentence.
- Give another word that is related to the word in some way and explain the relationship.

▶ Crossword Puzzle PAIRS or INDIVIDUALS

Create a crossword puzzle similar to the example below. Use vocabulary words from the unit. You can add other related words, too. Challenge your partner to solve the puzzle.

<table>
<tr><td></td><td></td><td></td><td></td><td>s</td><td>u</td><td>m</td><td></td></tr>
<tr><td></td><td>1 a</td><td></td><td></td><td>u</td><td></td><td></td><td></td></tr>
<tr><td></td><td>d</td><td></td><td></td><td>b</td><td></td><td></td><td></td></tr>
<tr><td>1 a</td><td>d</td><td>d</td><td>i</td><td>t</td><td>i</td><td>o</td><td>3 n</td></tr>
<tr><td></td><td>e</td><td></td><td></td><td>r</td><td></td><td></td><td>u</td></tr>
<tr><td></td><td>n</td><td></td><td></td><td>a</td><td></td><td></td><td>m</td></tr>
<tr><td>2 a</td><td>d</td><td>d</td><td></td><td>c</td><td></td><td></td><td>b</td></tr>
<tr><td></td><td></td><td></td><td></td><td>t</td><td></td><td></td><td>e</td></tr>
<tr><td></td><td></td><td></td><td></td><td>i</td><td></td><td></td><td>r</td></tr>
<tr><td>3 r</td><td>e</td><td>g</td><td>r</td><td>o</td><td>u</td><td>p</td><td></td></tr>
<tr><td></td><td></td><td></td><td></td><td>n</td><td></td><td></td><td></td></tr>
</table>

Across

1. _____ and subtraction are inverse operations.
2. To put amounts together
3. When you trade 10 ones for 1 ten, you _____.
4. The answer to an addition problem

Down

1. In 24 + 65 = 89, 24 is an _____.
3. A combination of the digits 0, 1, 2, 3, 4, 5, 6, 7, 8, and 9.
4. The operation that you can use to find out how much more one number is than another.

Vocabulary Activities (continued)

▶ Word Wall PAIRS or SMALL GROUPS

With your teacher's permission, start a word wall in your classroom. As you work through each lesson, put the math vocabulary words on index cards and place them on the word wall. You can work with a partner or a small group choosing a word and giving the definition.

▶ Word Web INDIVIDUALS

Make a word web for a word or words you do not understand in a unit. Fill in the web with words or phrases that are related to the vocabulary word.

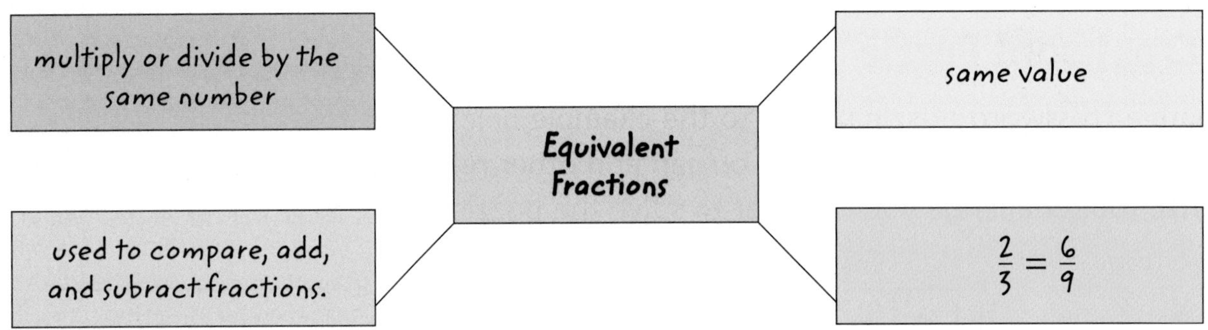

used to compare, add, and subract fractions.
$\frac{2}{3} = \frac{6}{9}$

▶ Alphabet Challenge PAIRS or INDIVIDUALS

Take an alphabet challenge. Choose 3 letters from the alphabet. Think of three vocabulary words for each letter. Then write the definition or draw an example for each word.

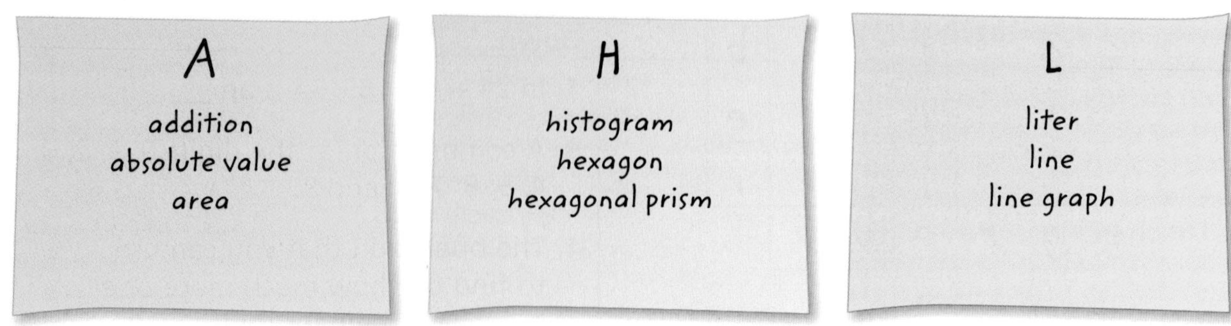

A
addition
absolute value
area
H
histogram
hexagon
hexagonal prism
L
liter
line
line graph

▶ Concentration PAIRS

Write the vocabulary words and related words from a unit on index cards. Write the definitions on a different set of index cards. Mix up both sets of cards. Then place the cards facedown on a table in an array, for example, 3 by 3 or 3 by 4. Take turns turning over two cards. If one card is a word and one card is a definition that matches the word, take the pair. Continue until each word has been matched with its definition.

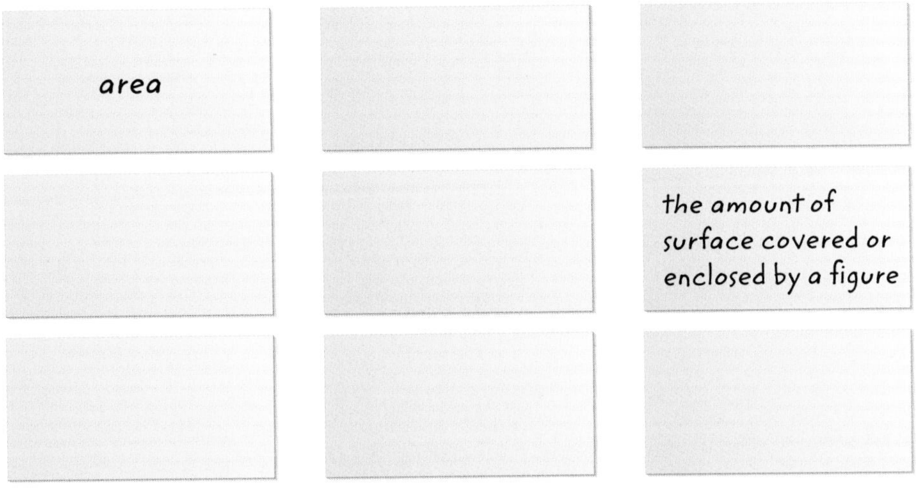

area
the amount of surface covered or enclosed by a figure

▶ Math Journal INDIVIDUALS

As you learn new words, write them in your Math Journal. Write the definition of the word and include a sketch or an example. As you learn new information about the word, add notes to your definition.

octagonal pyramid: Pyramid with a base that is an octagon and triangular faces that meet at a vertex.

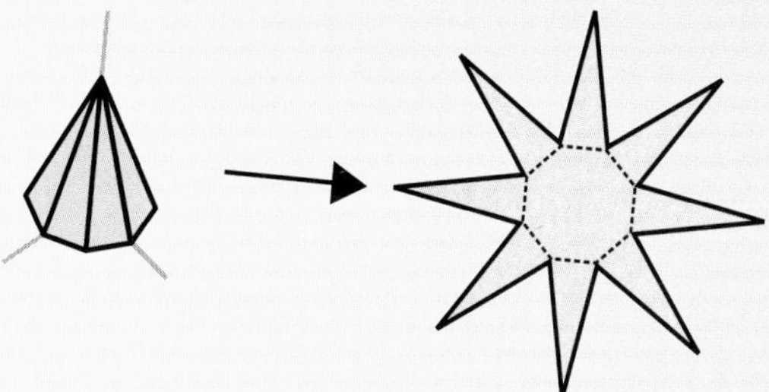

Surface area: the total area of all the faces of a solid figure.

▶ What's the Word? PAIRS

Work together to make a poster or bulletin board display of the words in a unit. Write definitions on a set of index cards. Mix up the cards. Work with a partner, choosing a definition from the index cards. Have your partner point to the word on the poster and name the matching math vocabulary word. Switch roles and try the activity again.

mean
median
box plot
dot plot
quartile
gap
first quartile
histogram
third quartile
range
cluster
outlier
mean absolute deviation
interquartile range

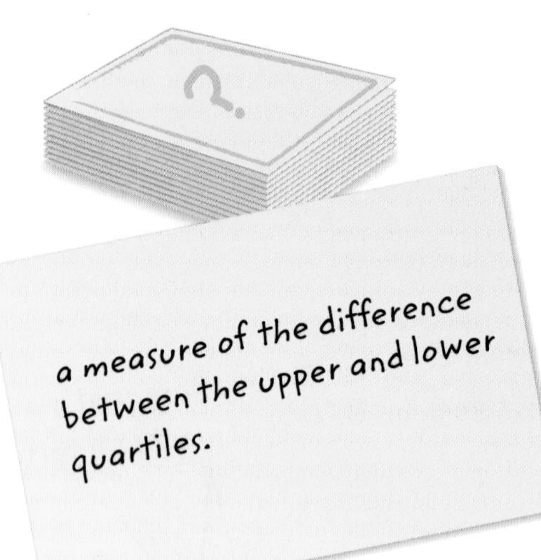

a measure of the difference between the upper and lower quartiles.

Glossary

A

absolute value A measure of the distance a number is from zero on a number line.

acute triangle A triangle with three acute angles. An acute angle has a measure that is greater than 0° and less than 90°.

Examples:

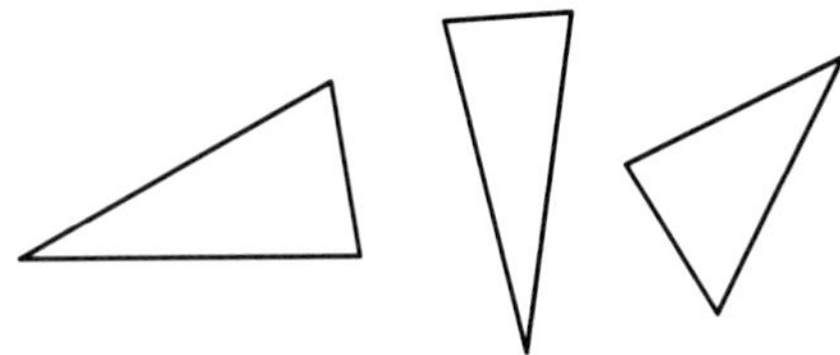

algebraic expression An expression that includes one or more variables.

Examples: $10(b + a)$
$7n$
$5x^2 - x$

area The amount of surface covered or enclosed by a figure. Area is measured by finding the number of same size units of area required to cover the shape without gaps or overlaps.

Associative Property of Addition The property that states that changing the grouping of addends does not change their sum. For any numbers *a*, *b* and *c*, $(a + b) + c = a + (b + c)$.

Example: $(7 + 8) + 2 = 7 + (8 + 2)$

Associative Property of Multiplication The property that states that changing the grouping of factors does not change their product. For any numbers *a*, *b* and *c*, $(a \cdot b) \cdot c = a \cdot (b \cdot c)$.

Example: $(9 \cdot 15) \cdot 20 = 9 \cdot (15 \cdot 20)$

B

bar graph A graph that uses the lengths of bars to show data. The bars may be horizontal or vertical.

Example:

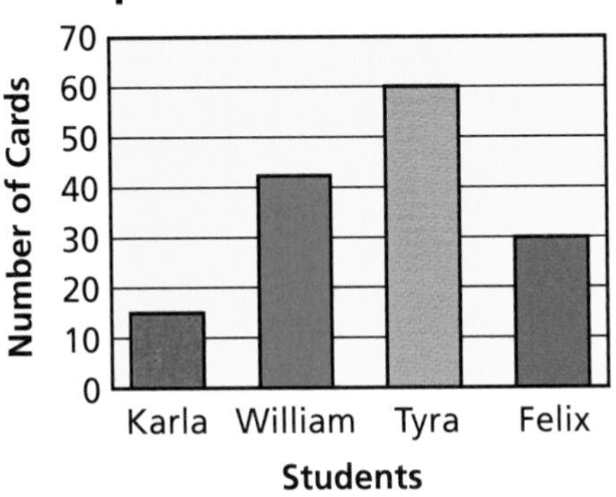

base of a figure For a triangle or parallelogram, a base is any side. For a trapezoid, a base is either of the parallel sides. For a prism, a base is one of the congruent parallel faces. For a pyramid, the base is the face that does not touch the vertex of the pyramid.

Examples:

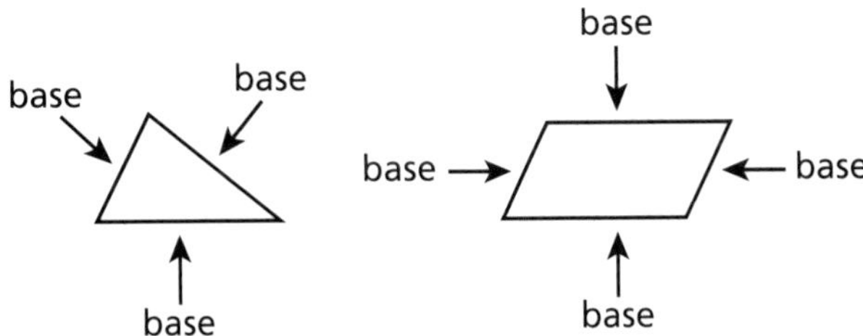

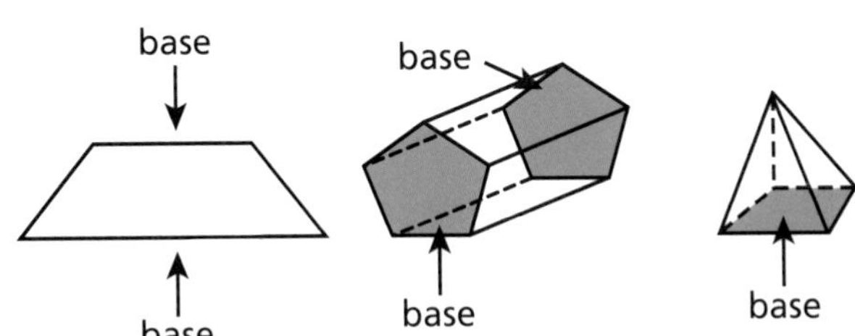

base of a number A number, variable, or expression that is raised to a power.

Examples: 4 is the base in the power 4^3.
a is the base in the power a^7.

basic ratio A ratio in simplest form.

Examples: The basic ratio for $\frac{25}{30}$ is $\frac{5}{6}$.
The basic ratio for $\frac{12}{24}$ is $\frac{1}{2}$.

box plot A graphic summary that shows the median, quartiles, and minimum and maximum values of a set of data.

Example:

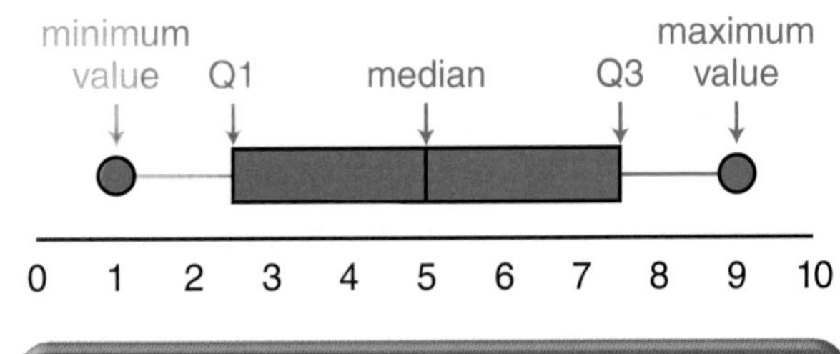

C

categorical data Data expressed as words that represent categories.

Example: Favorite sport: football, soccer, baseball, so on.

center of a polygon A point inside a regular polygon that is the same distance from each vertex.

Examples:

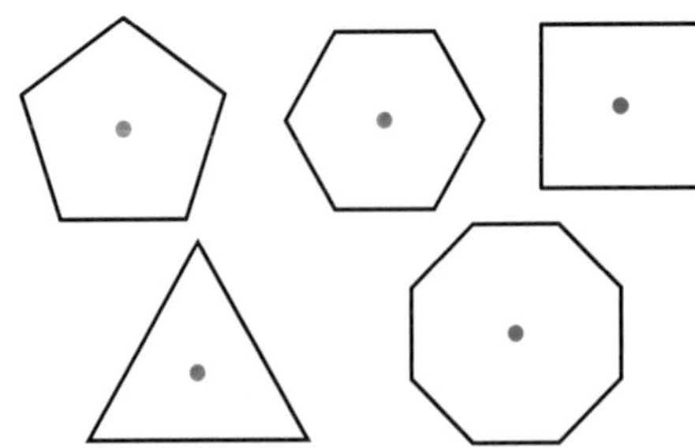

circle graph A graph used to display data that make up a whole. (Also called a *pie graph* or a *pie chart*.)

Example:

Sahil's Postcards from the U.S. by Region

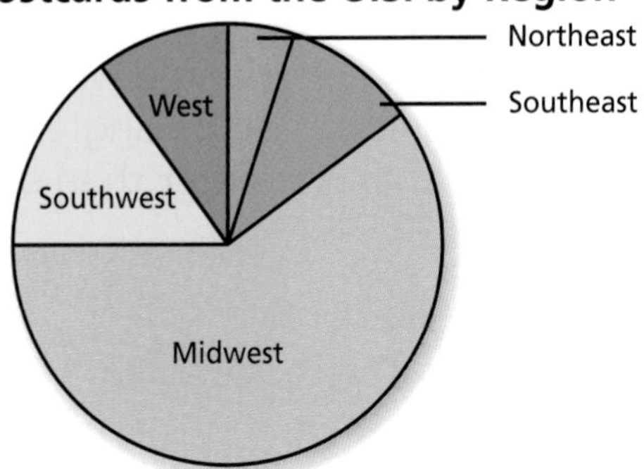

cluster A group of data values. A data set may have no clusters, one cluster, or more than one cluster.

Example:

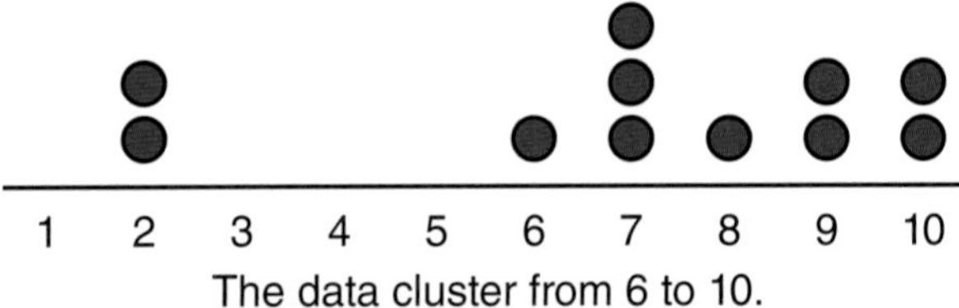

The data cluster from 6 to 10.

coefficient The number part of a term when the term is a number times a variable or a number times a product of variables.

Example: In $5x + 2xy$, 5 is the coefficient of the term $5x$ and 2 is the coefficient of the term $2xy$.

column In a data table, a vertical group of cells.

common denominator A common multiple of two or more denominators.

Example: 15 is a common denominator of $\frac{1}{3}$ and $\frac{2}{5}$.
$\frac{1}{3} = \frac{5}{15}$ $\quad \frac{2}{5} = \frac{6}{15}$
So, $\frac{1}{3} + \frac{2}{5} = \frac{5}{15} + \frac{6}{15} = \frac{11}{15}$

common factor A factor that two or more numbers share.

Example: 4 is a common factor of 12 and 20.

common multiple A number that is a multiple of two or more numbers.

Example: 24 is a common multiple of 8 and 6.

Commutative Property of Addition The property that states that changing the order of addends does not change their sum. For any numbers a and b, $a + b = b + a$.

Example: $18 + 21 = 21 + 18$

Commutative Property of Multiplication The property that states that changing the order of factors does not change their product. For any numbers a and b, $a \cdot b = b \cdot a$.

Example: $36 \cdot \frac{3}{4} = \frac{3}{4} \cdot 36$

compare ratios For two ratios, to state whether the amount of one quantity in a ratio is less than, greater than, or equal to the same quantity in the other ratio when the value of the other quantity in the ratios is the same.

complex figure A figure made by combining simple geometric figures, such as rectangles and triangles

Examples:

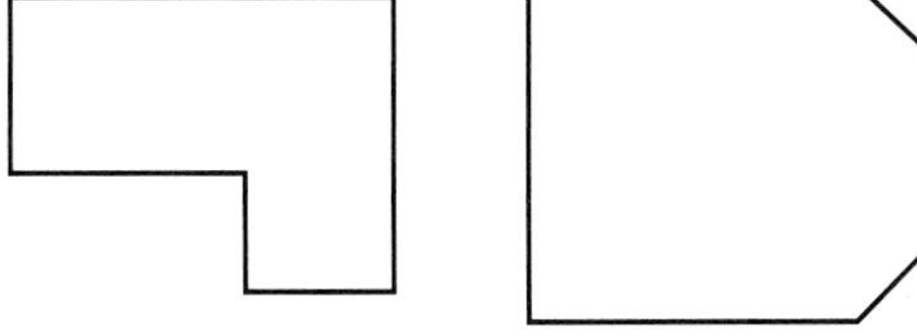

congruent Figures that are exactly the same size and shape.

Example: The bases of this pentagonal prism are congruent.

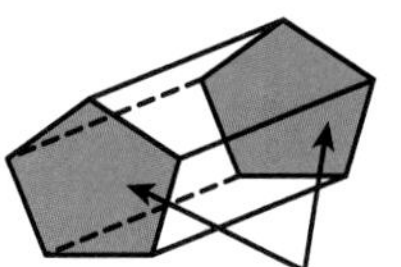

constant rate In a rate table in which the units are consecutive whole numbers, the constant difference in the values shown in the second column. Also the value in the second column when the number of units equals 1.

continuous data Data that represent an accumulation without interruption. Each data point is related to the data point before and after it.

Example: Temperature reading over a 24-hour period: 45°, 47°, 52°, and so on.

coordinate A number that determines the horizontal or vertical position of a point in the coordinate plane.

Example: The ordered pair ($^-7$, 3) gives the coordinates that determine the position of the point shown on the graph below. The first coordinate, $^-7$, determines the horizontal position of the point. The second coordinate, 3, determines the vertical position of the point.

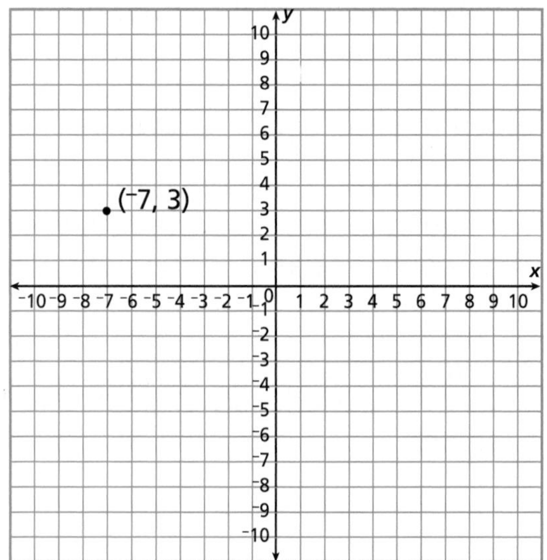

coordinate plane A plane together with a pair of perpendicular number lines that intersect at 0 on each number line. The perpendicular number lines are called axes.

Example: The coordinate plane is divided into four quadrants by the *x*- and *y*-axes. Below is the first quadrant of the coordinate plane.

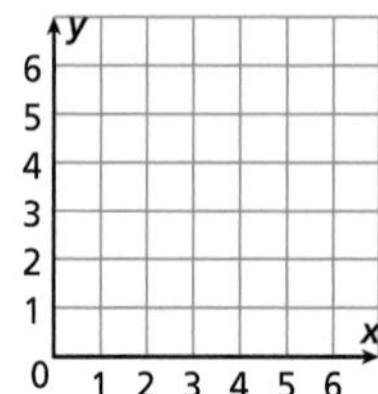

coordinates Each point in the coordinate plane corresponds to an ordered pair of numbers called its coordinates.

cross-multiplication A method used for solving proportions based on the fact that in a proportion, the cross-products are equal.

Example: $\frac{10}{15} = \frac{18}{27}$ is a proportion. The cross-products are equal.

$$\frac{10}{15} \times \frac{18}{27}$$

$$18 \cdot 15 = 10 \cdot 27$$

cube A rectangular prism with six congruent square faces.

cubic unit (unit³) A unit for measuring volume. It is the volume of a cube with each edge 1 unit long.

Example:

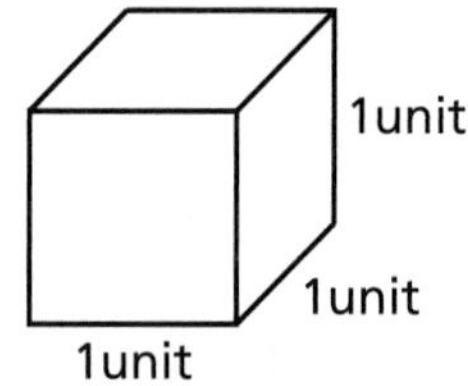

D

decimal A number with a decimal point in it. A decimal is another way to write a fraction. Some decimals are called decimal fractions because they represent fractions with denominators of 10, 100, and 1,000.

tenths	$\frac{1}{10}$ or 0.1
hundredths	$\frac{1}{100}$ or 0.01
thousandths	$\frac{1}{1,000}$ or 0.001

Example: The decimal 9.56 represents $9\frac{56}{100}$.

denominator The number below the bar in a fraction. It indicates the number of unit fractions made by dividing the whole into equal parts.

Example: In the fraction $\frac{3}{5}$, the denominator is 5.

$\frac{3}{5}$ ← denominator

It represents the 5 unit fractions (the 5 fifths) made by dividing the whole into 5 equal parts.

dependent variable In a relationship between two variables, the variable whose value depends on the value of the other variable.

Example: The cost of gas, c, depends on the number of gallons purchased, g. The cost, c, is the dependent variable.

diagonal A line segment connecting two vertices that are not next to each other.

Example:

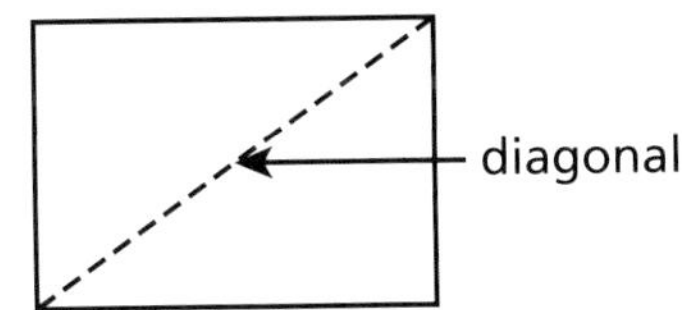

dimension The height, length, or width of a figure.

Examples: A line segment has only length, so it has one dimension.

A rectangle has length and width, so it has two dimensions.

A cube has length, width, and height, so it has three dimensions.

discrete data In a set of discrete data, each number is exact and the numbers are not related to each other.

Examples:

- The number of people who visit the library each day for a month.
- The number of books on each bookshelf at the library.
- The number of students in each grade in a school.

distance formula Distance (d) is the product of speed (r) and time (t).

Examples: distance = speed • time

or $d = rt$

Distributive Property Over Addition The property that allows us to distribute a factor to the terms of a sum or difference or to pull out a common factor from the terms of a sum or difference. For any numbers a, b, and c, $a(b + c) = ab + ac$.

Examples:

Distribute a factor:

$6(x - 2) = 6 \cdot x - 6 \cdot 2 = 6x - 12$

Pull out a factor:

$4y + 8 = 4 \cdot y + 4 \cdot 2 = 4(y + 2)$

dividend The number that is divided in a division problem.

Example:

$56 \div 8 = 7$ $\quad 8\overline{)56}$ with quotient 7

dividend

divisor The number that divides in a division problem.

Example:

$56 \div 8 = 7$ $\quad 8\overline{)56}$ with quotient 7

divisor

Glossary (Continued)

dot plot A display showing the frequency of numerical data. A dot plot uses a number line and dots to show how often the numbers in a set of numerical data occur.

Example:

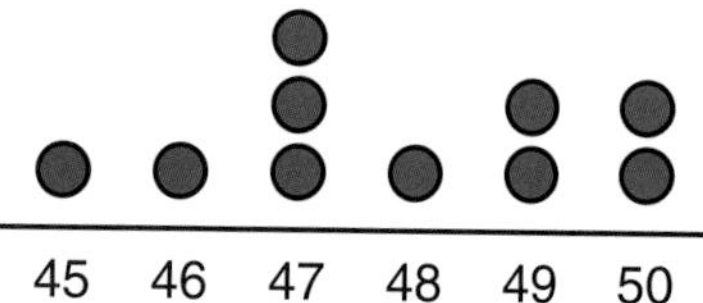

double number line A diagram with two number lines that shows how two quantities relate to each other.

Examples: The double number line below shows how distance and time are related for a person walking at a rate of 3 feet per second.

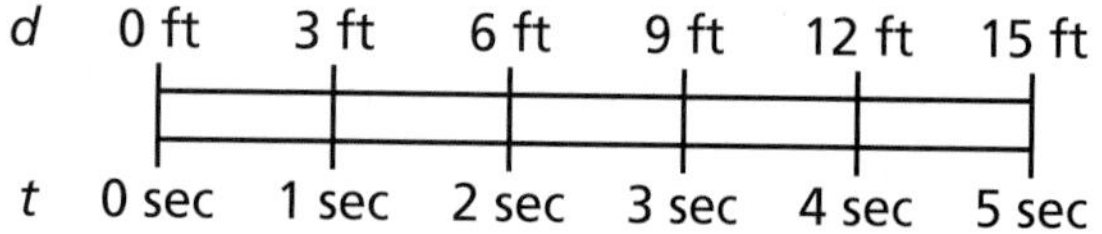

The double number line below shows what percent 0, 2, 4, and 6 millimeters are of 8 millimeters.

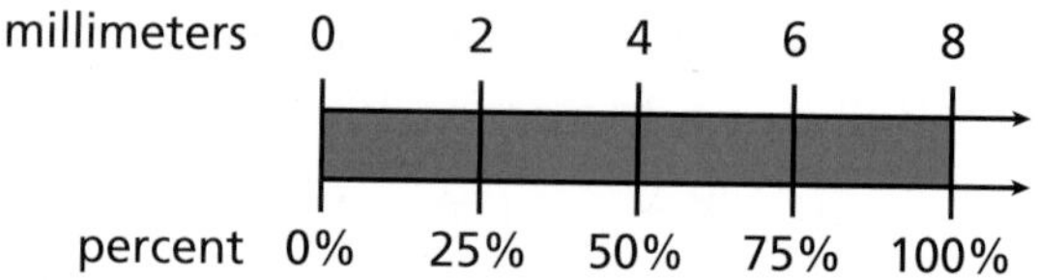

E

edge The line segment where two faces meet in a three-dimensional figure.

Examples:

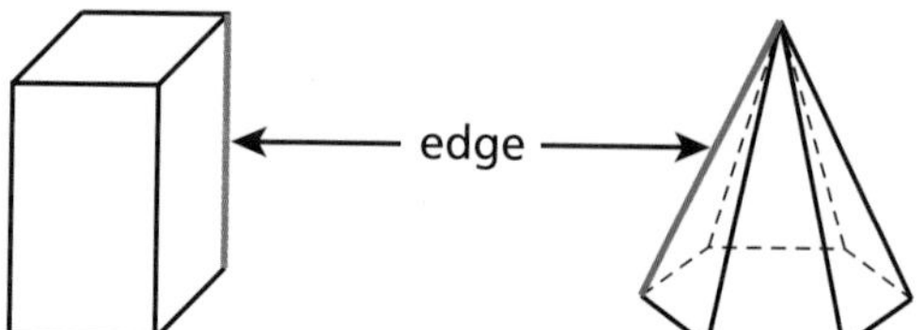

equation A statement that two or more expressions are equal. An equal sign (=) separates the two equal expressions in an equation.

Examples: $4 \cdot 2 = 8$

$x + 4 = 10$

equivalent expressions Expressions that always have the same value.

Example: $b + b + b$ and $3b$ are equivalent expressions.

equivalent fractions Fractions that represent the same number.

Example: $\frac{1}{2}$ and $\frac{3}{6}$ are equivalent fractions.

equivalent ratios Ratios that represent the same comparison. Equivalent ratios have the same basic ratio.

evaluate an algebraic expression Substitute values for the variables in an expression and then simplify the resulting numerical expression.

Example: Evaluate $10(b + a)$ when $b = 3$ and $a = 4$.

$10(b + a) = 10(3 + 4) = 10 \cdot 7 = 70$

exponent In a power, the small, raised number that indicates how many times the base is used as a factor.

Example: 3 is the exponent in the power 4^3.

$4^3 = 4 \cdot 4 \cdot 4 = 64$

expression A combination of one or more numbers, one or more variables, or both numbers and variables. An expression often includes one or more operations, but does not include an equals sign.

Examples: n

$x - 9$

$5 \cdot 2^2$

$\frac{1}{2} bh$

 F

face A flat surface of a three-dimensional figure.

Examples:

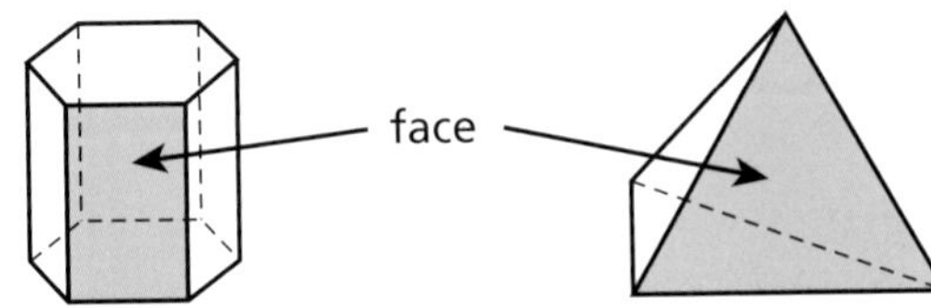

factor One of two or more numbers multiplied to make a product.

Example: $12 \cdot 4 = 48$

factor (12) factor (4)

factor of a number A number that divides evenly into the number.

Example: The factors of 18 are 1, 2, 3, 6, 9, and 18.

first quartile (Q1) The middle number, or mean of the two middle numbers, of the lower half of a set of data.

Example:

1 2 3 4 5 6 7 8 9 10 11 12

first quartile (between 3 and 4) median (between 6 and 7)

So, Q1 = 3.5.

fraction A number that is the sum of unit fractions, each an equal part of a set or part of a whole.

Example:

$\frac{3}{5} = \frac{1}{5} + \frac{1}{5} + \frac{1}{5}$ or $\frac{3}{5} = 3 \cdot \frac{1}{5}$

G

gap An interval with no data. A set of data may have no gaps, one gap, or more than one gap.

Example:

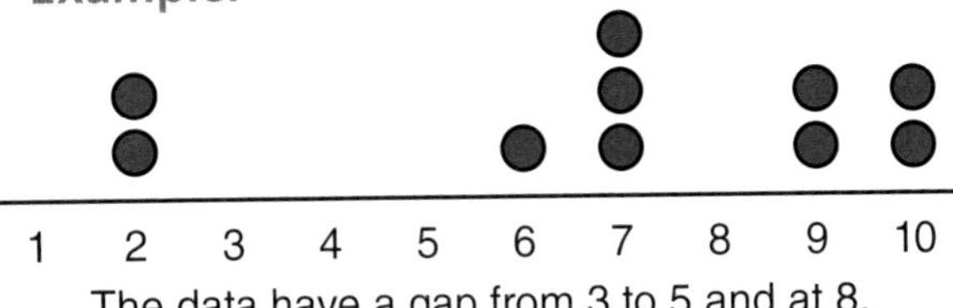

The data have a gap from 3 to 5 and at 8.

greatest common factor (GCF) The greatest factor that two or more numbers share.

Example: 15 is the GCF of 30 and 45.

H

height The height of a triangle or quadrilateral is the perpendicular distance from a base to a vertex that is not on the base. Finding this distance may require extending the base.

Examples:

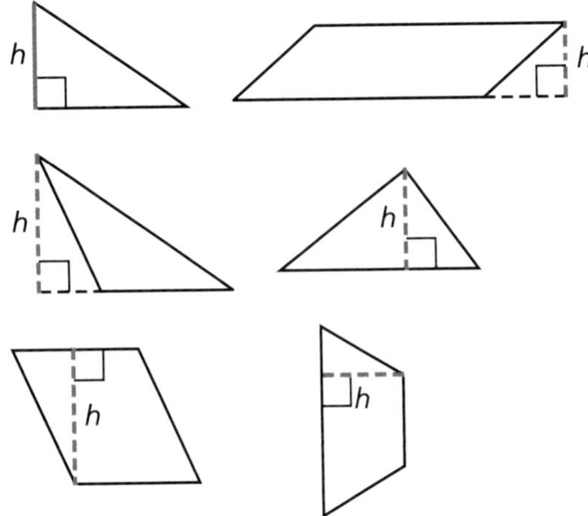

hexagon A polygon with six sides.

Examples:

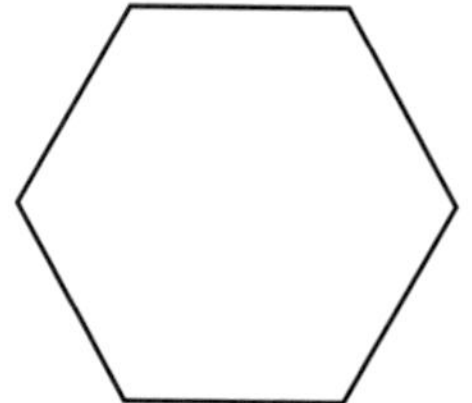

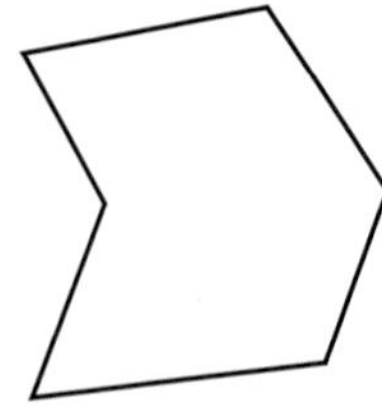

histogram A frequency display that uses bars to show the distribution of data in a set. Each bar represents an interval, or range, of data.

Example:

U.S. Population, 2000

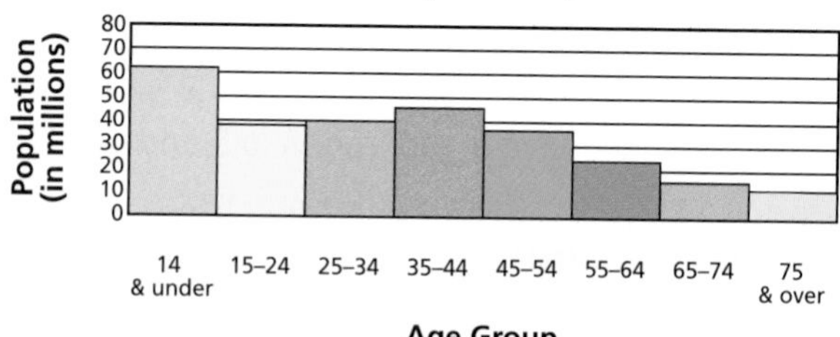

I

improper fraction A fraction in which the numerator is greater than or equal to the denominator.

Examples: $\frac{7}{5}$ $\frac{30}{8}$ $\frac{9}{9}$

independent variable In a relationship between two variables, the variable whose values influence the values of the other variable.

Example: The cost of gas, *c*, depends on the number of gallons purchased, *g*. The number of gallons purchased, *g*, is the independent variable.

inequality A statement that compares two expressions using one of these symbols: > (greater than), < (less than), ≥ (greater than or equal to), ≤ (less than or equal to), ≠ (not equal to).

Examples: $4 + 7 > 10$

$x - 2 \leq 8$

infinite Greater than any whole number; unlimited.

Example: $x > 3$ has an infinite number of solutions.

integers The set of integers includes whole numbers, their opposites, and zero.

interquartile range (IQR) A measure of the difference between the upper and lower quartiles. IQR is a way to describe the spread or variability of the data in a set.

Example:

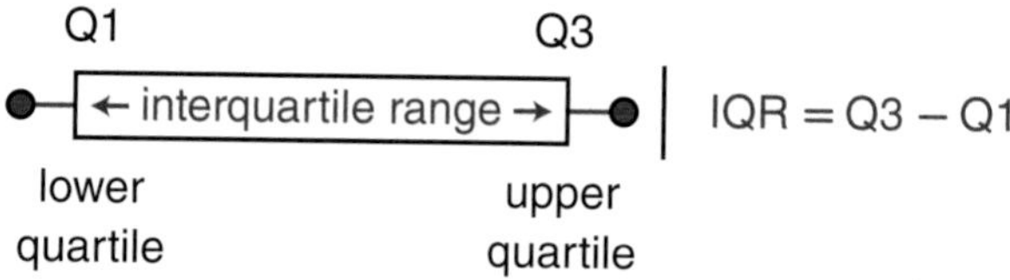

interval A range of numbers in a frequency display such as a histogram. An interval is sometimes called a *bin*.

inverse operations Operations that undo each other. Addition and subtraction are inverse operations. Multiplication and division are inverse operations.

Examples: $5 + 9 = 14$, so $14 - 9 = 5$.

$7 \cdot 9 = 63$, so $63 \div 9 = 7$.

L

lateral face A face that is not a base. Prisms have rectangular lateral faces and pyramids have triangular lateral faces.

Examples:

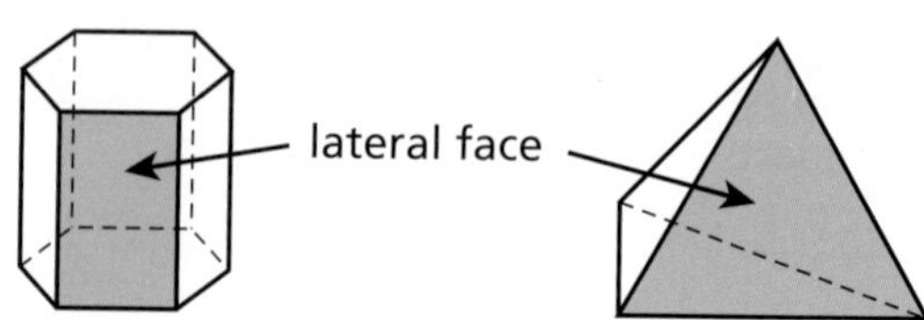

least common multiple (LCM) The least number that is a multiple of two or more numbers.

Example: 36 is the least common multiple of 9 and 12.

like terms Terms with the same variables raised to the same powers.

Example: In $6 + 2x + 1 + x$, 6 and 1 are like terms and $2x$ and x are like terms.

line graph A graph that uses a broken line to show changes in data.

Example:

Deer Population in Midland Park

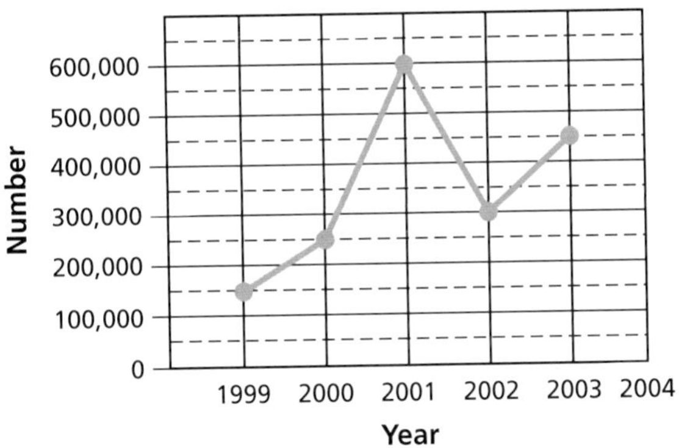

line of symmetry A line such that if a figure is folded on that line, the two parts will match exactly.

Example:

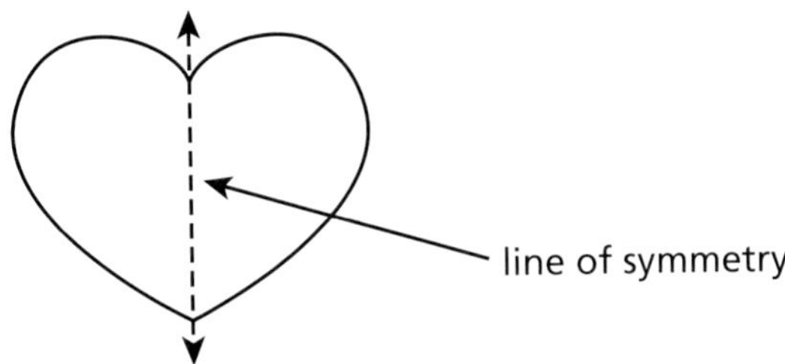

line plot A diagram that shows the frequency of data on a number line.

Example:

		X			
		X		X	X
X	X	X	X	X	X
45	46	47	48	49	50

linear equation An equation with a graph that is a line.

liquid volume A measure of how much a container can hold. Also called *capacity*.

M

mean A single number that summarizes all of the values in a set of numerical data. A mean is a measure of center that shows what the common data value would be if all of the data values were the same. A mean is calculated by adding the data values and dividing the sum by the number of values.

{8 3 1 9 14}	← A set of numerical data.
$8 + 3 + 1 + 9 + 14 = 35$	← Add.
$35 \div 5 = 7$	← Divide. The mean of the data is 7.

mean absolute deviation A measure of variability that shows the average distance the data values in a set are from the mean.

Example:

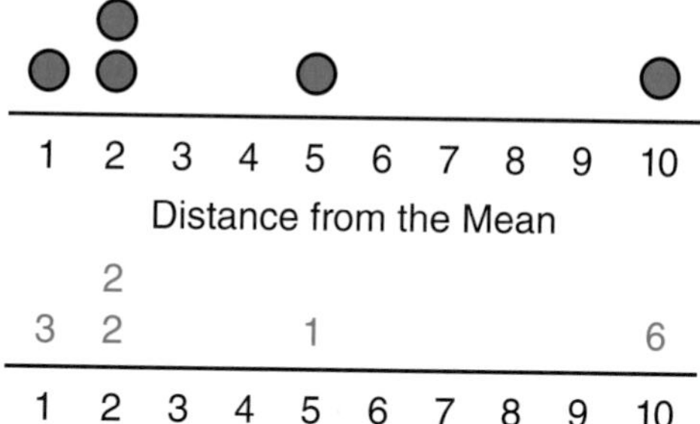

The mean absolute deviation is $(3 + 2 + 2 + 1 + 6) \div 5 = 2.8$.

median A single number that summarizes the center of a set of numerical data. The median is the middle number, or the mean of the two middle numbers, when data have been arranged from least to greatest or from greatest to least. After the median has been calculated, one-half of the remaining numbers in the set will be less than the median and one-half will be greater.

Examples:

2 5 7 11 20 — median = 7

39 26 24 3 — median = 25

mixed number A number represented by a whole number and a fraction.

Example: $2\frac{1}{5}$ is a mixed number. It means $2 + \frac{1}{5}$.

mode The number or category that occurs most often in a set of data. A set of data may have no modes, one mode, or more than one mode. The mode is often used to describe categorical data.

multiple The product of a given number and a counting number.

Example: 3, 6, 9, 12, and so on are multiples of 3.

multiplicative comparison A way of comparing two quantities using *as many* or two amounts using *as much*. A multiplicative comparison can be expressed in two ways.

Example: When comparing 2 circles and 6 squares, the comparison can be expressed as:

There are 3 times as many squares as circles.

or

There are $\frac{1}{3}$ as many circles as squares.

multiplicative inverse The product of a number and its multiplicative inverse is 1.

Example: 6 is the multiplicative inverse of $\frac{1}{6}$.

$6 \cdot \frac{1}{6} = 1$ and $\frac{1}{6} \cdot 6 = 1$.

N

negative numbers Negative numbers are to the left of, or below, 0 (the origin).

net A two-dimensional flat pattern that can be folded into a three-dimensional figure.

Examples:

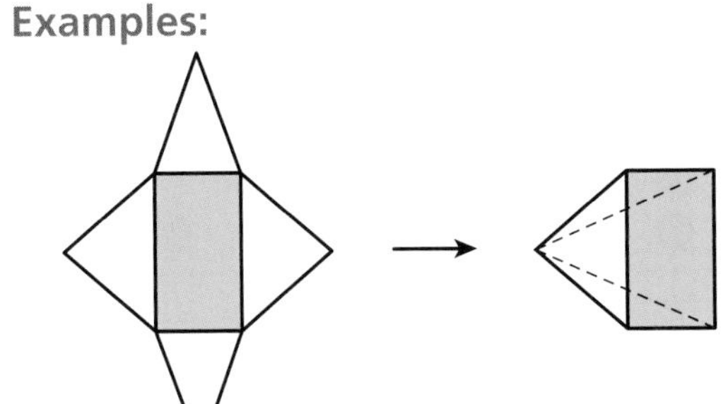

net of rectangular pyramid rectangular pyramid

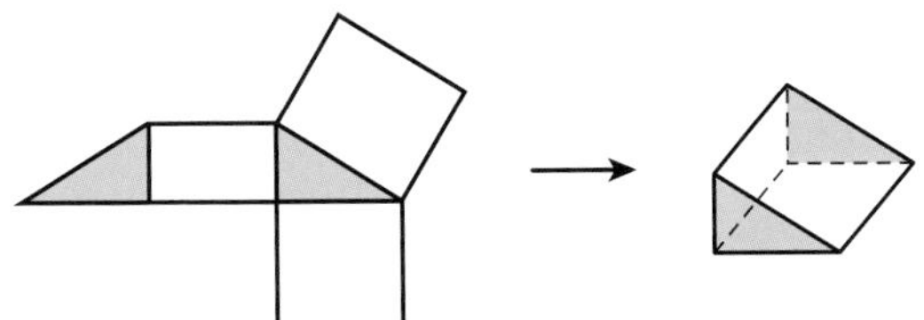

net of triangular prism triangular prism

number line A line that uses points to represent the distance and direction from zero of integers and other rational numbers.

Example:

$^-3 \quad ^-2\frac{1}{2} \quad ^-2 \quad ^-1\frac{1}{2} \quad ^-1 \quad ^-\frac{1}{2} \quad 0 \quad \frac{1}{2} \quad 1 \quad 1\frac{1}{2} \quad 2 \quad 2\frac{1}{2} \quad 3$

numerator The number above the bar in a fraction. It indicates the number of unit fractions the fraction represents.

Example: In the fraction $\frac{3}{5}$, the numerator is 3.

$\frac{3}{5}$ ← numerator

The numerator shows that the fraction represents 3 fifths: $\frac{3}{5} = \frac{1}{5} + \frac{1}{5} + \frac{1}{5}$.

numerical data Data involving numbers and quantities.

Examples:
- The number of students in each class in a school.
- The population of a city each year for the last ten years.

numerical expression An expression that does not include variables.

Examples: $36 - (2 + 9) \cdot 3$
$20 - 8 \div 2$

O

obtuse triangle A triangle with one obtuse angle. An obtuse angle has a measure that is greater than 90° and less than 180°.

Examples:

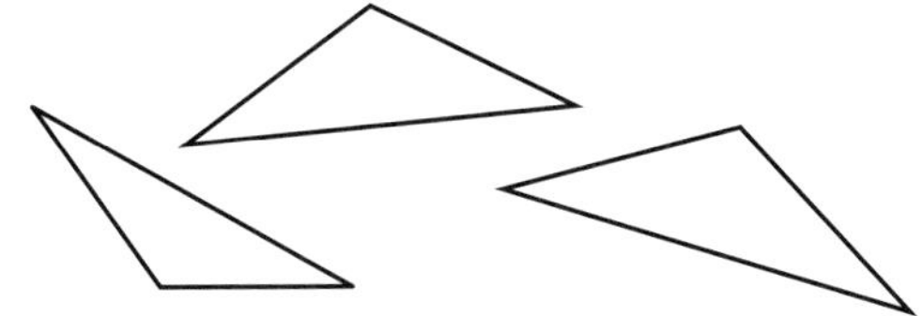

octagon A polygon with eight sides.

Examples:

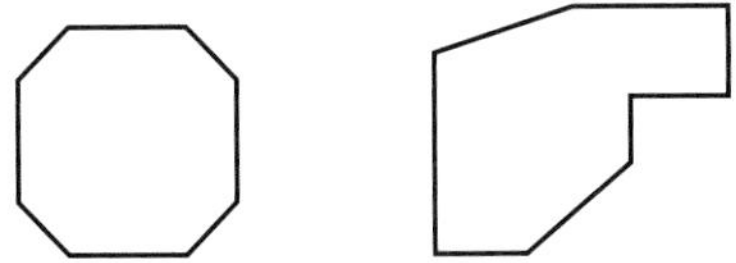

opposites Two numbers are opposites if they are the same distance from zero on a number line, but in opposite directions.

Examples: $^-5$ and 5
12 and $^-12$

ordered pair: Two numbers that are inside parentheses and have a comma in between them. Ordered pairs can represent points on the coordinate plane and are written as (x, y).

Examples: (5, 3) is an ordered pair, where $x = 5$ and $y = 3$.

Order of Operations A rule that states the order in which the operations in an expression should be done:

1. Perform operations in parentheses.
2. Simplify powers.
3. Multiply and divide from left to right.
4. Add and subtract from left to right.

origin The origin of a number line is the point at 0. The point of intersection of the *x*-axis and *y*-axis is called the origin of the coordinate plane.

outlier An extreme or distant value. A set of data may have no outliers, one outlier, or more than one outlier.

Example:

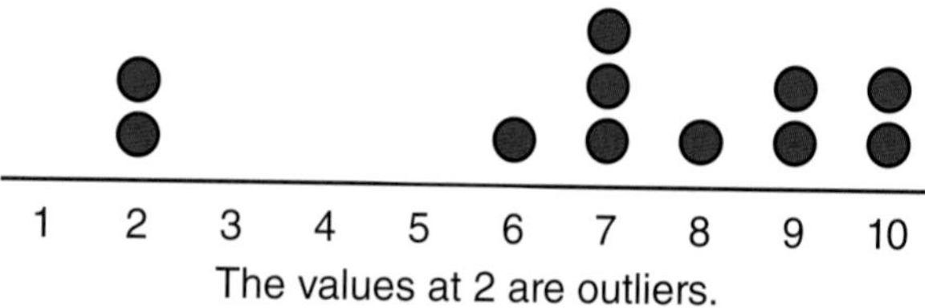

The values at 2 are outliers.

P

parallelogram A quadrilateral in which both pairs of opposite sides are parallel and opposite angles are congruent.

Examples:

peak The value (or values) that appear most often. A set of data may have no peaks, one peak, or more than one peak.

Example:

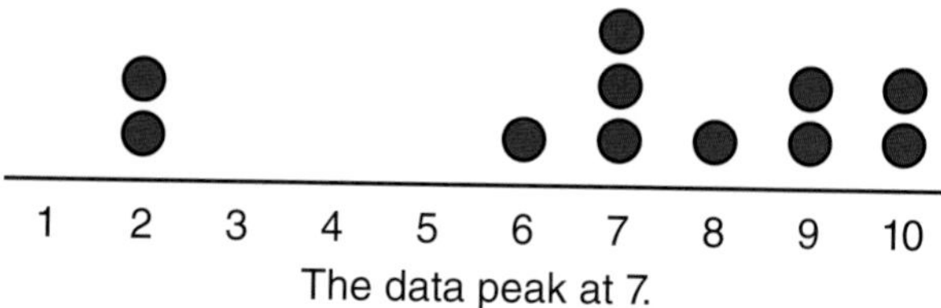

The data peak at 7.

pentagon A polygon with five sides.

Examples:

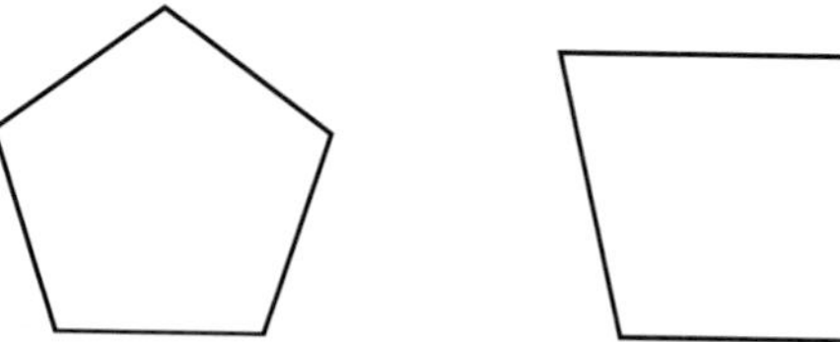

percent(%) An amount out of a hundred or per hundred.

Examples: $34\% = \frac{34}{100}$

$124\% = \frac{124}{100}$

perimeter The distance around a figure. It is the total number of same size units of length required to form the sides without gaps or overlaps.

perpendicular Lines, line segments, or rays are perpendicular if they form a right angle. A right angle has a measure that is equal to 90°.

Example:

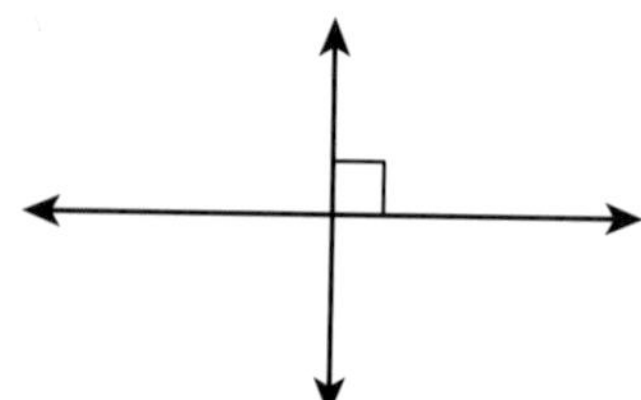

polygon A closed figure formed by line segments that do not cross each other.

positive numbers Positive numbers are to the right of, or above, 0 (the origin).

power An expression that includes an exponent and represents a repeated multiplication. The power of the expression is determined by the exponent.

Example: 4^3 (read "four raised to the third power") means $4 \cdot 4 \cdot 4$.

prism A solid figure with two congruent parallel bases.

Examples:

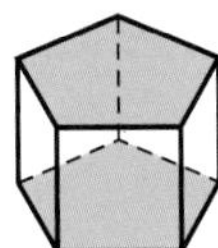
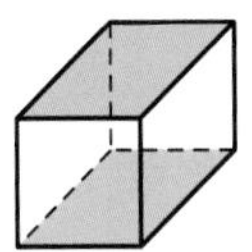
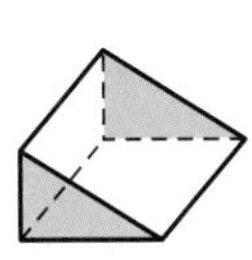
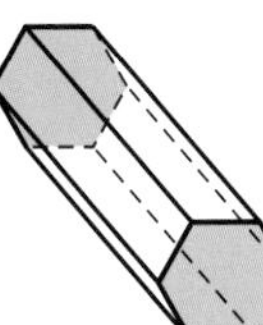

product The result of a multiplication.

Example: $12 \cdot 4 = 48$ ← product

proportion An equation stating that two ratios are equal.

pyramid A solid with a polygon for a base whose vertices are all joined to a single point.

Examples:

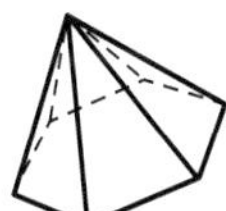

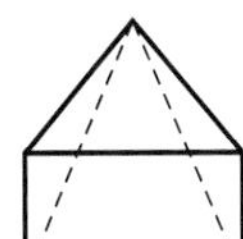

Q

quadrant The *x*- and *y*-axes divide the coordinate plane into four regions called *quadrants*. Beginning in the upper right quadrant and moving in a counterclockwise direction the quadrants are numbered using the Roman numerals I, II, III, and IV.

Example:

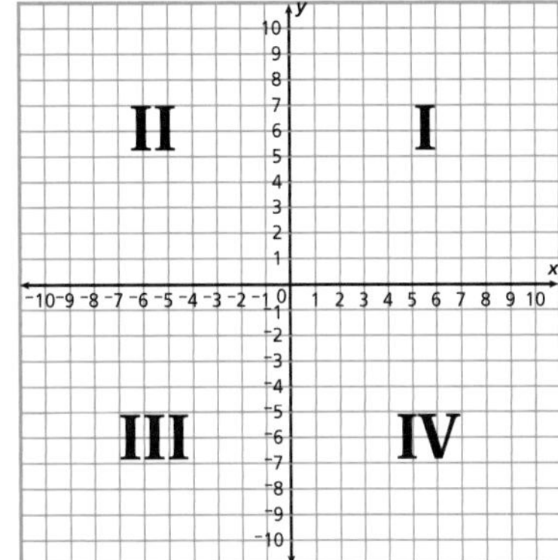

quadrilateral A polygon with four sides.

Examples:

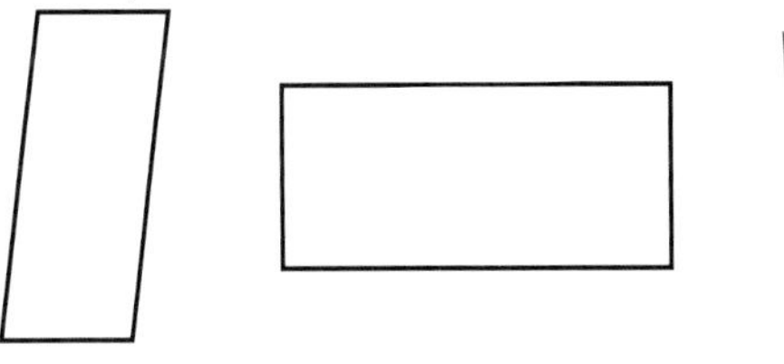

quartiles The values of the points that separate a set of data into four approximately equal parts.

quick drawing A sketch that summarizes a situation without showing unnecessary detail.

Example: Below is a quick drawing of the algebra-tile model for $3 + 2x$.

quotient The result of a division.

Example:

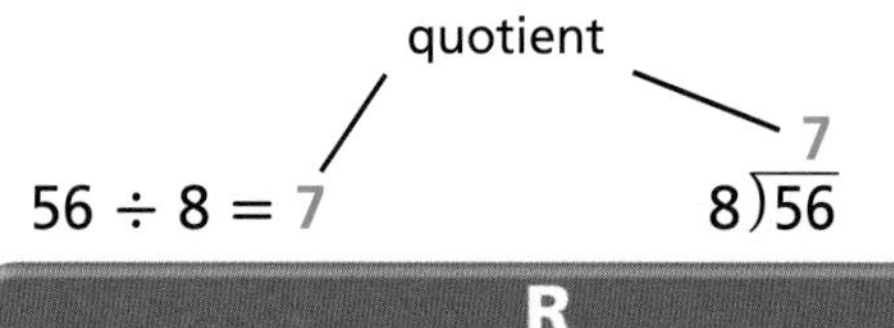

R

range A single number that summarizes the variability of the data in a set. The range is calculated by subtracting the least number in the set from the greatest.

Example: {5 2 16 10} ← The greatest value in this set is 16. The least value is 2.

$16 - 2 = 14$ ← Subtract. The range of the data is 14.

rate A special ratio in which the quantities may be described with different units (such as dollars and pounds).

rate table A two-column table showing the number of units in the first column and the value associated with each given number of units in the second column. When the units are listed as counting numbers in consecutive order, the values in the second column will show a constant difference; this constant difference is the unit rate.

Example: The rate table below shows how the unit days and the number of dollars saved are related. The constant difference is 3, and the unit rate is 3 dollars per day.

Number of Days	Dollars Saved
1	3
2	6
3	9
4	12

ratio Two quantities are in the ratio *a* to *b* if for every *a* units of the first quantity there are *b* units of the second quantity.

rational number Any number that can be expressed as a fraction $\frac{a}{b}$, where *a* and *b* are integers and $b \neq 0$.

ratio table A table showing equivalent ratios.

reciprocal The product of a number and its reciprocal is 1. The reciprocal of the fraction $\frac{a}{b}$ is $\frac{b}{a}$.

Example: $\frac{4}{3}$ is the reciprocal of $\frac{3}{4}$.

$\frac{3}{4} \cdot \frac{4}{3} = 1$ and $\frac{4}{3} \cdot \frac{3}{4} = 1$

rectangular prism A solid figure with two rectangular bases that are congruent and parallel.

Example:

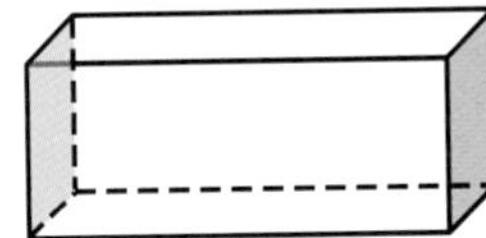

reflected point A given point and its reflected point are mirror images across the *x*-axis or *y*-axis of the coordinate plane.

Examples:

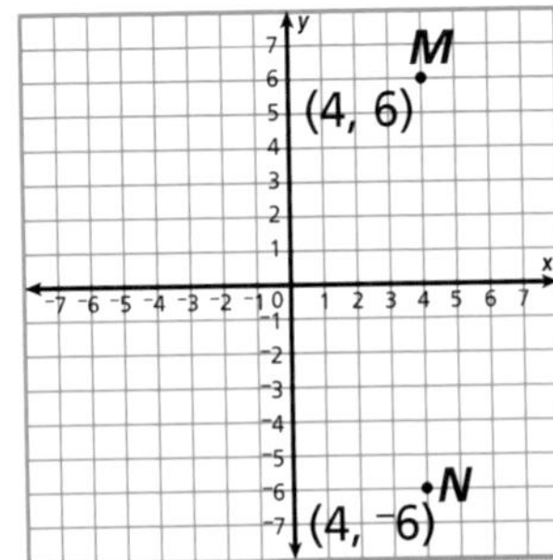

Point *N* is a reflection of point *M* across the *x*-axis.

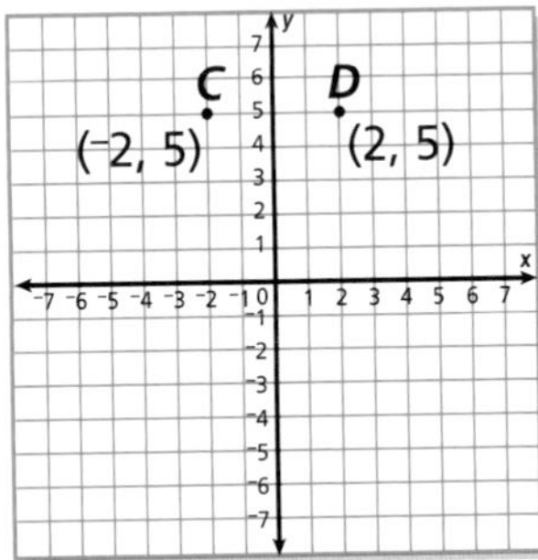

Point *C* is a reflection of point *D* across the *y*-axis.

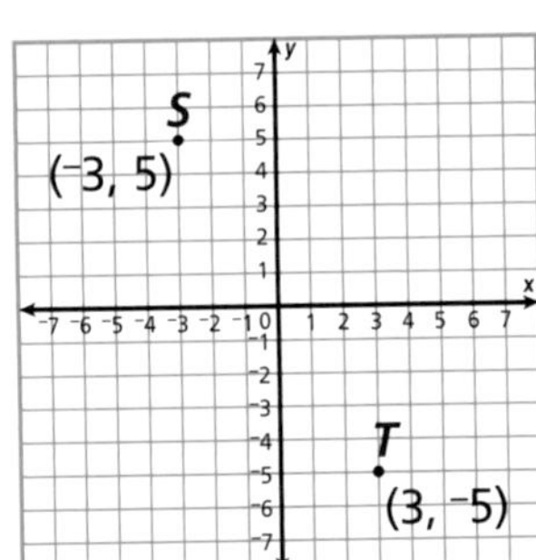

Point *T* is a reflection of point S across the *x*-axis and then the *y*-axis.

regular polygon A polygon with all sides the same length.

Examples:

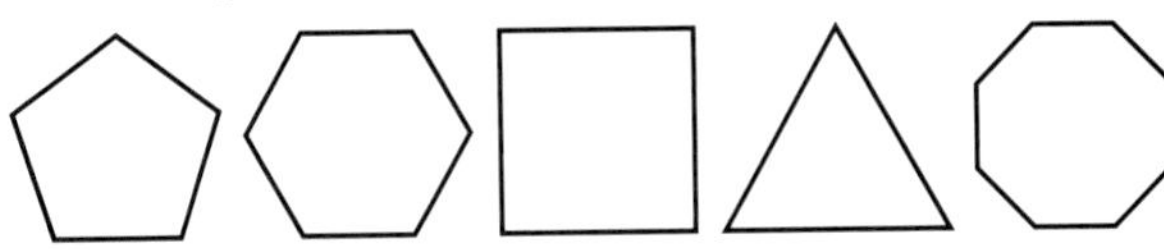

related parallelogram A parallelogram with the same base and height as its related rectangle or triangle.

Examples:

rectangle and related parallelogram

triangle and related parallelogram

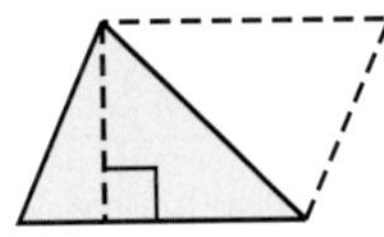

related rectangle A rectangle with the same base and height as its related parallelogram. A rectangle with the same base and height or half the height or base of its related triangle.

Examples:

parallelogram and related rectangle

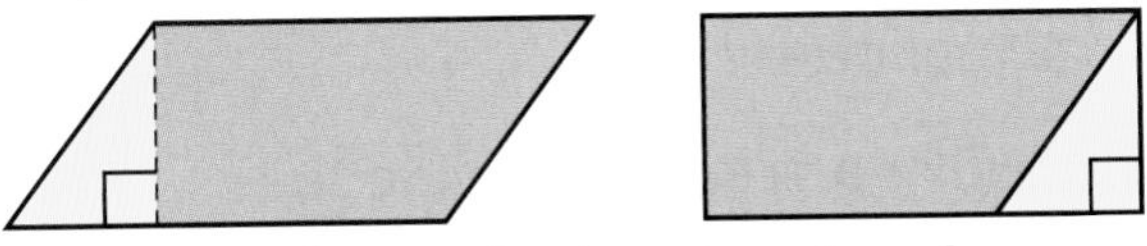

triangles and related rectangles

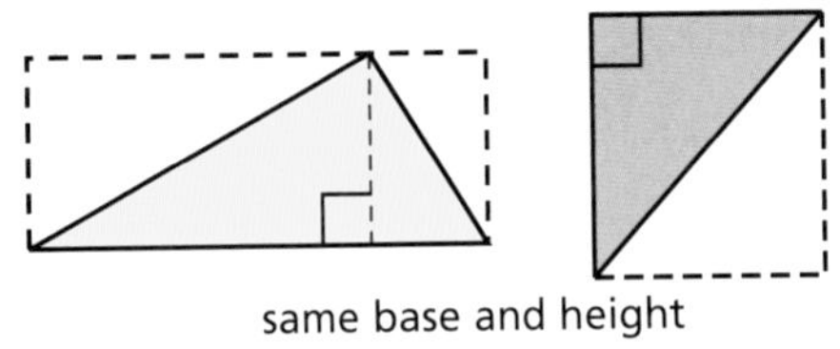

same base and height

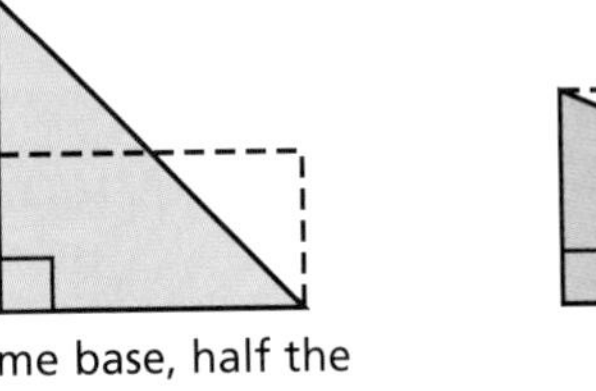

same base, half the height

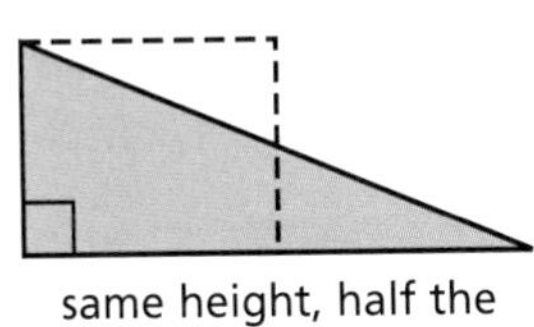

same height, half the base

remainder The number left over after dividing a number that is not evenly divisible by the divisor.

Example: $32 \div 6 = 5$ R2
The remainder is 2.

rhombus A parallelogram with all sides the same length.

Examples:

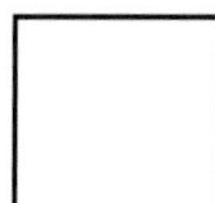

right triangle A triangle with one right angle. A right angle has a measure that is equal to 90°.

Examples:

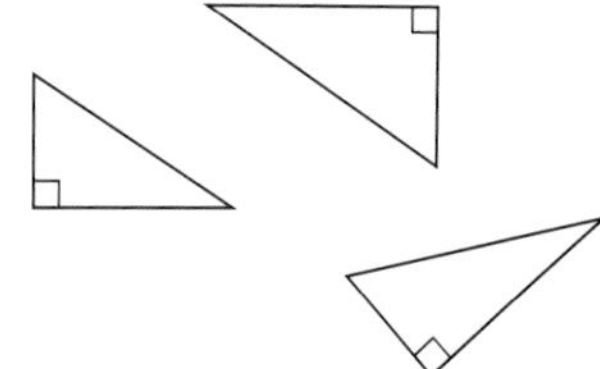

row In a data table, a horizontal group of cells.

S

scale of a model A ratio comparing the size of the model to the size of the actual object.

simplify a fraction Divide the numerator and denominator by a common factor to make an equivalent fraction that is made from fewer, but larger, unit fractions.

Example: Simplify $\frac{5}{10}$ by dividing both the numerator and denominator by 5.

$$\frac{5 \div 5}{10 \div 5} = \frac{1}{2}$$

simplify an expression Perform operations and combine all like terms.

Example: Simplify $3x + 5 + x + 2$.
$3x + 5 + x + 2 = 4x + 7$

slant height The height of a triangular face of a pyramid.

Example:

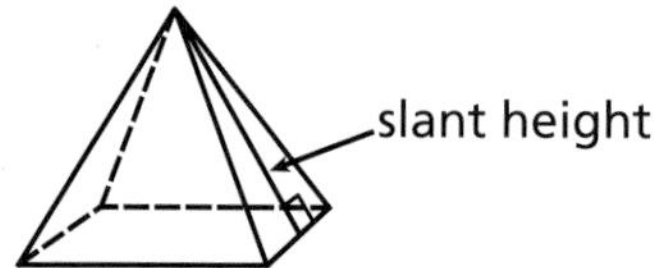

solution of an equation A number that can be substituted for the variable in an equation to make a true statement.

Example: $x = 4$ is a solution of $3x + 1 = 13$ because $3(4) + 1 = 13$ is true.

solution of an inequality A value that can be substituted for the variable in an inequality to make a true statement.

Example: $x = 10$ is a solution of $x + 3 < 20$ because $10 + 3 < 20$ is true.

solution set The set of all solutions of an inequality.

Examples:

This graph shows the solution set for $x > 3$.

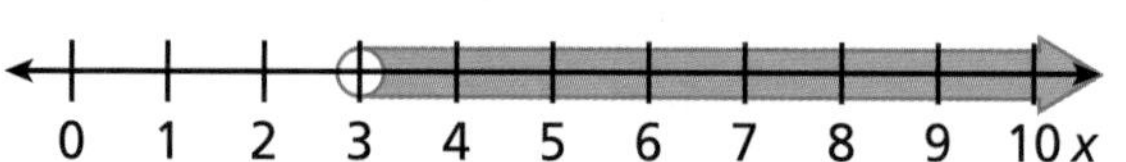

This graph shows the solution set for $x \geq 3$.

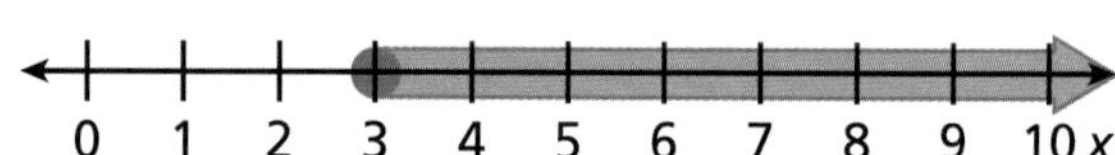

square unit (unit²) A unit of area equal to the area of a square with one-unit sides.

Example:

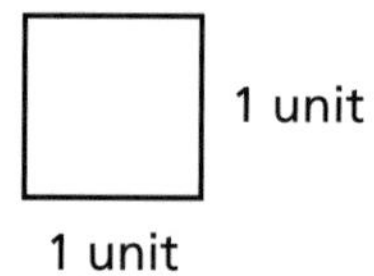

surface area The total area of all the faces of a solid figure.

symmetric data A data distribution that has a line of symmetry. The shape of the data on one side of the line of symmetry is the same as the shape of the data on the other side of the line.

Example:

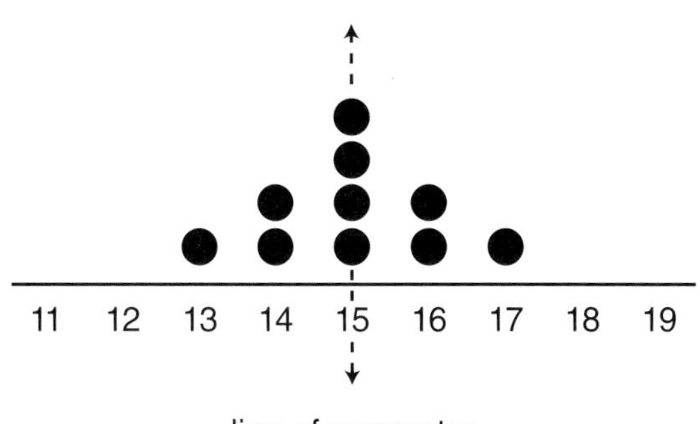

T

tape diagram A drawing that looks like a segment of tape used to illustrate number relationships. Also known as a strip diagram, bar model, fraction strip, or length model.

Example:

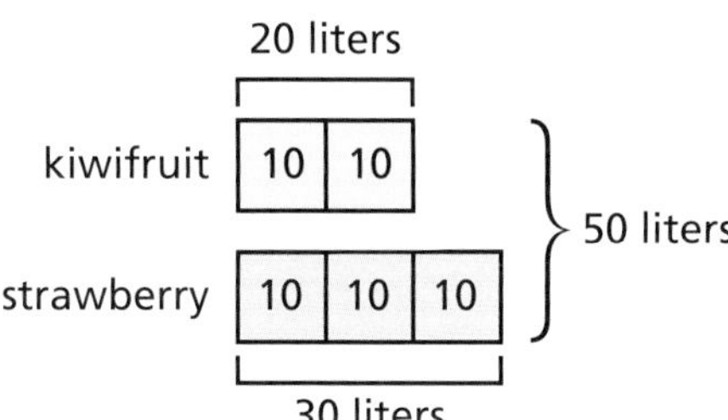

term Part of an expression that is added or subtracted.

Example: 4, $3b$, and b^2 are terms of the expression $4 + 3b + b^2$.

tessellation A pattern of closed figures that completely cover a surface with no gaps or overlaps.

Example:

third quartile (Q3) The middle number, or the mean of the two middle numbers, of the upper half of a set of data.

Example:

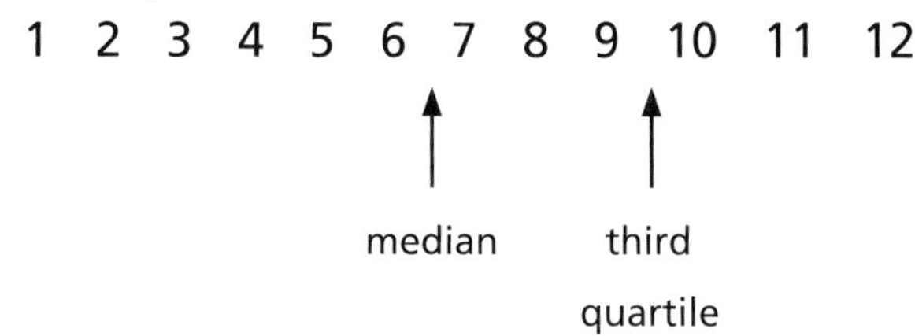

So, Q3 = 9.5.

trapezoid A quadrilateral with exactly one pair of parallel sides.

Examples:

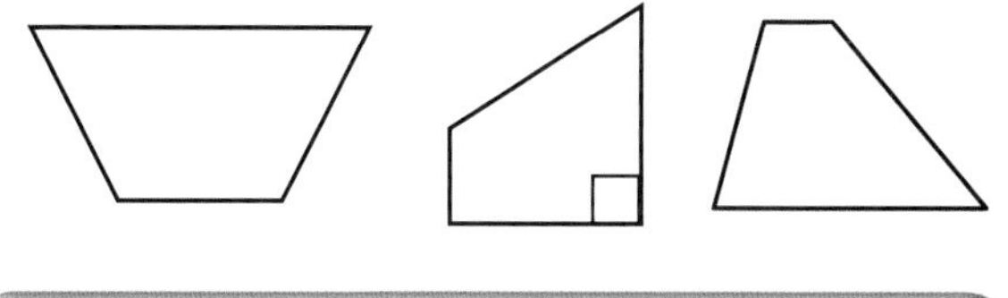

U

unit cube A cube with one-unit edges.

unit fraction A fraction with 1 in the numerator.

unit length The distance between tick marks of a number line.

Example:

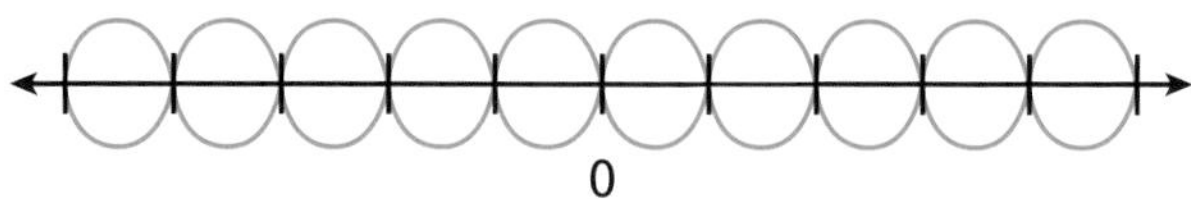

unit price The unit rate associated with a price or cost.

Example: 4 dollars per pound

unit rate The value associated with 1 unit.

Example: 5 miles *per* hour
3 dollars *every* week
2 apples *each* day

unit rate strategy A strategy in which a table is used to solve proportions.

Example: In this example, the unit rate, $\frac{3}{4}$ or $\frac{3}{4}$ to 1, is used to solve the proportion 3:4 = *x*:5.

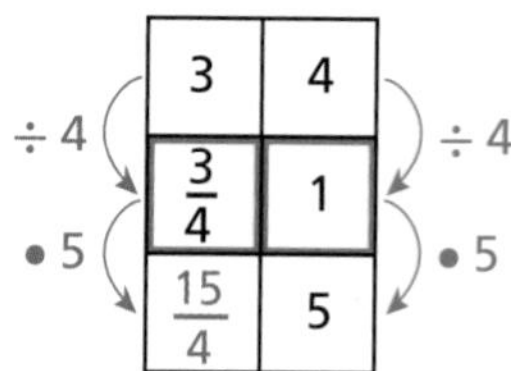

unit rate triangle When a rate situation is graphed in the coordinate plane, the unit rate triangle is a right triangle with base equal to 1 and height equal to the unit rate. The third side of the triangle is part of the line representing the rate situation.

Example: In the unit rate triangles in this graph, the base is 1 and the height is 3. The unit rate is 3.

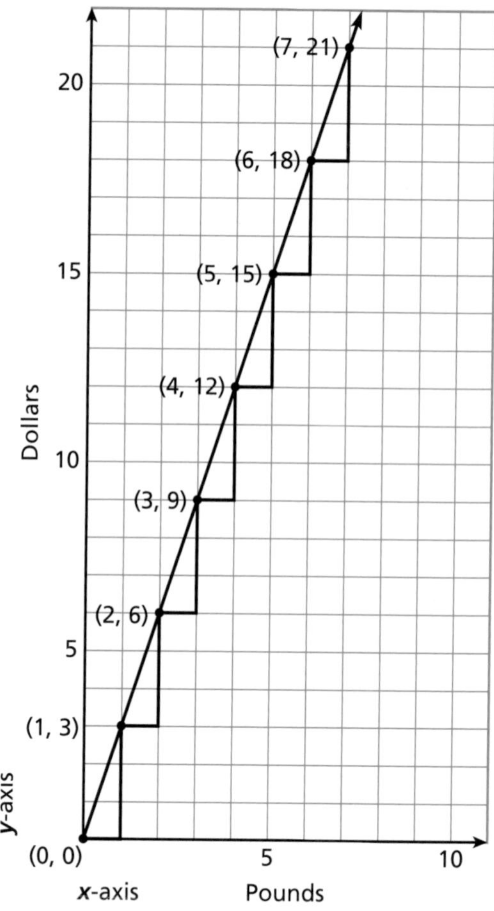

unsimplify Rewrite a fraction as an equivalent fraction with a greater numerator and denominator.

Example: Unsimplify $\frac{3}{5}$ by multiplying it by $\frac{6}{6}$.

$$\frac{3}{5} \cdot \frac{6}{6} = \frac{18}{30}$$

V

variable A letter or symbol used to represent an unknown number or a quantity that varies.

Example: $y = 2x$

x and y are variables.

vertex A point common to two sides of an angle or polygon, or three edges of a solid figure. The point of a pyramid.

Examples:

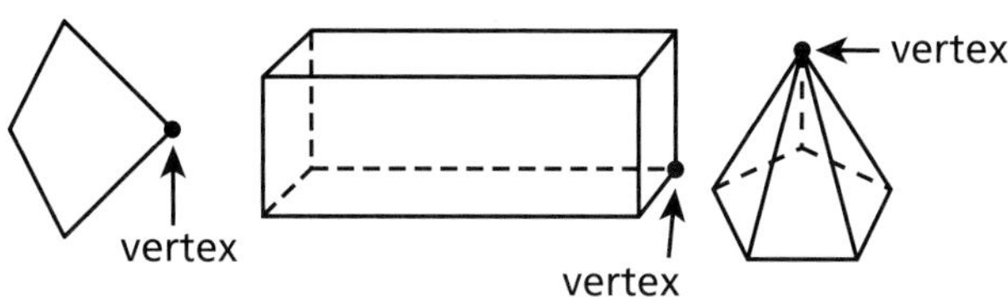

volume The amount of space occupied by a solid figure. Volume is measured in cubic units.

X

x-axis The horizontal number line in the coordinate plane.

x*-coordinate** The first number in an ordered (x***, y) pair.

Y

y-axis The vertical number line in the coordinate plane.

y*-coordinate** The second number in an ordered (x, ***y) pair.